# WILLIAM LAW

# WILLIAM LAW
## HIS LIFE AND THOUGHT

### A. Keith Walker

FOREWORD BY
## A. R. VIDLER
Honorary Fellow of King's College, Cambridge

Recommended by the Publications Committee of
the Church Historical Society

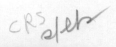

LONDON
S·P·C·K
1973

No. 94 in the
Church Historical Series

*First published in 1973*
*by S.P.C.K.*
*Holy Trinity Church*
*Marylebone Road*
*London NW1 4DU*

*Printed in Great Britain by*
*The Camelot Press Ltd, London and Southampton*

ERRATUM, *p. iv, acknowledgement should read*
This book has been published with the aid of grants from the
Bethune-Baker Fund of the University of Cambridge and the
Marc Fitch Fund.

SBN 281 02749 8

FOR
JOHANNA

*They that love beyond the world*
*cannot be separated by it*
WILLIAM PENN

AND
ANDREW AND SARAH

# CONTENTS

# ACKNOWLEDGEMENT

Thanks are due to the following for permission to quote from copyright sources:

Faber & Faber, Ltd, and Harcourt Brace Jovanovich, Inc., New York: *T. S. Eliot, Selected Essays* (1951).

# FOREWORD

It is *prima facie* likely that a writer who has been held in very high esteem by Christians of divergent schools of thought has teaching of permanent value to impart. Testimonies abound both from his contemporaries and from subsequent times to the profound influence that William Law has exercised. Let it suffice to mention here only two or three. George Whitefield wrote in his journal: 'Before I went to the University, I met with Mr Law's *Serious Call to a Devout Life*, but had not then money to purchase it. Soon after my coming up to the University, seeing a small edition of it in a friend's hand, I soon procured it. God worked powerfully upon my soul as he has since upon many others, by that and his other excellent treatise *Christian Perfection.*' And the latter he described as a book 'worth its weight in gold and which God has blessed to the conversion of many'. Then on a memorable occasion John Keble said to Hurrell Froude: 'Froude, you said one day that Law's *Serious Call* was a clever book; it seemed to me as if you had said that the Day of Judgment would be a pretty sight.' In more recent times, the great Scottish divine, Alexander Whyte, testified: 'It was a red-letter day when I first opened William Law. . . . The study of this quite incomparable writer has been nothing less than an epoch in my life.'

It is strange that there has hitherto been very little systematic study of Law's thought. The present book fills a serious gap in the history of English theology. It is based on a comprehensive, sympathetic, but not uncritical, survey of his life and work, and I am glad to have this opportunity of commending it.

If William Law is a teacher for our own time, that is largely because he goes against the grain of trends and axioms that are at present fashionable. A writer who could say that 'mortification, of *all kinds*, is the very life and soul of piety' (his italics!)

will not easily attract readers today. Yet his all-round rigorism may be not only a wholesome corrective of our easy-going ways but also a salutary pointer to a deeper kind of joy in believing than is commonly met with in this age of anxiety. It was Archbishop Benson who said that Law's *Serious Call* had helped him to realize how much his work was spoiled by his 'feeling its burden too much by far.'

Most readers today, however, who are charmed by what they discover in this neglected author, will also be repelled, and rightly so, by some of his attitudes and emphases. Law viewed the Church as a school for saints rather than as a home for sinners, and the old evangelical punster who said that 'Law came before the Gospel' hit a nail, even if he did not hit it precisely on the head. No doubt, Law had a 'soaring vision', but I must confess that of some of his teaching I do not know whether to say 'this is so lofty that I cannot attain unto it' or 'this is nonsense: away with it!' It is only fair to add that I am placed in a similar predicament by the writings of a good many other theologians.

This book has the merit of providing the necessary material in which one can distinguish the gold from the dross and also of enabling readers who are unfamiliar with Law's works to see which of them contain spiritual insight and nourishment of enduring worth.

*Rye*, 1973                                        A. R. VIDLER

# INTRODUCTION

The name of William Law is virtually unknown to the reading public. His writings, apart from the *Serious Call*, are almost unknown to educated Christians. We can find reasons for the present obscurity of this once popular author. Part of his work was a contribution to a debate whose content has changed significantly since the eighteenth century. Furthermore, his cultural environment prevented the best development of his genius. He lacked poise and his mystical works are cast in an eccentric phraseology, clothing sometimes unprofitable speculations. 'Vatiocinatory bosh' is the epithet Austin Farrer is reputed to have attached to the theories of Berdyaev. But Berdyaev was almost as captivated by Jacob Boehme as was Law. Would we be wise to let the ghost of Law lie?

For a number of reasons the answer must be No. Law was a genius of wide-ranging ability. Edward Gibbon praised him 'as a wit and a scholar', believing that, 'had not his vigorous mind been clouded by enthusiasm, he might be ranked among the most agreeable and ingenious writers of the times'.[1] Dr Johnson commended Law's *Serious Call* as 'the finest piece of hortatory theology in any language'.[2] John Wesley was fully conscious of the rare quality of Law's art and intelligence.[3] In each generation a few gifted men have continued to praise him. F. D. Maurice admitted his distinction.[4] Leslie Stephen remarked upon the 'controversial ability in which he had scarcely a superior in that time'.[5] H. P. Liddon was concerned that Law's *Three Letters to the Bishop of Bangor* should be reprinted. Charles Gore supervised the work and wrote an appreciative, if discriminating, Preface.[6] Dean Inge believed that in 'strength of intellect Law was Boehme's equal, and as a writer of clear and forcible English, he has few superiors'.[7] The numerous quotations from Law in Aldous Huxley's *The Perennial Philosophy*

indicate his interest in an author whose talents he rated higher
than Johnson's.[8] In 1944 he made the significant comments to
Alan Watts:

> I have been reading William Law—with the greatest
> pleasure and profit. What a really wonderful writer, when he
> is at his best. It is sadly typical of our education that we are
> all made to read the second-rate amiabilities of Addison and
> Steele—but that one of the great masters of devotion and of
> philosophical theology is passed over almost in silence.[9]

Law practised what he taught, and achieved deep sanctity.
An examination of his life and teaching should help us to
modify our views of the character of eighteenth-century
England. Law was as much a product of the times as Hume or
Chesterfield. Furthermore, a continuing importance is to be
given to mystical writers. Even an age as confused and material-
istic as ours witnesses a considerable and growing interest in
them. It is deeply instructive to follow the path along which the
High Church rigorist came to holiness.

Law's mastery of prose writing has always been admitted. We
shall comment briefly in the language that moved Caroline
Spurgeon to declare him 'our greatest prose mystic'.[10]

The present writer will contend that Law is a great—if
eccentric—theologian. He warrants a larger place in the
histories of Christian thought than he has been allowed; and he
can speak to us. His range is that of adequate religion, which,
according to von Hügel, combines the historical-institutional,
rational-critical and experimental-mystical.

John Wesley was first the pupil, then the critic of William
Law. Wesley's importance is undisputed, but most accounts of
his relation with Law are too biased in his favour. It is worth the
attempt to write a more objective record.

The standard biography of our subject remains J. H. Overton's *The Life and Opinions of the Reverend William Law*. Despite
Overton's fitness as an historian we have only to notice that his
book was published in 1881 to indicate the likely need for
reassessment. The author is grateful to A. W. Hopkinson,
H. Talon, and especially to S. Hobhouse for their contributions
to this end.

Various institutions and people have helped the author in his

effort to understand William Law: the public libraries of
Huddersfield, Slaithwaite, and Wells; Leeds University
Library and especially Dr Williams's Library; the late Canon
K. N. Ross and especially the Reverend Professor E. J.
Tinsley under whose tuition he prepared a thesis for the degree
of Doctor of Philosophy at Leeds University on this subject.
Special acknowledgement should be made to the Bodleian
Library, Oxford, where the author was permitted to examine
the unpublished 'Letters to a Lady' and miscellaneous manu-
script material on the Nonjurors.

It is mainly an intellectual biography. We know little of the
outward circumstances of Law's life. As it was comparatively
uneventful, the loss is not great. We may agree in any case with
Hester Gibbon that 'his life may be seen in his writing'.[11] Add
to his writings the testimony of Byrom, Tighe, Wesley, and the
labours of Walton and the image as well as the opinions of
William Law come before us.

# 1

## EARLY YEARS AND THEIR
## CULTURAL BACKGROUND

William Law was born in 1686 in the Northamptonshire
village of King's Cliffe. His father was a grocer and ranked as
a gentleman. William grew up in a locally respected and
genteel family. His mother, Margaret Farmery, came from
Lincolnshire. He was the fourth of eight children, the first five
all being boys.

During Law's lifetime the country's population increased
from about five to seven million. England remained largely
rural. As the century progressed, it became more powerful
politically and economically. A hierarchically ordered society
gave privilege to the middle and upper classes. The polish and
self-confidence in the appearance of the subjects of Gainsborough's portraits reflect a social reality.

A new this-worldly concern had been bred by the age of
Reason. Though moving slowly at first, the Agrarian and
Industrial Revolutions gathered momentum in fresh methods
of crop production, animal breeding, the invention of the steam
engine, the mechanization of cotton and wool production, the
development of the pottery, iron, and steel industries, the im-
provement of roads and canals, and other technological devices.
Typical of the times is the enthusiam of John Wesley for the
electrical experiments of Benjamin Franklin: 'What an amazing
scene is here opened for after-ages to improve upon!'[1] By 1757
Tucker could declare, 'Few countries are equal, perhaps none
excel, the English in the Numbers and Contrivance of their
Machines to abridge labour'.[2]

By contrast the political and religious upheavals of the seventeenth century had seemed to show that inadequate public
authority permitted disorder, chaos even, to disrupt social life.
At the same time the will to change became exhausted by too

1

long exposure to revolution, counter-revolution, and disorder. Social institutions tended to ossify and Sir Robert Walpole could admit, 'I am no . . . Reformer'.[3]

These cultural qualities helped to mould William Law. He became a confident author, who gravitated towards an experimental theology, but he saw little need for social engineering. At home or at school—in Oakham or Uppingham perhaps—he discovered the value of modest prosperity and the *status quo*.[4]

Rural charm still clings to King's Cliffe. The village is modest and substantial, the countryside quietly beautiful. The naturally introspective nature of young Law must have been confirmed and purified by such an environment.

With time very contrary impressions came to him. Medicine was still rudimentary. So bad was sanitation that the first recognizable feature of an English town was its stench. Of children born in London only one in four survived.[5] That ordinary citizens could find life nasty, brutish, and short is exemplified in the autobiographical sketch of Laurence Sterne (1713–68). The day after his birth his father, an army officer, found himself without work. He had a wife and two children to support. His sister married an inconstant man and died of a broken heart. Boat travel between England and Ireland almost cost the family their lives. Four brothers and sisters died in childhood. His father died in 1731 of a wound sustained in a duel, together with a fever. He became senseless some months before death. The woman Sterne courted almost died of consumption. He journeyed to Italy in 1764 for health reasons.[6]

The poor of those days were multitudinous and usually wretched. They tended to be ignorant and dirty. In towns their accommodation was overcrowded and mean. They had little or no money and when they obtained work it was usually drudgery. Individually weak, as mobs they could be formidable.[7] To George Crabbe (1783) village life was a 'life of pain'.[8]

Heavy drinking and gambling were national vices. Clients were assured that they could be drunk for a penny and dead drunk for twopence. Fortunes of up to £20,000 could pass hands in gambling at fashionable London clubs. Hogarth, as well as Gainsborough, illustrates the eighteenth century.

If the remarkable philanthropy of the age, which produced hospitals, schools, and social benefits of many kinds, to some

extent offset the bleakness of outlook likely to be engendered by
these adverse realities, we can think that they must have influenced Law in his formulation of the idea, unusual for his time,
that life without God is tragic. They must also have encouraged
the rigorist belief that friendship with the world is enmity with
God.

There are few extant allusions to Law's youth. It seems likely
that he received a strict, Christian, and happy upbringing. The
basis of a letter to his brother George in 1716, in which he expresses personal grief, is the warmth and harmony of their
family relations. Until this time, indeed, he believes that he has
'enjoyed a large share of happiness'.[9] It is quite possible that the
beautiful portraits of family affection and care in the *Serious Call*
owe something to his experience as a boy. Law's father's tomb-
stone states that he was a kind father, a tender husband, a true
friend, and a peaceable neighbour.

We can imagine Law imbibing the principles of the Bible and
Prayer Book at school and at home. In addition he would
learn at school some Latin and Greek, English, mathematics,
and possibly French.

That the seeds of rigoristic Anglican principles germinated in
his heart is clear from a list of rules Law drew up for himself,
possibly on going to Cambridge University at the age of eighteen
or nineteen. We shall give the list in full, as it embodies beliefs
and practices to which he remained faithful and which he
commended to others.

1. To fix it deep in my mind, that I have but one business
   upon my hands, to seek for eternal happiness, by doing
   the will of God.
2. To examine everything that relates to me in this view, as
   it serves or obstructs this only end of life.
3. To think nothing great or desirable, because the world
   thinks it so; but to form all my judgements of things from
   the infallible Word of God, and direct my life according
   to it.
4. To avoid all concerns with the world, or ways of it, but
   where religion and charity oblige me to act.
5. To remember frequently, and impress it upon my mind
   deeply, that no condition in this life is for enjoyment, but
   for trial; and that every power, ability, or advantage we

have, are all so many talents to be accounted for, to the
Judge of all the world.

6. That the greatness of human nature consists in nothing
   else but in imitating the Divine nature. That therefore all
   the greatness of this world, which is not in good actions,
   is perfectly beside the point.

7. To remember, often and seriously, how much time is inevitably thrown away, from which I can expect nothing
   but the charge of guilt; and how little where may be to
   come, on which an eternity depends.

8. To avoid all excess in eating and drinking. (The last
   three words are not fully legible on Law's script; 'eating
   and drinking' are a likely and usual conjecture.)

9. To spend as little time as I possibly can, among such persons as can receive no benefit from me, nor I from them.

10. To be always fearful of letting my time slip away without
    some fruit.

11. To avoid all idleness.

12. To call to mind the presence of God, whenever I find
    myself under any temptation to sin, and to have im-
    mediate recourse to prayer.

13. To think humbly of myself, and with great charity of all
    others.

14. To forbear from all evil speaking.

15. To think often of the life of Christ, and propose it as a
    pattern to myself.

16. To pray, privately, thrice a day, besides my morning and
    evening prayers.

17. To keep from public-houses as much as I can, without
    offence.

18. To spend some time in giving an account of the day,
    previous to evening prayer: how have I spent this day?
    what sin have I committed? what temptations have I
    withstood? have I performed all my duties?'[10]

This seems to be the earliest literary expression of William
Law's that we possess. In being logical, well-written, vehement,
and single-minded, it is typical of his adult character; in being
rigoristic and more reminiscent of the religious age that was in
fact giving way to a new order, it reflects his sheltered youth and
its Caroline character.

These rules might have been written by Richard Baxter, but we have no need to postulate Puritan influence on the author. He had been steeped in the Bible and Prayer Book. The New Testament affords ample opportunity for rigorist conclusions. Respecting the rigorism and humanism of Jesus, Kirk concludes: 'The two points of view lie side by side in the gospel; neither can be eliminated, yet no clue to their reconciliation is expressed.' The rest of the New Testament is of a similar character.[11]

Subsequent Christian teaching has contained rigorist and humanist elements with an official bias towards the rigoristic. This is certainly true of the Prayer Book (1662), as a perusal of the orders of service for Baptism and Marriage make plain.

Adherence to the school of the Caroline divines ensured that Law would strain biblical and other statements towards a rigorist position. Lancelot Andrewes believed that apart from church government he had the same religion as Puritans.[12] Bishop Ken's *Manual of Prayers* for Winchester scholars bids his readers remember their Creator and flee youthful lusts.[13] There is little humanity in the entire manual.

It is probable that Law met the popular book of devotion *The Whole Duty of Man* whilst he was young. It would encourage his rigorist tendencies. He would learn that marriage was a duty 'to him that cannot live innocently without it', or as a means of serving God better or saving our own souls.[14] Food is admittedly necessary for the preservation of life, but 'as men use not to take physic for pleasure, but remedy, so neither should they eat' for any other purpose.[15] The function of clothes is to hide our nakedness, fence off the cold, and distinguish the sexes.[16]

The Carolines insisted that the devout must live by Rule, which is what Law's eighteen rules purport to be. But they regarded the Prayer Book as providing the best Rule and would have criticized him for formulating a set of rules and thus increasing rigidity rather than genuine liberty.[17]

A devotional book which Law probably met early and which he came to prize only less than the Bible, was Thomas à Kempis' *Imitation of Christ*. Much of his later teaching on personal religion can be related to this work. It is rigorist. Enough for the moment to quote: 'When a man has perfect compunction, then the whole world is burdensome and bitter to him'.[18]

This narrow and stony path pursued so soon in life by Law

led upwards, at least in the sense that it must have strengthened
and purified his character. But the suppression of natural im-
pulses coincident with this probably contributed to that harshness of temper he was only to overcome with age.

Mention in the rules of 'the infallible Word of God' reminds
us further that Law was educated less to question than to obey.
Though biblical criticism 'came into its own' about 1678 and
with the work of Richard Simon,[19] Law remained a Fundamen-
talist and was partly led to Boehme in an effort to safeguard the
biblical text. He remained a Nonjuror longer than he should
have done and until supernatural charity possessed his soul,
felt irritated by unbelievers. There was an intellectual as well as
an emotional constriction in his upbringing.

He entered Cambridge in 1705 as a Sizar at Emmanuel
College. He took his B.A. degree in 1708, was elected Fellow of
his college and received holy orders in 1711, and took his M.A.
in 1712.

Oxford and Cambridge Universities partook of the moribund
condition of most institutions of the time. Gibbon was later to
compare them to old, infirm, and prejudiced people.[20] If we may
agree that the modern world-view came to birth between 1680
and 1715,[21] so that nature rather than God, reason rather than
tradition, Deism rather than Christianity, equality rather than
hierarchy became men's concern, we can see the significance of
Gibbon's analogy. But the aged may have virtues envied by the
young.

There was both scholarship and piety at the Universities.[22]
At Cambridge there had been a strong reaction against
Calvinism after the Restoration and a repudiation of Aristo-
telianism and patristic learning. After its publication in 1689
Locke's *Essay* came to be studied. The High Church tradition
remained strong only at St John's College. Emmanuel had been
a Puritan stronghold in the seventeenth century, but the
Cambridge Platonists and the Nonjuror William Sancroft as
Master (from 1662), had changed the ethos. It seems likely that
either chance or the reputation of Sancroft decided Law's
parents to enter him at Emmanuel.

We can think of Law applying himself to Latin, Greek, and
Hebrew,[23] learning about Greek and Latin culture, studying
the Bible, patristics, and Christian history and doctrine,[24]

discovering logic and philosophy. The revered name of Sir Isaac Newton, no less than the growing interest of the age, would ensure that he learned something of science and scientific method. Nor was Law unhappy in these pursuits. In 1740 he could tell Dr Trapp that when he was about eighteen he was fond of such writers as Virgil, Horace, and Terence, and that he would have been glad to have translated Milton had he been able to. But he adds characteristically, 'this *Ardour* soon wore off'.[25]

Law's attention to his rules was probably punctilious. His serious attitude is reflected in the recollection that 'he met Taulerus in the public library [at Cambridge], that he liked him'.[26] Tauler was an austere, otherworldly, medieval, and affective mystic. As Law would credit Tauler with having written the *Theologia Germanica*, it is possible that he learned something of use to combat the unorthodoxy of acquaintances. There is teaching in this book that could make one sympathetic to Boehme.

Unorthodoxy there certainly was. The changing feeling of the age, exemplified in the work of Hobbes, Bayle, Locke, and Newton affected everyone. In 1668 Daniel Scargull was expelled from Cambridge for atheistic utterances and only restored after public recantation. In 1710 William Whiston was expelled for his neo-Arian views.[27] Such instances indicate, of course, that the prevailing power remained Christian and Anglican. Whichcote could even contend that 'Wickedness produceth Atheism; and Atheism settles men in Wickedness'.[28]

The most significant influence upon Law at this time came from the writings of Nicholas Malebranche (1638–1715). He told Byrom in 1729 that it was because of Malebranche that he kept his act at Cambridge on 'Omnia videmus in Deo'. He had come upon him independently and immediately perceived his importance.[29] Even in 1729 Law declared himself willing to go to Paris to converse with anyone who had known Malebranche.

It is an indication of the poverty of intellectual life at Cambridge that Malebranche became known to Law only by chance, and it is an indication of Law's discrimination and independence that he did discover and relish him.

Born into a privileged family, Malebranche was destined early for the priesthood because of a spinal deformation. He

entered the Oratory founded by Cardinal Bérulle in 1611. He
learnt to venerate Augustine and Platonism. The influence of
Descartes was evident and Malebranche admitted his power.
He had a protected debate with Arnauld on the theory of grace
and his writing on the subject was put on the Index in 1690.
Fontenelle considered him a great geometrician and physicist.
In addition he was interested in anatomy and the life of insects,
declaring himself more moved by observing the ways of insects
than by the whole history of Greece and Rome. Though given
to meditation and love of the countryside, he was no recluse.
He was fond of children and included Leibniz among the distinguished men with whom he conversed.

We may briefly indicate his philosophical position. Respecting the problem of the union of mind and body, he held
that there was a correspondence between soul, traces in the
brain, and the emotions, with movements of the animal spirits.
The natural union of mind and body is caused by the will of the
Creator, the conjunction in time between ideas and brain
traces, and the will.

By the word 'thought' he sometimes meant the whole con-
cious life of the soul, but more generally pure spirit, which
is the essence of the soul, and in God. Sense, imagination
and volition are not of this essence. Only by a 'sentiment
intérieur' are we assured of the persistence of our own selves.
Because the soul is united with God the Word is spiritually
present in the soul.

In meditation and prayer all states of consciousness other than
pure understanding have fallen away. The soul can participate
in God undisturbed by the body and free like Adam.

Malebranche believed that only the intuitive proof of God's
existence was conclusive, but he used Descartes' ontological
proof on the necessity of the existence of God. We see all things
in God as essences and appreciate that their existence is possible,
but not necessary. God can be seen only in Himself, for nothing
finite can represent the infinite. To see God is to see that he
exists. Union with God permits us to have an idea of him. The
Christian religion assures us that Jesus Christ is the 'maître
intérieur' capable of enlightening us.

We cannot grasp the mode of God's power in our present
state. As we know that he is perfect we must trust that he is

omnipotent. His power is essentially general in expression and particular causes obtrude consequentially to the general cause. Because of this we can understand the appearance of evil. He rejected pantheism and described Spinoza as a wretched philosopher. A certain kinship with Spinoza's thought is found in his belief that the created world is contingent on God for its existence.

In knowledge we are given the idea of things only. Ideas are real and even resist the mind, for we cannot think of a circle that has two unequal diameters. We see all things in God. This must be so because before creation God was alone. Before producing the world he must have had an idea and knowledge of it. Thus all creatures are in God spiritually. Again, our souls are so united with him that the pure understanding thus constituted is the union of the soul with the ideas in God. It is interesting to note that when we begin to want to ponder a particular idea, a number of ideas flood into our minds. Ideas are not innate but present in the soul because of human participation in the divine.

Reason is united with the Word and consubstantial with God.

If it is true that it is infinite . . . immutable and necessary, it is certain that it is not different from that of God Himself; for only the universal and infinite Being can contain in itself a universal and infinite reason.

He nevertheless distinguishes between human reason and faith. While God is the source of all knowledge, science requires doubt, evidence, and progress. But faith denies doubt, authority replaces evidence, and progress often means error. Yet the Word speaks in reason as well as in faith. Before the Fall men lived according to reason and the life of reason will be one of the rewards of heaven.

By attention the perceptions of the soul grow clearer. Prayer helps concentration and good inclinations have their origin in God and help us to strive towards him. Bodily inclinations are really passions. They originate in God and so teach us to love our bodies and all that is useful to them. He does not condemn curiosity because it leads to natural science. Such science gives us power over nature, thus enabling us to live better the life of reason. Evil is the absence of good and therefore nothing.[30]

This brief outline of Malebranche's philosophy indicates that his importance lay not only in his innate brilliance and acquired learning but in his creative response to the intellectual crisis of the day. He was a student of science and of the philosophy of Descartes and, at the same time, a loyal son of the Church with an esteem for Augustine and Platonism. We draw the conclusion that Law was somehow conscious of the difficulties for orthodoxy and that Malebranche eased his position.

Prayer and mysticism were also important for the Oratorian. His order favoured Dionysius the Areopagite. His writings are suffused with the sense of the immensity of God, the nothingness of the creature, the absorption of the soul in God, and its adherence to Christ. On prayer he urges, 'Oubliez même, si vous pouvez, que vous avez un corps.' He was indebted to à Kempis and believed that as the Truth speaks inwardly, external direction is unnecessary. He rejected Quietism and the Fideism of Pascal who uses reason to reject reason. Reason pervades his mysticism. He considers that knowledge itself is the illumination of the soul by God. He commends asceticism on the grounds that Original Sin has drastically weakened the soul's perception of God.[31]

This devotional side to Malebranche must have impressed Law and encouraged his own spiritual efforts. He was also probably impressed by the fact that Malebranche was a celibate, had few personal possessions, and wrote beautifully.

As a Fellow Law resided at Emmanuel and took pupils. Against his name on the college register we read 'celebrated enthusiast'.[32] The occasion for this characterization was the conjunction of Law's vehement personality and his belief in the doctrine of the Divine Right of Kings.

In 1713 he was chosen as orator at the ceremonies attending the Bachelors' Commencement.[33] In giving what was customarily a burlesque oration from a three-legged stool Law took the opportunity to enforce his Nonjuror principles. He asked whether, when the Israelites made the Golden Calf the object of worship, they ought to keep to their god *de facto* or return to their God *de jure*. Some thought the speech reflected on the government. Mentioning the matter a week later Byrom recorded, 'He is much blamed by some, and defended by others; has the character of a vain, conceited fellow'.[34] At least Law's readiness of manner and speech had sufficiently impressed his contemporaries to honour him as orator. And it seems that Law's religion did not preclude playfulness, even on Ash Wednesday! The event proved his sincerity and rashness. He was degraded in University rank to undergraduate status.

His conviction remained. On the day appointed for thanksgiving for General Peace, he preached at Hazelingfield (7 July 1713). He said that subjects must not examine too nicely the affairs of their prince, 'an imprudent Curiosity is the common Fault of Mankind'. He asks:

Can we imagine that God's Vicegerent, to whom he has committed the Protection and Government of part of the Creation, may be treated with the least degree of Disrespect?

As government is providential, rebellion is really directed against God and is a sign of pride. The subject must exercise 'passive obedience'. He ends with a paean of praise for Queen Anne:

Thou Great, Dear Offspring of Great CHARLES, how do his Royal Virtues Shine in Thee.[35]

In view of the incompetence of the Stuarts generally, and the evil of James II in particular, this sermon indicates Law's ability to maintain a theory in the face of plain facts.

In 1714 Queen Anne died and George, Elector of Hanover, was invited to succeed to the English throne as George I, thus ensuring the Protestant succession and public peace. Rather than break his oath of loyalty to the House of Stuart Law resigned his Fellowship in 1716.

His decision was taken painfully and he appreciated that his prospects would be 'melancholy enough'.[36] His chances of advancement in Church or State were ended; daily sustenance might even be problematical. This action also meant that intercourse with contemporaries would be curtailed. As a great bishop he would have been in the midst of affairs and mixing with distinguished men. He was now restricted to the company of Nonjurors and ordinary persons. A mature criticism of his developing views was thus made more unlikely, and such criticism Law needed.

There seems to be no substance in the assertion that for some

years he proved a gay parson. He may have served as a curate
at Hazelingfield after 1711 and later associated with Dr Heylin,
who was vicar from 1714–19. Heylin was an authority on
mysticism.[37]

In 1716 in a letter to his brother George, Law claimed that he
could think about his folly without dejection. In the silent years
between 1716 and 1723 when he entered the house of Edward
Gibbon we may think that his Christian earnestness was
maintained. It is likely that he experienced indigence. Overton
discovered a reference to a Nonjurors' subscription made on
Law's behalf. But Law never refers to the difficulties of these
years.

# 2

# THE CHURCH AND THE BANGORIAN CONTROVERSY

Law left Cambridge as a Nonjuror in 1716. What kind of reasoning informed his conviction? In its complete form the theory of the Divine Right of Kings states that the monarchy is a divinely ordained institution; that hereditary right is indefeasible; that kings are accountable to God alone; that non-resistance and passive obedience to monarchs are enjoined by God.

Biblical texts were pressed into service: in 1 Samuel, 7.10–18; Proverbs 8.15; Psalm 51.4; Daniel 4.32b; Luke 20.25; John 19.1; Romans 13.1–7; 1 Peter 2.13–17, were to be found examples of kingly authority and the fidelity of subjects.

Appeal was also made to antiquity. Charles Leslie believed that 'All the ancient fathers are full of it'. The doctrine came into prominence in the fourteenth century as the Divine Right of Emperors, to enable the state to withstand the enlarged authority of the Pope. Richard II was the first English king to use the doctrine to support his absolutist aims. The English reformers believed generally in passive obedience to the monarch, but the *Homily on Wilful Rebellion* only mentions actual rulers. Hooker, with typical judiciousness, and in agreement with the best English lawyers, commended a constitutional monarchy. Reverence to the king he qualifies as follows: 'so is the power of the King over all and in all limited, that unto all his proceedings the Law itself is a rule . . . the King's grant of any favour made contrary to the Law is void'.

The chaos of the Civil War lent support to the doctrine and led men to distinguish between *de jure* and *de facto* authority. In 1681 Filmer published his *Patriarcha* and gave syllogistic expression of the doctrine. Thus: what is natural to man exists by divine right. Kingship is natural to man. Therefore kingship exists by divine right. By appealing to Natural Law rather than

13

to the Bible and tradition Filmer unwittingly prepared the way for the overthrow of the doctrine. Locke taught that the state was founded in compact and he allowed equal rights to all. This teaching was accepted increasingly, enabling Figgis to make the judgement, 'From 1688 the Stuart cause is the expression of the passion of the past'.

On biblical and traditional grounds the doctrine had been contested of course. Those that swore loyalty to William in 1688 said that obedience to the powers that be, inculcated by St Paul, referred to present powers; that kingly power changed hands violently and incongruously in biblical times without the doctrine being developed; that the teaching of the Fathers is inconclusive as power of the monarch changed hands as violently and incongruously as ever it did in biblical times without protest from churchmen; that later tradition gives no adequate support for the doctrine; that Nonjurors address themselves insufficiently to the duties of monarchs. What must subjects do when a monarch repeatedly and ruinously disregards his duty to God?[2] In view of Law's later development it is interesting to note Macaulay's point that the type of fidelity the Nonjuror had to Scripture ranked him with the Quakers. Neither party would admit of compromise with certain letters of Scripture.

In the eighteenth century the Nonjurors were no more than a small body of idealists. Tories such as Swift and Bolingbroke were against the doctrine; Berkeley argued from Natural Law only; Butler recognized no authority as absolute.

It is worth noticing that Nonjurors such as Dodwell, Nelson, and Brokesby returned to the national Church when Bishop Lloyd died and Bishop Ken resigned. Like Ken they recognized the vice in schism itself and wanted the separation to end. Lathbury, the historian of the movement, believed that after 1710 Nonjurors acted on rather different principles from their predecessors. He was less sympathetic to them.[3]

That Law should maintain this doctrine for so long and at such cost may be a tribute to his integrity, but it is also an indication of a certain narrowness and inflexibility. Coleridge had many of the talents of Law but that myriad-minded man would no more have been a Nonjuror than he would have been a disciple of Boehme.

There were high-minded and able members of the group of

course. But it was factious and over-concerned with non-essentials. The conversion of Bishop Brett's daughter to Roman Catholicism was attributed to the continual squabbles of Nonjurors. To the divisions that developed after 1717 Lathbury traced the ultimate reason for the extinction of the movement.[4]

They corresponded with representatives of the Orthodox Church with hopes of reunion. But in 1725 Archbishop Wake intervened to clarify the unrepresentative position of Nonjurors, and the correspondence stopped.

In the meantime the controversy over 'usages' erupted. Study of antiquity suggested to Hickes, Collier, and others that Anglican eucharistic form was defective. A petition was circulated among Nonjurors in 1716 recommending the removal of certain defects in worship and discipline and Law was a signatory. Respecting the Eucharist the petition stated four omissions: the oblation and invocation, prayers for the faithful departed and the mixing of water with the wine. It mentioned also the lack of uniformity in public worship, the too great variety of attitudes to the established Church, the lack of discipline and scheme of repentance.[5]

The gauntlet had been thrown down. In the ensuing controversy between 1717–25, forty tracts were written. Bishop Collier, head of the smaller Usagers section, excommunicated the Non-Usagers and published a revised Service Book in 1720 from the 1549 Prayer Book and ancient sources. The established rite was declared a 'nullity'. It provided for an expressed oblation of the elements to God the Father, the direct invocation of the Holy Spirit with the prayer that the elements be made the body and blood of Christ, prayer for the departed in the great intercession and use of the mixed chalice.[6] Triune immersion at baptism, chrism at confirmation and unction were prescribed also.

The Non-Usagers, led by Bishop Gandy, remained faithful to the 1662 Prayer Book. As a consequence, although the Nonjurors had founded the 'Catholic Church in England' in 1717, they were destined not to meet as a united body. At first Law seems to have sided with Bishop Collier.

Study of the Fathers and Liturgy with the accompanying anxious debate and decisions did not consume Law's energies at this time. In the growth of Latitudinarianism he perceived a greater challenge and threat than anything troubling Non-jurors.

The Caroline theological method gave priority to the Bible, as being the Word of God, in all matters of faith and practice. It honoured tradition, especially that of antiquity, as interpreting rather than as adding to, revelation recorded in the Bible. The earlist centuries of the Faith were the purest, it was argued, and the Holy Spirit guided the Church along the essential lines for its development. Within its proper domain reason was absolute, a gift of God for true discrimination.

Anglicans looked upon this method as refreshing theology and purifying the ancient Faith. But the Renaissance had affected men no less than the Reformation. Whilst the Renaissance was not anti-religious, and many of its stars were devoutly Christian, by its rediscovery of ancient Greece and Rome and its development of the critical faculty, as old manuscripts were studied, seeds were sewn for the nurturing of the anti-dogmatic principle and the supplanting of Bible and tradition by reason; a reason moreover that found its model in scientific method. Following the Septuagint for Isaiah 7.9, Augustine had taught that 'unless you believe, you will not understand'. Christendom endorsed his view. But the philosphers, embodying the Enlightenment, reversed the axiom.[7]

It was the traditional belief that the Bible consisted in propositional revelation. As the seventeenth century progressed the observation became more insistent that the text was inconsistent. For example, if Adam and Eve had only two children why is there reference to people finding Cain after he has killed Abel and been driven away from his parents? The work of Spinoza and Simon introduced larger difficulties and suggested a more dispassionate approach to Scripture.

As foreign travel became more common and men travelled further, the recognition that there were many ancient myths and that the Bible was but one book purporting to reveal truth brought more doubts to men's minds.

The question of biblical morality became insistent, not only before critical reason, but because of the injustice resulting from Roman Catholic and Protestant practice of some of its precepts. 'Must witches be killed?' 'Must unbelievers be compelled to come in?' 'Is hell to be so populous?' were some of the questions people were asking.

Tradition was also to be seen not so much as a channel through which the light of revelation was filtered as a weight upon the back. According to P. Hazard, 'The very notion of historicity was tending to disappear'.[8] Men sensed the difficulty of accurately estimating past events; they knew of the variety of interpretations and they were coming to think that the present should concern them more.

Most of all, reason was winning for itself a new importance. After the turmoil of the Reformation and Renaissance men were coming to an assessment of their place in the universe with new tools in their hands. Lord Herbert of Cherbury (George Herbert's brother), who lived from 1583–1648, considered authority an inadequate basis for religion; natural and rational religion seemed to him more just. He believed that there were five ideas innate in the human mind and that these constituted essential religion. They were: that God exists, that he should be worshipped, that the practice of virtue is a true means of honouring him, that sin should be abhorred and repented of, that there will be rewards and punishments in heaven. Religion was thus given a philosophical tone and reason was deemed able to arrive at adequate religious truth.

Hobbes' *Leviathan* (1651) helped the new movement by repudiating tradition and scholasticism and suggesting that the human mind might be the real source of religious belief. Spinoza wrote his philosophy according to geometric pattern, and the philosophy of Descartes was basically mechanical.

Bacon (1561–1626) had already bidden men turn to this world as natural philosophers. He is considered the father of modern science, and it is appropriate that the Royal Society should have been incorporated by Royal Charter by 1662. In the same century Malpighi invented the microscope, Torricelli the barometer, and the thermometer and telescope were much improved. By such new means reason upset old beliefs and promised to make a new world.

Newton and Locke were among the most distinguished, and were the most famous, exemplars of the Enlightenment in the first half of the eighteenth century. From a single formula Newton had been able to deduce everything in planetary theory.

By reason and observation he indicated the extent of law in the physical universe. One reason why the word 'light' captivated the eighteenth-century mind was because the work of Newton had so often centred upon it.

Locke was the philosopher to whom everyone referred. He was thought to have pursued reason in philosophy as Newton had in science. His work is marked by common sense and logical rigour. His few certainties include God, his own existence and the truth of mathematics. He ridiculed scholastic thought and 'enthusiasm'.[9] His belief, common, if sometimes unconsciously so, for the times that science provides the supreme form of proof emerges in a characteristic sentence, 'It is as certain that there is a God, as that the opposite angles made by the intersection of two straight lines are equal'.[10] His book, *The Reasonableness of Christianity*, commends simplicity in belief, and considers the unity of God and the truth of Jesus as Messiah to be the essence of the New Testament. Locke's pedestrian style and modest religion are typical products of his fundamental ideas.

Ernst Cassirer has written of the Enlightenment, ' "Reason" becomes the unifying and central point of this century, expressing all that it longs and strives for, and all that it achieves ... it constructs its ideal according to the model and pattern of contemporary natural science'.[11] As a generalization this is true, but there were notable dissentients.

For the Caroline divines and the Cambridge Platonists reason was an inclusive faculty. That no restrictive meaning was given to the word is clear from a remark of Jeremy Taylor's, '[It is] not guided only by natural arguments but by divine revelation and all other good means'.[12] G. R. Cragg defined the word as the Cambridge Platonists used it to mean 'the discipline of thinking exactly and philosophically about the things which are Real . . . [and] it involved the unification of the whole personality in the pusuit of truth'.[13] For such men as these reason is of the realm of eternal truth; reasoning is participation in God.

The Cambridge Platonists, because of their Platonism and the mean ends to which such things could be put, were not greatly concerned with dogma or ritual. John Smith spoke for them all when he confessed, 'True religion is no piece of artifice . . . it is a new nature informing the souls of men.'[14]

Their concern was for spiritual life and good conduct, which for them were the high points of the life of Reason.

They were followed, as the seventeenth century drew to a close, by the Latitudinarians. They shared with the Platonists an impatience with doctrinal wrangling and ecclesiastical functions. J. Beardmore could define them as 'persons that had no great liking for the liturgy or ceremonies, or indeed the Government of this [Anglican] Church, but yet had attained to such a largeness ... of judgement ... that they could conform'.[15] But they had lost the mystical nerve intensifying the religion of the Platonists. The restricted understanding of reason characterizing the Enlightenment was something to which they approximated. The value in this was to admit freely the self-critical element into orthodoxy, the impoverishment was that the numinous was distrusted and tradition only partly understood.

Archbishop Tillotson exhibits most of what is best in the movement. Although he wrote discourses against transubstantiation and Purgatory, most of his writing is concerned with ethical matters. He is lucid and moderate and inculcates a prudential morality and is as much at home in the classics as in the Bible. He was the friend of Locke and became a Fellow of the Royal Society because he thought that the study of nature gave solid support for religion. Reacting, as all the Latitudinarians did, against the religious fanaticism and squabbling of the seventeenth century, he held that 'the strongest opiates in the world are *Enthusiasm* and *Popery*'.[16] The spirit of the movement is maintained in Samuel Clarke, who could examine over a thousand texts of Scripture and find no basis for the doctrine of the Trinity; in Burnet's lucid, factual historical writing and tendency to Socinianism; in the 1771 Feathers' Tavern Petition to Parliament requesting that the clergy be allowed to interpret the Bible as they wished, that they should not be bound by the creeds or formularies.

Law was no Latitudinarian. As a descendant of the Caroline divines with remarkable potentiality for spiritual apprehension, he believed that they secularized the Faith. The writing of Benjamin Hoadly gave Law an opportunity to express his thoughts.

Hoadly (1676–1761) was educated at Cambridge and was a Fellow of Catherine Hall for a time. He was the friend of Samuel

C

Clarke and revered Locke. Though not a creative writer he effectively applied a good measure of common sense to political issues. He was prepared to champion the cause of Low Churchmen during the High Church period of dominance when Queen Anne reigned. He was something of an Erastian, and his ridiculing of church authority and praise of King George I ensured his elevation to the episcopacy. He became bishop of Bangor in 1715. As a cripple he preached in a kneeling position. However, he never visited his diocese and we must concur with the judgement of Norman Sykes that 'His elevation to the bench is the gravest offence against ecclesiastical propriety of the century'. Hoadly was mainly to blame for the matter.[17] Besides being a pluralist he moved with suspicious rapidity up the ladder of preferment, becoming Bishop of Hereford in 1721, Bishop of Salisbury in 1723 and Bishop of the rich see of Winchester in 1734.

He had already opposed the High Churchman Atterbury when, in 1716, the posthumous remains of the Nonjuror Dr Hickes were published. They provoked from Hoadly *A Preservative against the Principles and Practices of the Nonjurors both in Church and State*. The fundamental principle of the book was that a man's 'title to God's favour cannot depend upon his actual being or continuing in any particular method, but upon his real sincerity in the conduct of his conscience and his own actions under it'. Applied to the 1688 Revolution this meant that the revolution was necessary, that the state can deprive ecclesiastics of their function if they attack the regime, and that it is responsible to itself for its ordering; that Nonjurors are prohibited by just procedure of civil law, and that the successors to the clerics and laity faithful to William are the true members of the Church of England. He proceeded to the necessary conclusion: God does not require men to belong to the same external communion, his favour rests upon the sincere; private judgement is a more reliable guide in religion than tradition or dogma; power of absolution could not be granted to fallible men.

The authority of the Church was attacked further in a sermon published with the King's approval in 1717. He enlarged upon the words of Jesus, 'My kingdom is not of this world'. Christ's Church must be identified with his kingdom, it is not of this world. Further, he is the sole authority over the Church. To 'erect Tribunals' or to make Church declarations wrests authority from Christ. Men must be left free to come to their own decisions and not threatened by ecclesiastics.[18]

Hoadly's work was interpreted by most churchmen as subversive to the institution of the Church. It produced a literary fray that involved fifty divines and produced seventy-four pamphlets in July 1717 alone. For a couple of days the business of the City was brought to a halt. More heat than light was engendered, of course, leading Leslie Stephen to conclude sadly, 'This controversy . . . is one of the most intricate tangles of fruitless logomachy in the language'.[19] The attempts of the Lower House of Convocation to have Hoadly censured was prevented only by the king proroguing Convocation, with the calamitous result, indicative none the less of impoverished theology, that it never met again until the 1850s.

We do not know where Law lived at the time, between 1717 and 1719, when he replied to Hoadly in *Three Letters to the Bishop of Bangor*. He allowed his name to accompany his writing only to avoid the accusation of unfairly attacking the Bishop. But such was the acuteness, wit, and polish of his contribution that he rose from obscurity to fame in a moment.

There seems to have been three reasons why Law wrote. Hoadly was a Latitudinarian and his principles undermined the Church. He attacked Nonjurors. By his opinions he gave Law the *occasion* to fulfil a clamorous part of his nature. Denied a pulpit and possibly some social dignity, conscious of his latent powers, and reflecting his age in a love of argument, the urge to combat Hoadly must have been strong.

The *First Letter* briefly treats the whole question. He considers the inadequacies of sincerity and the importance of authority and prayer in religion.

Despite Hoadly's protestations even freethinkers believe his intention to be 'to dissolve the Church as a *Society*'.[20] If sincerity is enough to recommend us to God any or no form of religion will suffice. Intellectual convictions are unimportant. A churchman can only exclaim: 'Your Lordship is ours, as you fill a *Bishopric*; but we are at a loss to discover from this Discourse what other Interest we have in your Lordship.'[21]

Though sincerity is important the Bible requires more than

that. Christ stated that believers would be saved and unbelievers damned. Surely unbelievers are not all insincere?
Paul said that we can be saved only in the name of Christ,
but Hoadly has discovered 'an Atonement, more universal
than that of his Blood'.[22]

Sincerity itself can be morally ambiguous. It may 'be often
charged with Guilt. . . . It may have been from some ill Conduct
of our own, some Irregularities . . . that we conceive things
as we do.'[23]

Coming to the question of church authority Hoadly contradicts the teaching of the Church, of which he is a bishop, if he
regards ordination in conformity with the Apostolic Succession
as a dream and trifle.

> If there is no *Uninterrupted Succession*, then there are no
> Authorized Ministers from Christ; if no such Ministers, then
> no Christian Sacraments; if no Christian Sacraments, then
> no Christian Covenant, whereof the Sacraments are the
> Stated and Visible Seals.[24]

In fact men can no more make a priest than a sacrament as
both are 'positive Ordinances' created by God.

He cuts through the verbal tangle concerning Hoadly's statements on church authority by indicating that the 'Reasons
you everywhere give against this authority, conclude as strongly
against any Degrees of Authority, as that which is truly Absolute'.[25] He argues for the same authority as that of Christ and
the Apostles which was real without being absolute. Even the
sanctifying power of the sacraments is dependent upon the
manner in which they are taken. This principle should not
surprise Hoadly who has himself defended the limited authority
of the English government. Obedience to such authority is
rational and appropriate to 'Rational Creatures'.[26]

It is wrong to say that Christ, as king of his kingdom,
cannot delegate his authority. If this is true we could have no
civil government for God has declared himself king of all the
earth (Isa. 33.22; Dan. 4.17). Furthermore, we need authority
in addition to that provided by Bible and reason.

The *Letter* concludes with a sharp criticism of remarks made
by Hoadly on the subject of prayer. Hoadly defined prayer as
'*A Calm and Undisturbed Address to God*'.[27] Law replies that as

prayer consists chiefly in confession and petition it is odd that *'Perturbation* of Spirit' should be absent from confession and *'Fervour and Warmth'* from petition.

No doubt the intellect should be dispassionate in its exercise, but we cannot conclude that 'there is no such thing as the *Right Use* of our *Passions'*. Passion is no more a crime than understanding. 'It is nothing but mistaking the *Value* of Objects, that makes a criminal. An *Infinite Good* cannot be too *passionately* desired, nor a *Real Evil* too *vehemently* abhorred.'[28] Biblical support for these thoughts is forthcoming in such an expression as that of St Paul when he speaks about godly sorrow, or that where we are bidden to imitate Christ who prayed with such earnestness before his Passion. Law re-defines prayer as, 'an *Address* to *Heaven, enlivened with such Degrees of* Fervour *and* Intenseness, *as our* Natural Temper, *influenced* with a true Sense *of God, could beget in us'.*[29]

The *Second Letter* is concerned with much the same matter as its predecessor. He defends ecclesiastical traditions as a High Churchman. He appeals to Scripture (Acts 8.14; Heb. 6.1–2; Eph. 4.7; 2 Tim. 2.6), and 'Primitive Observance, and the Universal Practice of all succeeding Ages in the Church'.[30] He mentions the Councils and quotes St Cyprian and Bishop Beveridge, the eminent Caroline divine.

We should not reduce the Eucharist to the level of a memorial meal. The attempt to do so provokes from Law a Scriptural reference (1 Cor. 10.16) and the question 'are human Benedictions to be all despised, though by them the Bread and Wine become Means of Grace, and are made the spiritual Nourishment of our Souls?'[31]

Hoadly's 'novel Doctrine' contradicts the method of God's providence. The Jewish and Christian dispensations show the dispersal of God's blessings and judgements by human hands. Bishop Potter is quoted for support.

We should no more revile ministers with charges of priest-craft than did Jewish recipients of blessings revile Abraham or Job. The frailty of ministers is admitted: the treasure is in earthen vessels that the excellency may be seen to be of God.

All 'sacerdotal Power is derived from the Holy Ghost'.[32] Christ was consecrated before he began his ministry. He ordained the Apostles with the power of the Holy Ghost. As ministers are ordained to the same function as the Apostles it is necessary that they are ordained in the same way and by the same power. The Apostolic Succession guarantees that present ministers are in line with those originally ordained by Christ. We credit our Bibles because they can be traced back to ancient manuscripts. The Bible itself does not mention the possibility of corruption because it is obvious that the true script must be kept. Hoadly's attack upon the Apostolic Succession concludes equally against the Bible.

It is useless to advocate order for decency's sake. It is not what is authoritative but what is unauthoritative that can be dismissed as a 'Trifle'.[33]

Hoadly dismisses authoritative absolutions because fallible men cannot pronounce what is infallible. This argument declares against the sacraments and Christianity, for no one is infallibly sure that he is qualified to receive the sacraments or that he will be saved. Hoadly doubted whether the Matthaean text giving the Apostles power to bind and loose sins applied to the clergy. Law replies that the Church has always understood that the clergy succeeded to the office of the Apostles. Their power is effective only when the other divinely instituted conditions are in operation.

He will not allow that Christ did not claim to forgive sins. He states his exegetical principle to be that 'the first obvious Sense of the Words . . . [are] the true sense',[34] and analyses Mark 2.9–10 to find the traditional sense upheld. Excluding Christ because forgiveness belongs to God alone argues against his divinity.

There is nothing narrow about traditional Christianity. The Church has always taught that God's uncovenanted mercies reach sincere unbelievers.

In a Postscript Law answers various objections to his *First Letter*.

Some said that as the uninterrupted Succession was not mentioned in Scripture, it was not binding. But the authority of the Bible is not mentioned in the Bible. On this principle how are we to guess that the sacraments are to be the ordinary means of grace in all ages? The priestly office, Sabbath observance, and Sunday worship are not commanded in the Bible. Though not commanded they are well-founded, and therefore we accept them. It is the same with the Apostolic Succession.

To the objection that apostolic practices are not binding Law replies that we must discriminate. We decide which practices to retain from 'the Nature of Things, from the *Tenor* of Scripture, and the *Testimony* of Antiquity'.[35]

The question was asked, Had the Succession been broken? He admits that anything 'founded upon *historical Evidence*' is liable to this criticism. But is there evidence that it has been broken? He thinks not and can mention an excellent written defence of the institution. He believes it also '*morally impossible*' that it should have been.[36] Since the Church has taught the necessity of episcopal ordination there 'has been a constant Guard upon the *episcopal Succession*'.[37]

Law's third and longest *Letter* was published in 1719 and it replied to Hoadly's answer to the *Representation of the Committee of Convocation*. It contains disquisitions upon the nature of the Church, excommunication, external communion, sincerity, and the Reformation.

He begins with questions respecting the Church. Hoadly said it was invisible. No Church on earth can be invisible. The acts of Christians must be partly visible; therefore the Church is visible.

Scripture is in accord with this rational point. Christ's parables of the marriage feast and the fishing net describe an earthly, visible Church with good and bad members. In fact the Church does not differ from earthly government in point of visibility 'but in regard to the *Ends* and *Purposes* for which it is erected, viz., the eternal Salvation of Mankind'.[38]

Hoadly's description contradicts Articles xix and xxxix of the Thirty-Nine Articles since he reckons the invisible Church to be the only true one.

The words of his text have an 'indeterminate' quality. They tell us what the Kingdom is not rather than what it is. The context shows that Jesus is saying that his kingdom is not a 'Temporal Kingdom as the *Jewish* and other Kingdoms are'.[39]

He comes to Hoadly's view of church authority. '*Common* Reason, the *Laws* of God, and our *Country*' indicate the limits of obedience to the relative authority for which Law argues.[40]

Hoadly believes that the office of excommunication only registers the Church's disapproval of the excommunicated person. He also believes that the right of excommunication is invested in all Christians. Law contends that it is a judicial power belonging to particular persons. It is logical to suppose that those who officiate at worship and admit people to worship should have the right to exclude. The act of exclusion 'is *as effectual* towards the taking from them all the Privileges of Christians . . . as their Act of Admission . . . entitled them to all the Benefits of Church-Communion'.[41]

Scripture plainly teaches the office (Matt. 18.15–18; 1 Cor. 5; 1 Tim. 1.19). It is a judicial authority because of God's designation of it as such. The idea finds support also in Christ's promise to be present where two or three are gathered in his name. This statement occurs significantly after the recommendation that an offender should be brought before ordinary Christians.

The purpose of excommunication is to preserve the honour of God and the Church, to reform offenders, to preserve other church members from bad influence, and to act as a deterrent. It is a merciful institution and can be effective only so far as a human institution can be.

Accidental effects flow from the office. We may expect consequences to last into the next world from an office divinely instituted. Neglect by an offender of the meaning of excommunication could lead to terrible ruin. Again, as it is the most powerful means, short of the Last Judgment, of awakening the sinner, those who neglect it can only render themselves 'more odious in the Sight of God, and made ripe for a severer Punishment'.[42]

He rebuts again the assertion that no external authority can oblige us to external communion with the remark that we cannot otherwise appear to ourselves or to others as Christians but by external communion. We are as much called to worship in a distinct fashion as to serve others distinctly. Christianity implies external communion as walking implies motion.

If external communion is an indifferent matter schism would be no grievous sin, but according to the Bible it is (Rom. 16.17). The idea concludes against the sacraments for their intention is to graft people into the Body of Christ.

Private judgement is inevitably involved in the choice of a particular communion. This does not detract from the objective reality of external communion. People could accept or refuse Christ when he was on earth; Heaven and hell are no less real for the fact that people may judge of them as they please. Sincerity is not enough. We have a recommendation to God from our religion as well as from our sincerity. There is true and false religion.

Hoadly stated that if we are obliged to obey church authority the Reformation could not be justified. His false assumption is that only human laws oblige us to external communion. In great matters we must be prepared to obey God rather than men. The question at the Reformation was whether the true religion was 'with the *Reformers*, or with the *Papists*'.[43]

In a Postscript he refers to Hoadly's unwillingness to concede that an erroneous conscience may not wholly justify a man. The only source of proper justification before God is the merits of Christ. We can only add that a person applying more to that source will be more justified, and that a person unconscious of it may be partly justified.

Purely in terms of performance Law vanquished Hoadly and wrote the only piece in the controversy deserving to be read today.

But certain merits and demerits in the substance of the piece are worth mentioning. Law was probably right to see in Hoadly's work the ghost of secularism. Hoadly judged Christianity by reason and his reason was often the tool of the beliefs of an Augustan. After him were to come the agnostics. But we may doubt if Law had taken the full measure of the movement, of which Hoadly was only one representative. Criticism of belief can be the precursor of religious life as well as death. Rational examination of Bible and tradition have not only proved necessary, they have increased our understanding of the past, assisted faith, and enabled the Church to meet opponents on reasonable grounds. Reason correctly showed Hoadly that the position of the Nonjuror could not be maintained and correctly suggested doubts whether bishops were to succeed to the office of apostle and (we may presume) whether the Succession has been maintained. Research has since noted the distinction between apostle and bishop and the impossibility of knowing whether the Succession has been maintained.[44]

Law's High Church convictions are everywhere in evidence. He adheres to the Caroline method in theology.[45] Although this enables him to uphold a robust form of Christianity against the ambiguous assertions of Hoadly, he claims too much for the High Church tradition by identifying Anglicanism with it.

The *via media* of Anglicanism is both Catholic and Reformed and admits different strains of the same belief. Though Law was prepared to unchurch members of non-episcopal churches and maintain a Catholic view of sacraments and ministry we cannot say that Anglicanism, as such, does this. Stillingfleet as a young man supported the conception of a comprehensive Church and believed bishops unessential. Chillingworth and Hales were notably liberal on such matters and Jeremy Taylor drew the distinction between fundamental and non-fundamental articles of belief, considering it wrong to unchurch those who loved God and whom God evidently loved. Scripture and the Apostles' Creed are the minimal standards of belief for Christians.[46] A similar tolerance was maintained by the Latitudinarians, and they must be included within Anglicanism no less than the High Churchmen.

A notable merit of Law's *Letters* is his defence of genuine prayer. His plea for passion in prayer was hardly Augustan and is all the better for that. Whilst it may surprise us to find him making confession and petition the essence of the practice, we should remember that, apart from the influence exerted by his polemical spirit, what could more support the plea for passion than these things? Caroline teaching on personal religion emphasizes the reality of sin and the need for confession to the detriment sometimes of so Catholic an element as adoration.

Law's *Letters* were, of course, controversial pieces. He is argumentative rather than creative, and he is intent to demolish Hoadly. Whilst he quotes from his opponent fairly and is never abusive his use of *reductio ad absurdum* and *argumentum ad hominem* methods means that logic can be sacrificed to display, and wit serve for truth. Hoadly doubtless gave too exclusive an importance to sincerity. There is an essential objective element in Christianity that a merely sincere person may never grasp.

In stressing this, however, Law underestimated the importance of sincerity in enabling the Church genuinely to readjust itself in the Age of Reason. His own future career demonstrates his personal involvement in this very situation.

Law puts an effective question mark against Hoadly's ecclesiastical position, tempting us to submit to this point recollecting the ambiguity in Hoadly's case and crediting wit with understanding. But whilst Hoadly's version of Latitudinarianism reduced Christianity, Law's version could ossify it and did not escape a narrowing dogmatism. The truth lay somewhere between the two positions and Law's later career again demonstrates his admission of this.

# 3

## LIFE UNTIL 1723 AND THE REPLY TO MANDEVILLE

During the silence of these years Law must have made various friendships. One such was likely to have been with Mr Gibbon of Putney, into whose house he entered in 1723 as tutor of Edward (father of the future historian). Archibald Hutcheson, M.P. was later to request his wife to lead a retired life after his death and ask Law to guide her. That two men of the world should form so high an opinion of Law is some testimony to his integrity and lack of sentimentality.

There have been left to us two penitential prayers written by Law at this time. They remind us of his seriousness.[1] One is a 'Prayer of deep humiliation'. Though his confession is long and severe, he mentions no particular sin. We cannot determine if he had been ill-tempered with someone or whether he was making use of the penitential season in the Church Calendar. He accuses himself of being 'an unclean worm, a dead dog, a stinking carcase'. Even here he is faithful to the Caroline divines. The exact words are used also, not by Baxter or Bunyan, but by Andrewes who derived them from the Old Testament and medieval religion.[2] Both prayers are pervaded by biblical phrases and the Prayer Book petition: 'And be not angry with me for ever'. There is deep urgency in his petition:

> O God, let me never see such another day as this. Let me never again be so oppressed with guilt, as to run away from thy presence, and be forced to abstain from the society of thy children.

Nor is he a Pelagian:

> Extend the atonement of thy Son's blood to me, a forlorn creature; and let not my sins utterly separate me from thy mercy in Christ Jesus.

30

His second prayer was written 'on entering holy Orders'. As mature Christian expression came early to William Law, it is difficult to decide whether to date it 1711, when he became a deacon, or 1727, when he was made a priest. He mentions 'further office at thy holy table' and petitions for evangelical zeal for labour among his 'fellow-christians'.

These prayers may well have taken the place of auricular confession. Taylor, Hall, Cosin, Ken, the author of *The Whole Duty of Man*, and other High Churchmen commended auricular confession, without stipulating its necessity.[3] Law never refers to the practice and we have no record that he ever made use of it.

In 1718 his mother died, leaving George and William in trust to dispose of her estate. Why William was chosen as one trustee and not his elder brothers, Thomas or Giles, we cannot surmise. Possibly a specially intimate relation existed between William and his mother. At any rate she left her six surviving children £115 each.

Law's reading and thinking had certainly continued in these years and when an enlarged edition of Mandeville's *The Fable of the Bees* was published, he replied to it immediately.

Bernard de Mandeville (1670–1733) was born in Rotterdam, studied medicine, and after travelling settled in London for life. He married an Englishwoman and practised medicine. He was fond of the coffee-house and tavern, spoke easily and loosely, had the reputation of being a non-believer, and (without evidence) of being vicious.

His masterpiece was the book in question. It took him twenty years to complete.[4] His original doggerel poem, *The Grumbling Hive: or Knaves Turn'd Honest*, was republished in 1723 with a number of explicatory essays added. By 1732 the work had been much enlarged, though his opinions remained substantially the same.

These opinions became very clear with the 1723 edition of his work. They created a stir. The Grand Jury of Middlesex presented the book as a public nuisance. Law wrote his refutation.

Mandeville ranged widely through the fields of religion, politics, ethics, and economics. Though diffuse and paradoxical his prose breathes life. Like Hoadly and Law he responds to the

crisis of the times. His inspiration comes mainly from Renaissance scepticism. He refers often to Montaigne, for whom reason
and religion were antithetical, but his chief mentor was Pierre
Bayle.

Hazard correctly sees Bayle as an important influence in
bringing to birth the modern mentality. He honoured reason
and truth and, through his wide reading and aggressive spirit,
was able to cast a lurid light on the progress of the Church and
State through the ages. He believed that nothing could be
known with certainty and objected to religion because it
appealed to mystery; respect for which he believed was incompatible with a rational mind. An observer in 1729 recognized that Bayle had brought religious and moral unsettlement
to many people.

Mandeville was not a careful writer, and like Bayle could
not always be as explicit as he wished. His basic theme was that
what is often condemned as vice works for the good of society;
that ascetical virtue is incompatible with utilitarian standards
of living; that men are moved by passions, not reason; that
passions are actuated by self-love.

He imagines human society as a hive of bees. He finds
'Millions endeavouring to supply/each others lust and vanity;/
. . . no calling was without deceit.' With the result that 'every
part was full of vice/ yet the whole mass a paradise'. A cry went
up to make the people honest. In anger Jove answered the cry
and the hive languished through lack of economic demand and
competition. The moral is drawn that we should be content
with the moral *status quo*.

A variety of ideas emerge from his explicatory essays. Religion
masks the selfish nature of man to convince him that he is
virtuous. Pity is a weak passion, most in evidence in the weaker
sex, women. If our hearts were open to the public gaze, we
should be despised. Vice helps society to prosper. Thus smiths
would be out of work if thieves gave up their crime. Contrary
parties assist each other. The Reformers stimulated the Roman
Catholics to reform and prostitutes enable ladies to live virtuously. We should no more dispute men's morals than their
tastes. Epicurus considered pleasure the highest good. Charity
is a passion, not a virtue. Extensively administered it produces
sloth. Charity schools are to be condemned, for they educate

the poor above their stations; a prosperous nation needs poor labourers. Custom, not truth, determines social habits. We cannot determine the truth of religion for there are so many. Polygamy is right for the Mohammedan, wrong for the Christian.

Mandeville's work proved seminal. A variety of distinguished men, including Hume, Adam Smith, and Dr Johnson acknowledged their debt to him. Berkeley, Gibbon, Rousseau, and Kant gave him specific attention.

Law's *Remarks Upon a Book, Entitled The Fable of the Bees* was published in 1723.[6] Though an advocate for Mandeville, Kaye allows that Law's short book 'is the ablest of all the replies to Mandeville, and in some ways [it is] to be ranked, as literature, with the *Fable*. It is a masterpiece of controversial writing.'[7]

He limits his aim to 'the Examination of such Passages as expose *moral Virtue*, as a Fraud and Imposition'.[8]

Mandeville believed man an animal flattered out of his natural state by the craft of moralists. Law believes that man and morality are both destroyed by Mandeville's estimate of man.

He defines man as a '*Compound of various Passions, that all of them as they are provoked, and come uppermost, govern him by turns*'.[9] Such a definition, says Law, would fit a wolf as well as a Greek philosopher. Though Mandeville believes he has defined man, his definition makes us incapable of believing anything. He must conclude that Newton's 'Reach of Thought [was] only so many blind Sallies of Passion'.[10]

Men are moral because they are made in the image of God. We have been helped by various oracles sent by God, especially Christ, so that we may aspire to be as the angels.

It is absurd to say that his inquiry omitted Christian considerations and considered man in his state of nature only. There could only have been one origin of virtue. In any case Mandeville's man must have been without virtue or religion. Noah and his descendants were never in this position, and Mandeville founds his observations upon the only people of whom he has knowledge, that is, Christians.

Morality cannot have originated in pride. This would mean that the humblest man 'is the greatest distance he can be placed from moral Virtue'.[11] Nor can we say that the first moralists appealed to pride to inculcate morality. We might as well

argue that the appeal to pride first raised man from his original
creeping position to an erect stature.

> Were not the first Principles and Reasons of Morality
> connatural to us, and essential to our Minds, there would
> have been nothing for the moral Philosophers to have
> improved upon. . . . *Music* supposes a confessed Perception of
> various Sounds; and *moral Philosophy* supposes an acknow-
> ledged difference of Good and Evil. . . . It is thus in all
> Sciences; the rationality of our Nature contains the first
> Rules, or Principles, and it is the Speculation of Man that
> builds and enlarges upon them.[12]

Truth and reason never had a beginning. If they did they
must be temporal, whereas they are eternal. Moral virtue is
simply '*Truth* and *Reason*, considered in relation to Actions'.[13]
In itself moral virtue never had a beginning. Considered in
relation to man's knowledge it began with Adam.

As for the obligatory nature of morality, 'The reasonableness
. . . of Actions themselves is a Law to rational Beings, and the
sight of that reasonableness carries an Obligation'. God is good,
not because of some external coercive force, but because of the
excellence of goodness. Because God wills it moral virtue is our
law. If, in common with men of all generations, we ascribe
infinite justice, goodness, and truth to God we must admit their
force in our own lives.

Section II begins with Mandeville's claim that morality is
founded in education, natural temper, or blind impulse. A
humble man does a good action because of the pleasurable
feeling it gives him. To disprove this Law supposes the opposite:
the proud man performing an action to enjoy his vileness.
Therefore, 'Virtue is Man's Duty, not as a Task that is imposed
upon him, but as it is the only Practice, that is the natural
Pleasure and proper Good of his being'. It is the nature of virtue
to give happiness and it loses none of its value because some
can perform it 'with Delight'.[14]

Against Mandeville's conception of ascetic virtue Law says
that it is duty and not self-denial that constitutes virtue. God
united man's rational nature with a physical body so that they
should generally act together. The body is meant to be an
'agent' for the rational nature. Pleasure is the body's reaction

to a delightful thought conceived in the mind. Such bodily assistances no more lessen the merit of virtuous action than 'Fasting and Prayer make our Piety less excellent, because it was assisted by them'.[15]

To say that habit makes people virtuous is to say that no principle of reason or duty prompts our action. But if we admit these principles in human action, it is impossible to prove that temperament has a greater share in it than reason. The presence of reason in an action can be proved from the fact that a bad action committed in the heat of kindled emotion brings sorrow after the subsidence of emotion. The origin of this concurrence between body and reason in good action is attributed to 'the Remains of that primitive Rectitude of Body and Mind before the Fall'.[16]

Law will not admit the degradation of pity. It springs from right judgement. To say that women have most of it because they have the weakest minds is to make an assertion without proof. In any case he tacitly agrees that women are pitiful from some principle of judgement.

But Law is no simple-minded rationalist. Reason has a thousand impediments diverting its force. A man can be wise one moment and foolish the next. The weakness of reason is evident even in speculative matters. Though Descartes had demonstrated many solid truths Newton was able to prove a vacuum where he had supposed a plenum. An additional difficulty with moral actions is the variety and hiddenness of motive.

This section ends with a display of irritation at free-thinkers and the observation that there is no argument on their side and that they only eclipse their fellows in arrogance.

In Section III Law notes that Mandeville dismissed inquiry into religious truth because the pursuit worked so much mischief and because so many answers were forthcoming. He replied from the Bible that God commands men to seek him and that the greatest happiness is promised to Christians. The very fact of false religion suggests the possibility of true religion. There is variety of good food and false money, but we allow the genuineness of both.

Many of his objections to religion and morality spring from his dislike of religion. But the Deist and free-thinker have as

D

many articles as the Christian 'and require a much greater Suspension of our Reason to believe them'.[17] If faith is 'an Assent of the Mind to some Proposition, of which we have no certain Knowledge', the Deist is more credulous than the Christian. Take the question of the resurrection of the dead. Supposing it to be true the Christian's belief is supported by all possible evidence. By contrast the Deist needs great faith for his disbelief, and has no evidence. Thus 'the *Christian* is the rational Believer, and the *Deist* the Blind Bigot'.[18] Those who laugh at religion have the strongest argument against it. Only if we think soberly will it seem important, and we are so little affected by it because 'The Concerns of the World keep our Spirits in a constant Hurry'.[19]

In Section V Law attacks Mandeville's belief that a 'certain hope' is nonsense. He indicates that 'Hope, or Expectation, does not imply *Uncertainty*, but *Futurity*'. It is certain or otherwise as the thing hoped for is certain or not. Applied to the future life we can be certain as God has informed us of it.

Law recognizes the fundamental difference between himself and Mandeville. He believes that the consequence of Mandeville's philosophy will be the destruction of civilization. Thus: 'Should I now lament the miserable Fruits of *Free-thinking*, which thus tend not only to set us loose from the Regards of Religion, but to destroy whatever is reasonable, decent, or comely in human Nature, though as a Friend of Religion I might be censured by *some*, yet surely as an advocate for the Dignity of Man, I might be pardoned by *all*.'[20]

He also rejects Mandeville's condemnation of charity schools. 'Whilst we can preserve but the very Name of Religion, a charitable Contribution to educate Children in it, must be reckoned amongst our best Works'.[21]

In a skilful Postscript Law draws on the works of Bayle, whom he recognizes as Mandeville's chief source, indicating his contradictoriness. He states that no law can be given concerning the human mind, but elsewhere gives one. He says that religion and belief do not affect conduct, and elsewhere the opposite.

We may trace Law's literary sources to the Carolines and Malebranche in particular. The Carolines accepted a rational, idealist philosophy. They believed in natural theology and that reason is in God. Thus Taylor's chief ethical work assumes that 'God is in our hearts by his laws'.[22]

Malebranche's thought is pervasively present in this work. We have noted previously his remarks concerning the concurrence between body and mind and his belief that reason is a transcendental faculty. We may add a few characteristic quotations from Law's underlined copy of Malebranche's *A Treatise of Morality*. 'The *Reason* of Man is the *Word*, or the Wisdom of God himself; for every Creature is a particular Being, but the Reason of Man is Universal.'[23] Order is the rule by which God acts.[24] Self-love is inherently evil.

As against Descartes and Duns Scotus Law sides with Malebranche and the Platonists in believing that there is an eternal fitness in things. They had argued that a thing is right only because God willed it to be so.

Apart from an occasional asperity of tone this is an admirable writing of Law. The close shrewd argument and frequent wit, no less than his psychological observations, make excellent reading. We cannot determine the victor in the debate for it is not resolvable at the rational level. Though guilty of rash words Mandeville represents secular man with the courage to draw the consequences of his belief. Law is a religious man conscious of the crisis in belief. That there was only a limited meeting of minds is evident in the discussion of virtue. Law upholds the traditional concept, Mandeville uses the familiar word to substantiate something different. But that the confrontation was not simply between the new and the old, is evident from the fact that although Law sometimes quotes the Bible to refute Mandeville (and really the Bible is in question), it is Law and not Mandeville who champions women and the education of the young poor.[25]

# 4

## LIFE AT THE GIBBONS' AND
## 'STAGE ENTERTAINMENTS'

In 1723 Law entered the house of Edward Gibbon, as chaplain and private tutor of Gibbon's son, Edward, who was then about thirteen years of age. Gibbon had some sympathy with the Stuart cause.

His dwelling was 'a spacious house, with gardens and lands, at Putney, in Surrey, where he resided in decent hospitality'.[1] Law resided there until 1738–9, his employer having died in 1737. The appointment brought Law a much needed degree of worldly security. That the advantage was not felt to be all on one side emerges from Gibbon's testimony; 'In our family he had left the reputation of a worthy and pious man, who believed all that he professed, and practised all that he enjoined'.[2] It seems that the care of Edward's sister, Hester, passed in some measure to Law. She was about seventeen when Law came to Putney. According to Low she had something of her father's manly understanding and a certain rigidity and moroseness of temper.[3] Her relation with Law endured. She joined him at King's Cliffe with Mrs Hutcheson in 1743/4.

Edward went up to Emmanuel College in 1723. He remained in residence until 1725, returning to Cambridge in 1727 and remaining this time until 1734. Law accompanied Edward to the university.

He seems to have been dull and wayward. We find him leaving Law and Byrom when they exchange ideas; agreeing, after procrastinating, to learn shorthand from Byrom but so busying himself with cards and other diversions that he makes no progress in the skill. He wrote badly and slowly. There is mention of Law intervening to reconcile father and son in a disagreement about smoking.[4] It has been suggested that he served as a model for Flatus, the inconstant man, in the *Serious Call*.

Living for years as virtually a member of the Gibbon family, Law was no recluse. Through the elder Gibbon the practical life of the business man impinged upon him; through the family generally, and Edward and Hester especially, domestic care and affection. His circle of correspondents and visitors increased with time. His activities among Nonjurors continued, as when he witnessed the consecration of Henry Hall as Non-juror bishop in 1725. Association with Cambridge University continued through Edward's education. Then there was London!

Of course he saw London through the spectacles of his time and beliefs. Middle-class life and the life of churchmen he assesses shrewdly, but the metropolis could show much more than these. There were the trash and filth littering the streets, inadequate drainage and sewerage. There were the brutal amusements and hard drinking of the poor, disease, and death. The social system meant that the poor were downtrodden. They often lived in cellars because they had no houses. Often they went without employment. Boys could work in difficult dull jobs for thirteen hours a day. Lack of decent amusement and free time drove the deprived to brutality.[5] Law must have known about all this and the knowledge contributed to his evaluation of human life. We know that he was always chari-table and that he became a notable philanthropist. But we look in vain in his writings, as in those of most of his contem-poraries, for a genuine understanding of social conditions and a plan for social betterment.

Of his personal appearance and social habits we know little. Jeremy Taylor usually adorned his works with his portrait, for he was handsome. It is typical of Law that he refused to have his portrait painted. There was reticence and humility in this, reminding us of St John of the Cross. There was also a certain distaste for the body. The attitude is typical of some Platonists. Plotinus had refused any physical likeness to be made of him because he 'seemed ashamed of being in the body'.[6]

Happily, we have some verbal accounts of his appearance. Tighe learned from residents at King's Cliffe that he was 'in stature rather over than under the middle size; not corpulent, but stout made, with broad shoulders; his visage was round, his eyes grey; his features well proportioned, and not large;

his complexion ruddy, and his countenance open and agreeable. He was naturally more inclined to be merry than sad.'[7]

A contributor to the *Gentleman's Magazine* in 1800 confirmed that Law was 'remarkably cheerful in his temper'.[8] Against this we have the remark of Wesley's sister that he was 'the picture of the Law itself, for severity and gravity'. She mentioned his adverse comments on women's dress in the *Serious Call*. Low quotes Charles Wesley's biographer, T. Jackson, to the effect that Law was stern, sour, and repulsive. It seems likely that until after middle life Law could be stern and occasionally sour, but that Jackson exaggerates. His strictures on women's dress and general gravity sufficiently explain Wesley's sister's view. We must remember also the odd simplicity of his own dress. He usually wore a clerical hat with the loops down, a grey wig, and a black coat. On first acquaintance Byrom described him as a 'poor happy man' and 'unfashionable'. But he adds significantly that 'Our young brethren were mightily pleased with him'. Not so Byrom's friend, Mr Green, who reported that Law was about to stop wearing a wig and that he was considered half-crazy.[9]

It is worth remembering that Law had little money to spare on clothes, inclination apart, and that his introvert temperament and bachelor carelessness may have made its contribution to a certain whimsicality of appearance. It would be interesting to know how much the practice of mortification, chosen and otherwise, contributed to sharpness of manner. At the same time favourable reports, the general direction of his life, and the wit and spiritual understanding apparent in his writings suggest that his affability and joy were real.

His writings suggest also what we know from other sources, that Law was a strong personality and ready speaker. Considering Wesley's own powers the following brief reflection is remarkable: 'I spent an hour with Mr Shelton, I think, full as extraordinary man as Mr Law; of full as rapid a genius; so that I had little to do but to hear; his words flowing like a river.'[10] According to Hester Gibbon he kept good health and we may believe that fact mingled with idolatry in her testimony that 'His eye was piercing, for it was the organ of his immortal soul, filled with divine light'.[11]

His personal habits were less rigorist than his writings might lead us to suppose. When Law and Byrom met for the first time, at Putney in 1729, they availed themselves of the amenities of the house and shared a bottle of French wine. When Byrom told Law that he was turning part of the *Serious Call* into verses, 'they laughed, and Mr Law said he must have a copy of them, and desired I would not put the whole book into verse, for then it would not sell in prose—so the good man can joke'. He proceeded to interest Law in shorthand. At dinner in 1737 he noticed that Law ate soup, beef, etc., and drank two glasses of red wine, toasting Church and King, and 'all friends'.[12] By the time he retired to King's Cliffe we know that he smoked a pipe of tobacco before going to bed. He offered Byrom tobacco at Cambridge in 1730.[13]

There is no need to emphasize that his scholarly habits continued. He told Byrom that well before 1735 'he had perhaps rummaged every bookseller's shop and bookstall in the metropolis'.[14] He was looking for religious and some philosophical writers of course. Sparse references in his writings to Plato Epictetus, Descartes, and such thinkers suggest that his early interest in the broader field of philosophy was maintained. But we cannot imagine William Law regaling himself with Horace or Shakespeare.

Law's authorship was also maintained. All that is bad or useless in his thought comes out in his pamphlet, *The Absolute Unlawfulness of Stage Entertainment* (1726). Though it excited well-earned opposition, and some support, Law so little repented of it that he had most of it reprinted in *Christian Perfection* and upheld its value in the *Serious Call* (p. 77).

In order to appreciate his condemnation of the stage we may outline the historical traditions bearing on the subject. Only through hellenistic influence did the Jews interest themselves in drama. The Church inherited the more usual Jewish ideas, and the memory of Salome and the Court of Herod Antipas confirmed the Christians' suspicions. Hope of Christ's imminent return kept Christians away from the amphitheatre as from a triviality often sordid, but as that hope declined, they were to be found there. The Church generally did not support the drama, and gladiatorial shows were condemned for their brutality and coarsening influence. It was thought that contact with other spectacles might bring contact with idolatry. Athletic shows were considered wasteful of time and money. In fact indecency often attended dramatic performances. In Imperial times copulation and executions took place on the stage. It is also true that the acting profession drew many members from the riff-raff of society. In the sixth century, Justinian, influenced by the Church, closed the theatres.

In medieval times the Church initiated drama. The Bible-History and Morality brought the drama out of the Church and eventually into the market-place. The Tree of Knowledge, as conceived by the schools of Hugh of St Victor, Abelard, and others, ranked the theatre as a practical science along with medicine, defence, etc., helping to heal the wound in man caused by sin. Great progress had been made by Elizabethan times. Queen Elizabeth attended a play in 1562 and we read of eminent persons giving their patronage to actors. The sixteenth-century play-goer was often a more disciplined person than his eighteenth- and nineteenth-century counterpart.

With the Puritans in power the theatres were closed by parliamentary ordinance in 1642, because they raised political and social objections. Under the Stuarts the London theatre had become attached to the Royalist cause. In the time of the Commonwealth the theatre had become a convenient meeting place for subversive purposes. Moral objections were based on the circumstances of Elizabethan times. Plays were connected with the way in which the medieval Church popularized itself. Elizabethan drama was identified with an Italianate habit of behaviour. Even so, we find that the first English opera, *The Siege of Rhodes*, was publicly performed with Puritan approval in 1656.

The theatre was revived under Charles II. The introduction of actresses increased the notoriety of the profession, sometimes with good reason. Though Restoration drama in the person of Congreve could rise to subtle and polished heights, coarseness and abuse were frequent. Thus Manly in Wycherley's *The Plain Dealer* (staged 1674) asks someone to 'pimp' for him and threatens a woman, 'I will lie with her out of revenge'. The just comment of E. Legouis on Restoration comedy is that 'If it were not tainted with an astonishing grossness or hinted obscenity, it would be one of the glories of the English theatre.'

The audience was not only interested in drama, however. Riff-raff filled the cheaper part of the house and the fashionable world loved to gossip and display themselves there.[15]

Modern drama was first attacked with vigour by the Puritans. W. Prynne considered popular stage plays to be 'sinful, heathenish, lewd, ungodly spectacles'. Anglicans took up the attack. Law himself refers to the work of Collier, Blackmore, and Bedford.[16] We can believe Law to be in virtual agreement with the Nonjuror, Collier. About Shakespeare Collier informs us, '[he] is too guilty to make evidence . . . when there is most smut there is least sense'. Plays erred in showing priests or criticizing the upper classes. He took exception to an irreverent use of biblical phrases. So popular was Collier's pamphlet that the King issued a proclamation against vice and profaneness. Congreve and D'Urfey were prosecuted. A writer in *The Oxford Companion to the Theatre* comments very fairly that Collier said a number of courageous and true things; that his work aided overdue reforms of the stage; that it was marred by ignorance, pedantry, and the failure to recognize that immorality on the stage reflected rather than encouraged immorality in life.[17]

Another Nonjuror, Robert Nelson, together with the Society for Promoting Christian Knowledge, remonstrated against the plays of the day. In 1703 he read Tillotson's words against plays to the Society. They printed them for distribution to ladies of quality. In a footnote it is asked whether *The Tempest* is suitable for acting after a storm.[18]

Concern for the effect of plays on public morals was widespread in Law's day. In 1737 Barnard, an ex-Quaker merchant, introduced a bill into Parliament to limit the number of playhouses in London. Walpole supported the measure and tried to secure the power of the Lord Chamberlain to license plays. When Barnard realized that Walpole's aim was to prevent plays attacking him he withdrew his bill. By reading the most offensive parts of *The Golden Rump* to the House Walpole gained his end!

It is evident that Law was only subscribing to well-known arguments in criticizing and even in outlawing plays. He begins by appreciating that some will regard him as a 'fanatic'. However, a sin remains the same whether committed in Church

or in the playhouse. 'The Stage . . . is condemned, as Drunkenness and Lewdness, as Lying and Profaneness are to be condemned, not as Things that may only be the Occasion of Sin,
but such as are in their own Nature grossly sinful.' What you
hear—and apparently only hear—in the playhouse are
'*Ribaldry* and *Profaneness*; that you entertain your Mind with
extravagant *Thoughts*, wild *Rants*, *blasphemous Speeches*, *wanton
Amours*, *profane Jests*, and *impure Passions*'.[19] As the purpose of
religion is to purify our corrupt natures, plays must be deemed
grossly sinful as they seek only to foster corruption.

The Bible teaches us that only good communications should
be spoken and warns us not to grieve the Holy Spirit (Eph.
4.29–30). Such teaching condemns playhouses. Actors may as
well be thieves as mouth the blasphemies they must. To become
part of the audience for their performances makes one a party
to their sin.

Playgoers need not be as immoral as the plays they watch of
course. '*Prejudice*, the Force of *Education*, the Authority of
*Numbers*, the Way of the World, the example of *great Names*'
sway the reason.[20] That familiarity disguises the evil in play-
going becomes apparent if we consider the use of cosmetics or
masquerades. Most people see that reason and religion condemn
these, and they do so because they have been practised only
recently. There follows a summary of a popular, contemporary
play. He compares its sentimental and trivial scenes with the
more rigorous parts of the Bible.

The pleasures we approve indicate the state of our minds.
If we are inwardly corrupt we will approve of corruption on the
stage. Otherwise we should be offended by stage productions.

An innocent play can be imagined no more easily than
innocent lust. At the moment the state of things in the theatre
is very bad. He quotes the mild Tillotson to the effect that
attendance at plays today contradicts the profession of Christianity.

It is no use excusing play-going on the grounds that it is a
small sin. To talk of a small sin is like talking of a small law of
God. 'Every Sin, as it is a Transgression of some Law of God,
must needs be a great one.' Only sins of '*Infirmity*, *Ignorance*, or
*Surprise*' carry less guilt. Wilfully persisted in, play-going becomes
a great sin.[21]

Small sins easily grow in their significance. 'Perhaps, as many People have lived and died unaffected with Religion, through a Course of *Diversions* and *Pleasures*, as through Gluttony and Intemperance'.[22] We should be careful of the diversions we indulge in as they 'take such deep hold of us'. Nor should we stress their importance because 'they have no necessary Foundation in Nature, but are our own Inventions . . . so many *Blanks in Life*'. At best they are methods of losing time, and the most innocent have something in them 'that seems to want a Pardon'.[23]

We have mentioned obvious sources for Law's views on the stage in the High Church and Nonjuror tradition. In distinction to some, for instance Collier, who absolved Molière from grave fault, it is notable that Law condemns the stage in the most rigorist fashion.

In some measure he could find support in the Caroline divines who refused the traditional distinction between mortal and venial sins. Such a distinction was held to be unbiblical and too conciliatory towards venial sins. But it is another matter to say that diversions in general and plays in particular are sinful. According to Jeremy Taylor, 'Natural necessity and the example of St John, who recreated himself with sporting with a tame partridge, teach us, that it is lawful to relax and unbend our bow, but not to suffer it to be unready or unstrung'.[24] Even John Wesley could speak of the 'noble game of quarter-staff' and recommend the value of poetry, music, history, and the rest. He believed that others, though not himself, might be able to play cards and attend the theatre with a clear conscience.[25] We find Byrom attending plays appreciatively.[26]

It is likely that Law knew of Bossuet's *Maximes sur la Comédie* (1694), in which a cleric was refuted who contended that the presentation of comedies was not necessarily harmful to public morals. Drawing support from Augustine, Chrysostom, and other Fathers he thundered against the evils of Comedy, that through laughter open the door to licence. Though God intends us to be happy, the delight of the play-goer is vain and may be compensated for by an eternity of torment. As the spectator must associate himself with the characters impersonated, fictitious sin is encouraged to become real in people's lives.

Francis de Sales had permitted Philothée to attend the theatre
so long as she did not allow the pleasure to absorb her. That the
French Church agreed more with Bossuet than with de Sales
is suggested by the fact that comedians were refused the sacraments in their life-time and Christian burial at death. Molière
was refused Christian burial.[27]

The extremity of Law's views suggests an origin, not only in
a church tradition, but also in his intemperate nature. Personal
unbalance and harshness find expression in this pamphlet. Such
a thought is strengthened when we notice that he is guilty of
misrepresentation. He enlisted the support of Tillotson in his
condemnation of plays. Read in context, however, Tillotson's
words state that present-day plays are to be condemned, but
that if they were improved in moral quality they could be
innocent, diverting, and useful. John Dennis pointed out Law's
error. But with every new edition of the work and of *Christian
Perfection*, in which much of it reappears, Law's original use of
Tillotson remains.

Together with misunderstanding the importance of play in
life, Law's main error lay in misunderstanding the purpose of
drama as the portrayal and criticism of life. That drama can
also transfigure life with an inspiration akin to religion would
be a view incomprehensible to Law and Bossuet, despite the
work of Shakespeare and Racine.

# 5

## 'CHRISTIAN PERFECTION'

We proceed to a much worthier publication which came out in the same year of 1726, namely *A Practical Treatise upon Christian Perfection*. Law was about forty years of age when he wrote it and had he written no more, his reputation as a prose writer and ascetic theologian would have been established. The title of the book also illustrates two dominant traits in his personality, the concern to be practical and the primary importance of growth in holiness.

The perfection he recommends 'calls no one to a *Cloister*, but to a right and full performance of those Duties, which are necessary for all Christians, and common to all States of Life'.[1] It is the heart that finds expression in our actions, and it is the heart, therefore, that must be made perfect. Though some men are more gifted than others and may accomplish more for God, he is equally pleased with the total dedication of the ordinary person.

A latent Pelagianism is discernible in the reflection that 'Perhaps it cannot be said of the best of Men that ever lived, that they performed their Duty in such Perfection in all Instances, as they might have done'.[2] At any rate we must endeavour after perfection, otherwise we might find ourselves in hell in the life to come.

After this Introduction Law begins by considering the design of Christianity to wean us from our disordered state to an enjoyment of the divine nature. Christianity has shown us the infinite goodness of God. We have been granted

A Revelation made to the World by his Son Jesus Christ. This Revelation has laid open the great Secrets of Providence from the Creation of the World, explained the present State of Things, and given Man all the Information that is necessary to quiet his Anxieties, content him with his Condition, and lead him safely to everlasting Rest and Happiness.[3]

Previously 'Man was a mere Riddle to himself, and his Condition full of Darkness and Perplexity'.[4]

This revelation teaches us that 'we have a Spirit within us, that was created after the Divine Image, that this Spirit is now in a fallen corrupt Condition, that the Body in which it is now placed, is its Grave . . . where it is enslaved to fleshly Thoughts, blinded with false Notions of Good and Evil, and dead to all Taste and Relish of its true Happiness . . . the world . . . is also in a disordered irregular State, and cursed for the Sake of Man . . . Devils also, and evil Spirits, have here their Residence . . . seeking whom they may devour'.[5]

He summarizes his point in words permanently important for him: the fundamental truths of Christianity are 'the deplorable Corruption of human Nature, and its new Birth in Christ Jesus. The one includes all the Misery, the other all the Happiness of Man'.[6]

Only by continual vigilance will we better our condition. Because our senses only make contact with this world we are easily deceived as to the truth. Our bodies are struck out of the account of happiness by our Lord's statement that we should not fear those who can kill the body and no more (Luke 12.4). We must adopt an attitude suitable to the greatness of our condition. We are to be present at the end of all visible things, appear before the judgement seat of God, and spend an eternity in heaven or hell.

The insignificance of the honours of this life appears from these honours themselves. But 'Every man sees the Littleness of all Sorts of Honours, but those which he is looking after himself.'[7]

With heaven as our aim we should pass through this life like an arrow through the air.

He moves to a consideration of the changed nature required of us. The doctrine of the new birth is at the centre of our faith. (He quotes such texts as John 1.12; 3.5; Romans 8.9; 1 Cor. 6.17.) Thus:

It is not therefore any Number of moral Virtues, no partial Obedience, no Modes of Worship, no external Acts of Adora-

tion, no Articles of Faith, but a new Principle of Life, an
entire Change of Temper, that makes us true Christians.[8]

There are certain marks indicative of the new birth. St John
tells us that if we are born of God we shall overcome the world.
We must, therefore, be in opposition to all vain worldly projects.
The same writer also tells us that if we are born of God we will
not commit sin. This means that we are to hate sin and try to
overcome it. Christ tells us that if we would be called the children of God we must love our enemies. Our only foe is the Devil.

The great change Christianity introduces us to is also represented in the Bible as death (Col. 3.2; Rom. 6.4, etc.).

> We are to enter into this State of Death at our Baptism . . .
> so that Christian Baptism is not only an external Rite, by
> which we entered into the external Society of Christ's Church,
> but is a solemn Consecration, which presents us an Offering
> to God, as Christ was offered at his Death.[9]

The rite is ineffective, however, unless our lives are changed.

He comes to a matter of crucial importance, the renunciation
of the world and of all worldly tempers. There is 'entire Enmity'
between the gospel and the world.[10] The parable of the Great
Supper shows that 'Christianity is a Calling that puts an End to
all other Callings'. Everything is trifling apart from the one
thing needful.[11] He allows that there are just wants of nature,
but we must pursue them 'with a kind of Indifference' so that
'our Souls may be truly sensible of greater Wants'.[12]

Law will not admit the argument of Latitudinarians that
the different position of the Church in the world—the world
having been Christianized—makes a rational piety sufficient.
There has only been an external change. If we match ourselves
against the Sermon on the Mount or listen to our Saviour's
advice to the Rich Young Ruler we shall admit the fundamental
change required. He will allow, however, that miracles are an
accidental feature of the gospel no longer needed.

Christ requires the inward, not necessarily the outward,
renunciation of wealth. Such renunciation is the very heart of
piety and we can check the legitimacy of a possession or action
by seeing if we can make it the subject of prayer.

He does not wish the privileged classes to disappear, for

distinctions in civil life have their use and even necessity. But
the rich must not use their money selfishly. It must be devoted
to 'the Relief of their distressed Brethren'.[13] The poor should
not be discontented for the rewards of religion should make
them thankful. There is no room for snobbery among men,
however, since 'Sin is their only Baseness, and Holiness their
only Honour'.[14]

It is not easy to live virtuously amid worldly splendour. In
fact 'every Virtue . . . is a progressive Temper of Mind, and
always equally labouring to preserve itself'.[15] If we object that
the advice is more fit for angels than men it remains that God
requires such striving from us.

He begins his meditations upon self-denial and mortification
with a phrase often used by Nonjurors in adversity: 'Christianity is a *Doctrine of the Cross*'.[16] We are reminded thus of the
proper foundation of the Faith, namely, the Atonement, and
that Christians must 'make themselves Sufferers for Sin'. If
suffering is the necessary atonement for sin we cannot think
that sinners will be excused from it.[17] We must 'labour to be
*holy* in order to be accepted of God'.[18]

It is true that the Prayer Book says that Christ's sacrifice is
a sufficient sacrifice for sin. It is so in that it supplants the need
for legal sacrifices; in that it need not be repeated; in that it
allows God to accept us on the terms of the New Covenant.
But the way of Jesus Christ is a way with atonement in it.
Our sufferings, in imitation of him, have atoning value. Death
is a suffering for sin, and we must all die.

The command to take up our crosses and follow Christ refers
to the sufferings we are to inflict upon ourselves. Self-denial
is as important as the gospel-sacraments. They have value
because Christ instituted them but acts of self-denial 'have an
*internal* and *essential* Relation to Holiness and Purification in the
*present State* of Man'.[19] Because we are corrupt mortification is
as important as the virtues which will last for ever. Indeed,
'All our Self-denials as Punishments of Sin, as Expressions of
Sorrow for Guilt, and as Preventions of Temptation, may be
considered as so many Instances of our Love of Purity.'[20]

Mortification should be regular and may extend even to
denying ourselves the benefits of the civil law out of obedience
to the Sermon on the Mount.

Opposition to mortification usually stems from those false ideals of life that seek to add religion to worldly living. But our souls need desperately to be saved.

Such self-denial is reasonable because it is the biblical requirement and 'When God speaks, we are as sure that infinite Reason speaks, as we are sure there is a God.'[21] As we are rationally offended by the antics of a madman, we may reflect that God is offended by the follies and stupidities of mankind.

> Religion is our *Cure*, it is God's merciful Communication of such Rules and Discipline of Life, as may serve to deliver us from the *Infatuation* and *Ignorance* of our fallen State.[22] Like madmen we are pleased with our corrupt state, so that God must impress his instructions upon us with terrors and threatenings. As he is Love he can 'only love such Things as are Lovely'.[23]

As we live in the unloveliness of sin we should not be surprised that God cannot make us happy now.

Fasting has a scriptural basis (Matt. 6.17–18) but it is also reasonable. Over-eating stupefies us and makes us reluctant to engage in spiritual activities. 'The Fall of Man consists very much in the Fall of the Soul into the Dominion and Power of the Body, whose Joy, and Health, and Strength, is often the Slavery, Weakness, and Infirmity, of the Soul.'[24] If the body is weakened the soul is more at liberty to act reasonably. A midnight reflection goes deeper because the body is tranquil. Eating can be an excuse to keep us from church and thus prove as harmful as notorious sins. The strictness with which we fast must, of course, be varied with our state of health.

After this treatment of renunciation and self-denial Law proceeds to treat of the necessity of divine grace and the duties to which Christians are called.

Our whole being is founded in and supported by 'some *invisible Union* with God', though in 'these dark Houses of Clay' we cannot comprehend the fact.[25] Jesus likened the Spirit to wind, which is as much as we can say. We should be able to think of all Christians as inspired persons for inspiration only signifies 'an *invisible Operation* . . . of God's Holy Spirit'.[26]

But the bestowal of grace is not indiscriminate. Scripture tells us that God resists the proud and gives grace to the humble

E

(Jas. 4.6). What a person receives of grace, in addition to God's primary sustaining power, depends upon his fitness to receive. Not only debaucheries deprive us of grace but 'poor *Amusements*, vain *Arts*, useless *Sciences*, impertinent *Learning*'.[27] The drift of the point emerges in Law's verbal portrait of *Titius*, who is so engrossed in mathematics that he forgets when Sunday arrives. He might as well be a merchant as a Christian.

Christians live by the wisdom of the Holy Spirit. We should give our time to the need for rebirth, mortification, and inward attentiveness to the Holy Spirit rather than to ordinary cultural activities. Properly speaking, the wisdom of prayer alone deserves to be called learning.

Being careful not to grieve. God's Spirit can be applied not only to the words we speak, but also to the reading of vain and impertinent books. For example, 'Books of *Wit* and *Humour*, *Romances*, *Plays*, and other Productions of the *Poets*.'[28] In addition to what he wrote in *Stage Entertainments* (much of which is reprinted here), we learn that books other than those of devotion are diversions, and indeed corrupt diversions. Our mirth should be our joy in the Lord. The spirit of Sunday should be spread to the rest of the week. After prayer, reading of devotional books improves our hearts best. Such reading 'enlightens our Minds, collects our Thoughts, calms and allays our Passions, and begets in us wise and pious Resolutions'.[29]

The life of the Christian should be one of constant prayer and devotion to God. Mention is made of Christ's perpetual intercession with the Father in heaven. Law allows that our prayers can be united with his and also that those offered at the altar are most to be desired since 'the Body and Blood of Christ are joined with them'[30] But he uses the image of Christ's intercession as a spur to us: prayer is efficacious in removing sin and bringing us near to God.

As God is the fountain of all happiness and men are weak and full of want we may define prayer as 'an *earnest Application or Ascent of the Heart to God, as to the sole Cause of all Happiness*'.[31] On this definition it is easy to see how humility, self-denial, and the renunciation of the world will enable prayer. Indeed the possession of these qualities is essential. Church-going, fervour in prayer, a multiplicity of devotional books are uncertain signs of devotion.

Whilst every biblical text calling us to God is an exhortation to prayer, may put us into a prayerful state, and make any place a chapel, *'Hours* and *Forms* of Prayer' are not to be slighted. Indeed the prayerful spirit is disposed to set times of prayer and such times enliven heartfelt devotion. Prayer begets prayer, because 'things which we make *constant* and *familiar*, will by Degrees steal the Approbation of the Heart'. We should cultivate those circumstanccs that wc find helpful. Meaningful prayer combats sin. We cannot long remain hypocrites when we sincerely regard the attributes of God and the condition of our lives. The reward of prayer is unique: 'a holy and happy Life'.[32]

The book ends, apart from the final exhortation, with a chapter urging the imitation of Christ. He is the way, the truth and the life. Unless we learn to conform to his example we cannot expect to inherit eternal life. Such imitation should be our 'Rule of Life',[33] and we must be at pains to imitate the spirit and temper of Christ, not particular actions of his. Such qualities as Law has in mind are humility, meekness, renunciation of the world, and his single-minded dedication to the Father. Through the medium of verbal portraits he contrasts the failings of Christians, such as our unwillingness to mix with thc impious for their good.

In the final exhortation Law insists that our happiness lies in holiness, and that all pursuits that do not further holiness (he includes study as well as indulgences) are to be considered as 'the Wanderings and Impertinences of a *disordered understanding*'.[34]

A second reason for the necessity of aiming at Christian perfection is that we do not know what 'Abatements of *Holiness* God will accept on Judgement Day'.[35]

Again, Christian labour is never in vain. Whatever discomforts we suffer, we know that every action can contribute to the building of an eternity to be spent in glory with God. By meditating on the glories of heaven the Christian can replenish his zeal for proper endeavours in this life.

Though books of devotion sold well in the eighteenth century, and the rigorist note was usual in them, we cannot help thinking that *Christian Perfection* must have come with the force of an explosion to many in the polite world to whom it was addressed

and among whom it found popular acceptance. We find the
saintly Bishop Wilson writing to Lady Elizabeth Hastings in
1729 of his providential meeting with it; how his recommendation to a friend near London led to him procuring eighteen
copies for parochial libraries; how this book in the hands of his
clergy will be 'the likeliest way to bring them to a serious
temper'.[36] Though later overshadowed by the *Serious Call* it
continued to make an impact on many, including John and
Charles Wesley, George Whitefield, and John Byrom. The fourth
edition came out in 1737.

Despite the humour sometimes lightening it, it is the harshest
book that Law wrote. We have already noted material in his
environment contributory to such rigour. There is a resonance
between this book and the eighteen rules he wrote for himself
in adolescence. The Caroline heritage leaves ample room for
sin and renunciation. Confession and penitence occupy a
prominent place in the private prayers of Lancelot Andrewes.
The author of *The Whole Duty of Man* advises his readers to
'Endeavour . . . to bring yourselves to this melting temper, to
this deep, unfeigned sorrow.'[37] Law's abrupt reference to man
as an animal and the conclusions based on this respecting the
value of this life find as easy parallel in words of Robert Nelson,
that contemplation of the brevity of existence will 'depreciate
and vilify all the entertainments of this animal life'.[38]

Yet the Carolines, especially Jeremy Taylor, were less harsh
than Law. His remarks about learning, for example, find no
support in the library of Bishop Ken where copies of Plautus,
Aristophanes, thirteen volumes of Horace, and volumes of
English literature and history are to be found.[39]

We may suspect the additional influence of Thomas à
Kempis and the fourteenth-century German school of mystics.
They asserted the uselessness of learning, an affective rather
than an intellectual approach to God, and the importance of
the new birth, rejection of the world, and inward communications of God.[40] Law probably knew nothing of Eckhardt. His
work was virtually unknown in England in the eighteenth
century, except derivatively through some of the other writers
of the school.

Something of the Stoics' assessment of life's vanity and the
stress upon detachment also informs Law's rigorism. His copy

of Marcus Aurelius' *Meditations* (published 1735, but he doubtless encountered it earlier; still in the library is Epictetus'
*Morals* (1721) and Seneca's *Morals* (1705) where the same
philosophy is inculcated) is much underlined. Section 2.8 where
the Emperor argues that we must do our duty as if we were to
die immediately and that nothing touches us but what makes
us better or worse personally, is annotated by Law 'excellently
reason'd'. He considers 'excellent advice' the remark in
Section 3.8 that we should occupy ourselves with rational virtue
and be indifferent to the body. He rewrites in the margin the
dictum 'all worldly things are but as the smoke' (10.31).
Books 2 and 12 are specially underlined. They teach Stoic
withdrawal from the world, indifference to the body, belief in
gods, and attention to virtuous and rational ideals.[41]

With the exception of Malebranche, who also could write
caustically about learning and who lived austerely, Law does
not seem to have been specially influenced by the French school
of ascetic writers. Bossuet would support something of Law's
harshness, but we miss from his writing the humanism of
St Francis de Sales and Fénelon.

Though the doctrinal motifs of Law will be considered later
we should notice his emphasis upon the fact that God can only
love what is lovely. There is here the Dionysian influence,
partly masking the gospel paradox that God does love the
unlovely, which is varyingly present in most mystics and
Catholic writers.[42]

Most writers of the Enlightenment period stressed the importance of happiness. A fruit of this stress is the enshrinement
of the right to the free pursuit of happiness in the American
Constitution. Law was doubtless aware that some of his contemporaries were beginning to expect happiness only from the
earth. His belief that happiness can only be the result of devotion to God is a belief common to Christians and much emphasized in the seventeenth and early eighteenth centuries.
Puritans, Caroline divines, Cambridge Platonists, and Latitudinarians are full of it.[43]

He says little about organized religion and its forms. He is
at pains, indeed, to notice how devotion to externals may go
with impiety. He is at variance here with the main tradition of
Christianity. The Caroline divines taught the value of the

Prayer Book system of devotion,[44] and a writer such as St Francis de Sales, who wrote for a similar audience to that of Law, and who united genius and sanctity with a profound grasp of theology, emphasized the importance of religious forms.[45]

Part of the harshness and unbalance in the book probably stem from the author's personality. By nature vehement, Law was in the purgative way, and he was conscious of the widespread religious formalism of the day. He thus confesses in a private prayer, 'Lord, my sins have made me odious in Thy sight . . . make me odious in my own sight. . . . Bless it O Lord to the Purification and humiliation of my Body and Soul.'[46]

The value of the work can be stated summarily. It impresses the reader as a manly plea by a vigorous, intelligent and single-minded writer for a reformation of life in accordance with what he understands the Bible to say. It is beautifully and strongly written. In his concern to be true to the Bible, to urge men to live by rule, to be Christian in a practical way he reflects Caroline ideals. The same applies to his belief that all men are called to perfection. He follows here the Anglican and Protestant rejection of the Tridentine double standard for clerics and laity. But we must not press the rejection too much. St Francis de Sales, as well as William Law, says, 'Wherever we are, we are able and ought to aspire to the perfect life.'[47]

Two further values can be mentioned. Law at this stage of his writing has reminded some of Pascal and Kierkegaard. Like them he has a vivid sense of the tragedy of life apart from the gospel; like them he makes violent demands upon Christians. Law knew Pascal and a volume including his *Thoughts* (1704 edition) rests on King's Cliffe library shelves.[48]

The book is not all harshness and gloom. If he despaired of natural man Law glorified in God; if he saw no hope rising from our selves he saw much from the condescension of God. There is a touch of experience in the words, 'There is a Time when our Hearts are more than ordinarily raised towards God, when we feel the Joys and Comforts of Religion, and enjoy a Peace that passes all Understanding.'[49]

# 6

## THE PERIOD OF THE 'SERIOUS CALL'

'Mr Law is not a deacon; it was a work of many years to persuade him to enter Priest's Orders but he at last submitted to the commands of his superior.' Thus, Bishop Smith to his fellow Nonjuror, Bishop Gillan in 1733.[1] He was ordained by Bishop Gandy in 1727. The record seems to have been written by Thomas Deacon.[2] Law's reluctance to assume responsibility in the Nonjuror Church seems to have been due to doubts about its authority in relation to the established Church, with which he had firm connections. The dangers of sectarianism and factiousness seem also to have been in his mind.

1727 was also the year in which he founded a girls' school at King's Cliffe. The means to do this, according to Tighe and Walton, came from a bank note for £1000 received by Law from an anonymous admirer.[3] The story is probably true and if so, it is characteristic of Law to take the question of charity with sacrificial seriousness and also to say little about the matter. Fourteen girls were to be trained in reading, knitting, and needlework. They were to receive clothing, if necessary, and taught religion and good manners. A salary was provided for a mistress. According to Tighe he erected an almshouse for the maintenance of two old women at this time. The women were to be unmarried, widows, or otherwise helpless.

Law's ordinary income seems to have come from what Gibbon gave him and the royalties received for the sale of his books. His arrangement was that the publishers should have the profit on the first edition and that all succeeding profit should go to him. His principal books ran through six or eight editions.

The publication of 1729 was more than usually successful. Law's immediate and eventual fame has been determined by *A Serious Call to a Devout and Holy Life, adapted to the State and Condition of all Orders of Christians.*

His theme is the Good Life. Covering again, though not repetitiously, much of the ground of *Christian Perfection*, he considers the meaning of Christian devotion, asks why so many Christians are undevout, relates his message especially to the condition of the leisured classes, gives a method of daily prayer and concludes with a panegyric on the excellency of the devout spirit.

Devotion is defined simply as 'a life given, or *devoted* to God'.[4] The spirit with which we pray should accordingly spread to the conduct of our entire lives. Some people give special importance to the time and place of public worship but we should note that 'there is not one command in all the Gospel for *Public Worship*; and perhaps it is a duty that is least insisted upon in Scripture of any other'. What the New Testament constantly insists upon is that our ordinary actions should be governed by a devout spirit.[5] For this to come about we need a changed heart that chooses God, rejects the world, and is concerned with neighbourly love.

A particular sin, like swearing, indicates why men live contrary to the gospel. They do not have 'the *intention to please God in all their actions*'.[6] If we test ourselves against this measure we shall discover our fault more completely than by reference to 'the weakness of our nature'.[7] Recognizing the Pelagian conclusions that could be built on this foundation, Law insists that his concern is with human response to God. He presupposes grace for the very possibility of Christian living.

Sins springing from ignorance or surprise will be covered by the 'goodness of God, and his rich mercies in Christ Jesus', but we cannot expect similar mercies for sins resulting from want of intention.[8] Since we are fallen creatures, 'born in the dregs of time', no angelic perfection is required of us but that 'of our *best* endeavours'.[9]

We are invited to consider our approaching death. At the point of death we would surely wish for the utmost perfection. To have neglected in life the pious warnings of God and man means that we die 'a death of great stupidity'. He impresses the fact that 'The greatness of those things which follow death, makes all that goes before it sink into nothing.'[10] The verbal sketch of *Penitens* enforces the argument. He believes that the example of *Penitens* will give the reader food for meditation.

A reason for his verbal sketches is evidently to stir the reader's imagination so that points stressed in argument may penetrate more deeply.

The form of duty required by clergy and laity differ, but not the substance. Indeed:

> Things spiritual and temporal, sacred and common, must, like *men* and *angels*, like *heaven* and *earth*, all conspire in the Glory of God. As there is but one *God* and *Father of us all*, whose Glory gives light and life to everything that lives; whose presence fills all places, whose power supports all beings, whose providence ruleth all Events; so everything that lives . . . must all with one spirit, live wholly to the praise and glory of this one God and Father of them all.[11]

Whilst most of our employments can be made a part of our duty to God, we should only engage in them so far as they are suitable to beings that are to live above the world whilst they live in it. It is the fact, rather than the form, of sin which is disastrous. Irregular tempers in trade are as bad as irregular tempers in drink.

We should remember that the purpose of dress is to 'cover our shame'.[12] Nor should we indulge in eating, which is 'one of the lowest actions of our lives, it is common to us with mere animals'.[13]

Free from the common necessities of men, the leisured classes have special obligations. They must 'imitate the *higher* perfections of *angels*'.[14] As Christianity is the 'refinement, and exaltation of our best faculties . . . a life of the highest Reason', we should not think it grievous.[15]

The main difficulty is that most people have a religion of the head, while their hearts are occupied with quite contrary desires. Further, the indiscreet use of lawful objects leads them astray rather than any fall into debauchery. The 'trifling spirit' of *Flavia* illustrates a point to which Law continues to return. We should live by 'a *religious rule*, observed upon a principle of duty to God'.[16] If we begin with the mildest rule we will find religious sentiment penetrating all our life. Time and money need to be brought under rule especially, for these 'talents are continual means and opportunities of doing good'.[17]

*Miranda* illustrates Law's womanly ideal. She takes no part in social diversions; uses little money on herself; distributes alms frequently and discreetly; is always 'neat and clean', dressing in the 'cheapest things'; observes a strict rule of daily prayer, studies daily the Bible, especially the New Testament; emulates the saints and cares for the needy and sinful. *Miranda*, as Law paints her, is loving and earnest rather than censorious and frigid, despite the lack of humanist virtues. She is an archetype of George Eliot's Dinah Morris in *Adam Bede*. (It would be interesting to know if Law's portrait helped to create Dinah. George Eliot observed real Methodists for her creation, and Methodists were encouraged to read the *Serious Call*.)

The importance of virginity in the pursuit of perfection is not to be overlooked. The example of the Early Church can guide us. Eusebius 'who lived at the time of the *first general council*, when the faith of our *Nicene Creed* was established, when the Church was in its greatest *glory* and *purity*, when its Bishops were so many holy *fathers*, and eminent *saints*', distinguished a first and second order of Christian.[18] The first order rejected marriage and possessions to devote themselves wholly to God. The second order adopted a lower form of life. They married, engaged in business, and devoted only some of their time to prayer and religious instruction. Christ said that the Rich Young Ruler must reject everything in order to be perfect. Thus virginity was esteemed in the Early Church. Not fear of this life, but a burning zeal for God and a joyous expectation of heaven, propels aspirants of the higher order. He ends this section with the words of Christ, 'He that hath ears to hear, let him hear.'[19] The same words appear on the title page of the book. Clearly Law sees a special importance in some form of the monastic life.

He will not allow that a constant regard for God makes life uneasy or dull. The new birth means that we exchange childish satisfactions and sickly passions for the real happiness of a sound mind. To root out passions that religion opposes is to free oneself from the unrest and dissatisfaction they cause. Meat, drink, and clothing supply our few wants in this life, beyond them we quickly fall a prey to false ideals.

Religious rules are not burdensome. They allow us to use things well. 'The strictness of these rules, only consists in the exactness of their rectitude.'[20] Their observance does not lessen enjoyment of this life. The effect of fasting, even, is to lessen the war in our nature and to increase our taste for spiritual joy, thus adding to 'the comfortable enjoyment of our lives'.[21] Nothing can lastingly help man but religion.

> Wisdom . . . appealeth to all our senses, teaching us in everything, and everywhere, by all that we see, and all that we hear, by births and burials, by sickness and health, by life and death, by pains and poverty, by misery and vanity, and by all the changes and chances of life, that there is nothing else for man to look after, no other end in nature for him to drive at, but a happiness which is only to be found in the hopes and expectations of Religion.[22]

Beyond death lies judgement, heaven, and hell. These too should affect us.

Having proved the necessity and advantage of devotion Law considers methods of prayer. 'Prayer is the nearest approach to God, and the highest enjoyment of him, that we are capable of in this life.'[23] Hence the importance we should attach to it. As sleep is a dull animal existence a Christian lying late in bed is more odious than a tradesman late for work. Beyond what is necessary sleep softens the personality and deadens the sense of devotion. 'Mortification, of *all kinds*, is the very life and soul of piety' and must have its effect in the matter of sleep.[24] The examples of Christ, Anna, Paul and Silas, and the '*primitive Christians*' show how sleep may be interrupted to make time for prayer. Such self-denial 'is the only royal way that leads to a kingdom'.[25]

Public worship requires set forms of prayer, but those who are proficient in private prayer and find that their 'heart is always ready to pray in its own language' should not restrain themselves. In words that suggest personal experience he continues,

> Sometimes the light of God's countenance shines so bright upon us, we see so far into the invisible world, we are so affected with the wonders of the love and goodness of God, that our hearts worship and adore in a language higher than that of words, and we feel transports of devotion, which only can be felt.[26]

So changeable is the human heart, however, that it is wise to have set forms of prayer available and rise above them when we can.

We should place ourselves quietly in the presence of God before speaking, and then use splendid words about God so as to affect the heart rightly. The '*stated hours* of prayer' he describes as follows:

Early morning: Praise and Thanksgiving
9 a.m.: Humility
Noon: Universal love and intercession
3 p.m.: Resignation to God
6 p.m.: Confession and Penitence
On retiring: The certainty of death

Before detailing these hours Law mentions the flexibility of the regimen; how, for example, we can add to our early morning devotion such petitions as our situation demands. Devotional books, of which the Bible is the best, find their place in private prayer, and the Bible should be used in any case.

Prayer should always begin with the chanting or singing of a psalm. Melody clears away dullness and opens heaven as nothing else can. Singing a psalm is as proper as speaking a prayer. It does not matter if our voices lack quality for we sing as rejoicing in God, not for the sake of other people.

Body and soul are kept in unity by God. Though they do not mix in substance they are so held together that they affect each other. For this reason we sing a psalm and reckon that those who 'have resolved all religion into a *quietism*, or *mystic* intercourse with God in silence' are mistaken.[27]

We should also use our imaginations to bring reality into prayer. If we imagine the multitude in heaven, for example, we will find it easier to praise God remembering their praise.

Though the hour of prayer at 9 a.m. is not commanded in Scripture the custom of saints, pious Jews, and primitive Christians is sufficient 'to make this hour a constant season of devotion'.[28] Humility is the special concern here for 'an humble state of soul, is the very state of Religion, because humility is the *life* and *soul* of piety, the *foundation* and *support* of every virtue and good work, the best *guard* and *security* of all holy affections'.[29] Pride is more deeply rooted in our nature than any other vice, it is the disorder of a fallen world. He counsels the contemplation of a crucifix when we find ourselves delighted by ourselves. We must not think of Christ 'suffering in *our stead*, but as our *representative*, acting in our *name*, and with such particular merit, as to make our *joining* with him *acceptable* unto God'.[30]

By making us proud the world can defeat our religion. Education can have a like effect. Sound instruction of the young should consist in inculcating the words of saints and wise philosophers. As the aim of education must be to alleviate the vicious effect of the Fall upon our rational natures, it must have a spiritual and moral basis. But pride is the first quality contemporary education seeks to waken. The child learns to scorn to be outdone. He must seek high office for the esteem in which it is held. It is useless to plead that the appeal to ambition stirs the young from idleness. In that case humility could not be taught to the middle-aged and Christ and the holy Apostles must be conceived as bringing the young into dullness and idleness.

The discourse of *Paternus* to his ten-year-old boy gives Law's ideal for boys' education. Though rigoristic, paternal love and tenderness glow through its words. The boy must think of God as his 'Friend', and think of him 'magnificently'. The Last Judgement is quietly introduced under the conception of a book in which is recorded all our actions, and for which we must one day answer. Referring to his future adult life *Paternus* hopes the boy will care for the bodies as well as the souls of those on his estate under his charge. He is taught Latin and Greek so that he might read of the action of God in old times and fortify his mind with the sayings of sages. He must aim at being 'all of a piece'; plain and truthful in speaking, rational in life, sober and clean in dress, temperate in eating. Humility, not pride must guide him, and the only man with whom he is to have a perpetual contention is himself.

He proceeds to attack the contemporary education of women. The question is important, not only because of its effect upon girls but because women are so influential with the young. He cannot admit that woman are innately inferior to men. For the most part he believes them to have clearer minds and gentler dispositions. *Eusebia* and her family illustrate Law's ideal for girls' education.[31] Her daughters are brought up as 'five virgins for the kingdom of Heaven'. Housewifery is the art upon which they concentrate and the moral and spiritual emphasis is upon humility and the rejection of the world. The girls are taught that what is really themselves is 'spiritual and rational . . . as contrary to all fleshly or corporeal beings, as *life* is contrary to *death*'. The body is like infected clothing and the reason has been so darkened by the Fall that we incline to 'that which is hurtful'. Marriage is acknowledged as a 'proper gift of God', but the higher perfection of the virgin state is proposed to the girls. Whilst children they were permitted to indulge in harmless amusements; now they must despise them. Upon the practice of charity no limits are put and in a phrase of peculiar beauty the girls are counselled, 'Love *poverty*, and reverence *poor people*'. Patching and painting, i.e., the use of cosmetics, and the love of dress are strictly forbidden. Christ's condemnation of the adulterous look (Matt. 5.28) is reckoned to allow no temporizing in such matters.

The subject for prayer at noon is universal love. Intercession is especially fitting here and we are encouraged to frame as our greatest thought of God 'a Being of infinite love and goodness; using an infinite wisdom and power, for the common good and happiness of all his creatures'.[32] We must imitate God in such 'universal tenderness and affection'.[33] Reason and piety will give us this quality.

It is significant that Law considers the effects intercession will have on the intercessor rather than the effects on those for whom intercession is made. We cannot hate those for whom we pray. The word 'tender' is used frequently in this section and he perceives that '*haughty, angry* language generally proceeds from some *secret habits* of pride in the heart'.[34]

Resignation to God's will is the special prayerful concern at 3 p.m. As God is universally active, there is always cause for thankfulness. The supposed chances of life are part of the fore-ordaining will of God moving all things to their best advantage. Of course we cannot see things as God does, so we must sometimes believe where we cannot prove. If we cultivate this practice we will learn to be moved by common things as by miracles.

At 6 p.m. the subjects for prayer are self-examination and confession. This is fitting as daily employment is usually ended by this time. A daily and particular confession is to be preferred to a weekly and general confession if we are to face our sins seriously. Our Rule of Life provides a useful check. We are bidden to recollect how odious sin is in God's sight. Creation was the work of a moment, 'the redemption of the world has been a work of longer labour'.[35]

Before retiring for the night we are recommended to consider death. We should reckon up the terrors and importance of death, consider the bed our grave, and, remembering the likeness of darkness and sleep to death, commit ourselves into God's keeping.

The book ends with a fine eulogy on the excellence of the devout spirit. In words that could be used as Law's epitaph he thus defends piety:

> *Great* devotion is the *noblest* temper of the *greatest* and *noblest* souls . . . they who think it receives any advantage from *ignorance* and *poorness* of spirit, are themselves not a little, but entirely ignorant of the nature of devotion, the nature of God, and the nature of themselves.[36]

As a man shows his nobility by being grateful to a parent or benefactor, or by being able to acknowledge a fault, so he shows the highest quality by praising God and beseeching his forgiveness. If we acknowledge the authority of Christ and the Apostles we must acknowledge the importance of devotion, for they were devout. Distress, sickness, and the fear of death usually expose our deepest needs and we become devout. We should accordingly cultivate the devout spirit though the desperate need for it is not always apparent. The favour of God must be the most worthwhile of all goods. He who does not labour to secure it is like a judge who knows much about painting but little about equity.

He contrasts worldly bravery with devout humility. The bravery of a soldier without humility is only the fury of a tiger. Devout humility 'contends with greater enemies, is more constantly engaged, more violently assaulted, bears more, suffers more, and requires greater courage to support itself, than any instances of worldly bravery'.[37]

Almost immediately the *Serious Call* took its place in the sequence of major works of Anglican devotion.[38] It has overshadowed

*Christian Perfection* because of its completeness, serenity, and
portraits. It is a deeper testament to Law's own spirit. The
agnostic, Leslie Stephen, rightly avowed, 'The power can only
be adequately felt by readers who can study it on their knees.'[39]

The authors to whom Law was indebted in writing *Christian
Perfection* are apparent in the *Serious Call*, and we can extend the
list. St Francis de Sale's *Introduction to the Devout Life* and more
particularly Jeremy Taylor's *Holy Living* and *Holy Dying* are
two obvious examples, and these were important to Law, not
only on account of their spiritual teaching, but because they
exhibited the art of communication to the social classes for
whom he also wrote.

The tenderness of the family portraits should not surprise us,
despite Law's rigorism. His own youth had been happy and he
doubtless experienced and noticed family affection in the
Gibbon household. The theme is consonant with High Church
teaching. Jeremy Taylor counsels parents, 'be tender-bowelled,
pitiful, and gentle, complying with all the infirmities of the
children'.[40]

He uses the word 'reason' more than 340 times. The age in
which he lived had a fondness for the word and deep respect
for the idea it represented. His mentor, Malebranche, fully
accords with the age in this matter. In what Law says about
the association of body and soul we can discern again an intellectual preoccupation of the day and again he is indebted to
Malebranche.[41]

Law returned to the Bible and the Middle Ages for his
advocacy of hours of prayer. The Caroline divines made much
of the Prayer Book pattern of two hours of prayer, though the
recommendations in the breviaries and primers were not
altogether abandoned. John Cosin published *A Collection of
Private Devotions: in the Practise of the Ancient Church, called
The Hours of Prayer . . . Taken out of Holy Scripture, the Ancient
Fathers and the divine service of our own church*, in 1627. He advocated seven hours. Lewis Bayly's *The Practice of Piety* (1612)
ran into its fifty-eighth edition 1734 and advocated prayers for
different occasions. He gave directions for prayer and was little
concerned with hours. The author of *The Whole Duty of Man*
believed that all public and family acts of worship should be
according to the Prayer Book, but he also advocated private

individual prayers for ordinary and extraordinary occasions. He has prayers for the time we wake and morning and evening. He mentions appreciatively the hours of prayer and contrasts the fervour of the first Christians with contemporary practice. Those who can, should use four hours and the two services of the Prayer Book.[42] Law must be faulted for neglecting to integrate the Prayer Book into his scheme, but earlier church practice, a continuing tradition within the Church of England, and his understanding of the sanctification of daily life made him the advocate of five or six hours of prayer.

We can sense the influence of the seventeenth-century French ascetic writers in this book. His emphasis upon the seat of religion in the heart, the importance of inspiration and the dangers of Quietism, no less than his remarks later, suggest that he had deeply meditated the words of Fénelon, and Madames Guyon and Bourignon. In his copy of Madame Guyon's *Moyen Court* we find him noting the words that it is necessary to pray 'en tout tems . . . l'*Oraison du Cœur*'.[43] Mortification must accompany prayer as we can bear it.[44] We must die to ourselves so that God can live in us.[45] God is already in the depths of our hearts, his presence can be experienced, he imparts essential virtue, we must listen attentively to what he says. In her *Autobiography* she calls marriage burdensome and praises chastity and the single life. She relates how, with the growth of piety, she gave up society, dancing, amusements, and how reading books other than the Gospels seemed disgusting to her.[47]

It is remarkable that so lucid a thinker as Law should produce a book less than fully coherent. He praises the present glory of God in created things, but is austere and otherworldly. He extols the heart, but also the reason. There is an unsettlement in the soul of the writer resulting from the cultural crisis of the time being enacted in his own life. His otherworldliness and affective devotion result from his interpretation of the Bible and Prayer Book, from favourite mystical writers and from his Caroline heritage. But the Enlightenment delighted in the creation and respected reason—both factors are prominent in Malebranche—so that Law's mind is caught in the confluence of two streams.

Law's personality is present in much of his writing. But a

F

disvalue as well as a value results from this. It is odd that in a
dissertation on devout living the Prayer Book is unmentioned
and no directions are given respecting the sacraments. His
statement that the New Testament is silent concerning the
duty of public worship is notorious. Part of the answer lies in
the just aim of Law to challenge a public that paid lip-service
to formal religion but evaded the personal commitment that
religion entails. Hence his emphasis on prayer itself and moral
virtue rather than upon particular prayers such as the old
manuals contained. [48] But the vehemence of Law's own nature
is also involved. His disapproval of the religious habits of his
day prevent him from commending the proper development of
those habits, even though they meant much to himself. The
cultural crisis, to which we have called attention and in which
Law was involved, may also be influential here, since with him
the Caroline system breaks down. He even strains its rigorism.
His strict Sabbatarianism may be compared with the equable
advice of Jeremy Taylor that we must abstain from all but
essential servile work, joyfully participate in public worship,
visit the sick, care for those in our charge, take our ease in
lawful games and the like, and beyond this enjoy 'our Christian
liberty'. [49]

Yet there is no denying the power of the *Serious Call*. It passed
into the twentieth edition in 1816. Byrom records that Lord
Lyttelton, who had not been encouraged to read it, was so
'fascinated' that he sat up at night to finish it. [50] Dr Johnson,
as we have seen on p. xi, believed it the finest piece of hortatory
theology in any language and described his experience on taking
up the book as a sceptical undergraduate. He expected to find
it a dull book 'and perhaps to laugh at it. But I found Law quite
an overmatch for me; and this was the first occasion of my
thinking in earnest of religion, after I became capable of
rational enquiry.' [51] Gibbon's view as a sceptic writing a
generation after its publication is interesting.

> Mr Law's master-work, the *Serious Call*, is still read as a
> popular and powerful book of devotion. His precepts are
> rigid, but they are founded on the Gospel: his satire is sharp,
> but it is drawn from the knowledge of human life; and many
> of his portraits are not unworthy of the pen of La Bruyère.

If he finds a spark of piety in his reader's mind, he will soon kindle it to a flame; and the philosopher must allow that he exposes, with equal severity and truth, the strange contradiction between the faith and practice of the Christian world.[52]

It benefited more than the educated. A letter from Scarborough to Lloyd's *Evening Post* in 1771 by a clergyman records the apparently fruitless labour in his parish until he read the *Serious Call* and was so impressed that he gave a copy to every member in the parish. There must be some truth in the euphemistic conclusion that the people were reclaimed 'from a life of folly and impiety, to a life of holiness and devotion'.[53] Methodist artisans certainly looked upon it as an improving book.

Its characteristic defects were felt of course. Byrom found that some of his young friends considered Law 'an impracticable, strange, whimsical writer'. Mrs Lloyd and her sister thought it a silly, ridiculous book because of its commendation of Eusebia's plain dress. It is amusing and instructive to repeat Byrom's record of Mr Gyles's opinion that 'Mr Law has grown a mere cynic, etc., but drank his health'.[54]

The *Serious Call*, and to a less extent, *Christian Perfection*, influenced the leaders of the Evangelical Revival and helped to nurture converts. In America in 1736 Charles Wesley found that the name of Law was known and confessed to friends, 'all I knew of religion was through him'.[55] In about 1777 he advised his daughter that she was ready to relish à Kempis and the *Serious Call*.[56]

In the autobiographical preface to the entry in his *Journal* recording his conversion, John Wesley writes, 'meeting now with Mr Law's *Christian Perfection* and *Serious Call*, although I was much offended at many parts of both, yet they convinced me more than ever . . . of the Law of God. The light flowed in so mightily upon my soul, that everything appeared in a new view.'[57] The *Serious Call* was made a text book at Wesley's Kingswood school. He also recorded, 'All the Methodists carefully read these books [the two mentioned previously] and were greatly profited thereby.'[58] Evangelicals influenced included Henry Venn, Thomas Scott, John Newton, Thomas

Adam, and George Whitefield (who mentions 'many others' whom the books helped, and weekly Communion, fasting, alms-giving, and sobriety in dress and eating which became a part of his religion because of Law's writing).[59]

Denominational barriers were crossed by the *Serious Call*. The Quaker, Fanny Henshaw, was clearly influenced by it, and the Quakers who wrote to Law admitted profiting by the book.[60]

The appeal of the *Serious Call* remains. It frequently appears in cheap editions. An American paperback abridgement was published in 1955 in consequence of a group of Presbyterian ministers and laity discovering that Law 'seemed to speak directly to us'.[61] This has been the experience of many. The judgement of the *Oxford Dictionary of the Christian Church* can probably be sustained. It 'has probably had more influence than any other post-Reformation spiritual book except the Pilgrim's Progress'.[62]

# 7

## 'THE CASE OF REASON'

The publication of the *Serious Call* secured Law's fame and he found himself increasingly the object of attention. People came to agree, to disagree, and to consult. Byrom came in a spirit of reverence and with the intention of doing anything but openly disagreeing. Because of his *Remains*, which can be read with pleasure for various reasons, we know much about Law that we would not know otherwise. Byrom was a man of parts; he had studied medicine, was an expert linguist, and the inventor of a method of shorthand, by imparting which he gained a living. He was a Fellow of the Royal Society, usually benign, but a trifle short-tempered and whimsical; he was also one of the tallest men in England. He had a genuine, intelligent interest in religion, being a High Churchman with a taste for mystical writers. He had read Boehme before Law had heard of him, and described himself as a 'disciple' of Malebranche.[1]
We meet Bentley, Butler, Newton, and the Wesleys in his pages. The unconscious charm of his narrative, as well as his chief distinction from Law, emerges in such a passage as the following: 'Jan. 31, 1730. Supper at Mitre with Chilton, Hough, etc.; talked about Hebrew points, happiness, Mr Law, stage plays; we paid 2s; I had two bottles—too much for a defender of Law to drink!'
We have mentioned that Law seems to have agreed at first with the Usagers section of the Nonjurors. He sided then with the Non-Usagers, not so much because of a change of view respecting the contended question, but because he realized that the question did not touch fundamentals. It divided Christians, and the established Church, though imperfect, observed a legitimate form of worship.[2]
In July 1731, Law and other Nonjurors met to discuss the Usages controversy. They declared that Brett and other Usagers

violently began the schism and required them to return to the
Non-Usagers. The Usagers' demands were unreasonable.
Mixing water with the wine at the Eucharist was forbidden and
at variance with the practice of the Church of England. The
policy of the Usager bishops, especially Bishop Smith, was
objectionable. This Declaration, of which Law may have been
the penman, only exacerbated the situation. In October 1731
we find Law stating that he agreed with the Usagers' points but
not with the idea that the Church no longer embodied them.
The Oblation can be observed without a particular form of
words. There is no authority for the mixed chalice. The Church
Militant prayer does not exclude the departed. The prayer of
consecration intends to bless the elements; special invocation is
therefore not necessary. The traditional rite should be employed.
After correspondence with Bishop Smith we find him submitting
proposals for peace among Nonjurors. He proposed that water
should be used with wine at the Eucharist; that the Church of
England be considered conformable to the Ancient Church at
the oblation, invocation, and prayers for the faithful departed;
that they should abide by the rulings of the Church of England
until further reform prove possible; that they should meet
with the kiss of charity and burn all records of the controversy.

In 1732 the Nonjurors reunited substantially on the terms
proposed by Law. About this time it seems that vestments such
as the cope were introduced, as well as cross and candle-
sticks for the altar. These innovations not only took up pre-
Reformation practice but that of such Caroline divines as
Lancelot Andrewes.

Law's deep involvement in these events produced different
views about his character. His abruptness made Bishop Smith
alter his opinion and declare Law 'one of the proudest men
living'. At one stage Law had to ask Rawlinson to take his
place in negotiations. Rawlinson wrote to Brett that Law
suffered from his 'too great forwardness'. But during the same
period Gordoun could write to Brett that 'This Good Man seems
full of humility and Repentance . . . a true primitive Christian
Spirit'. At one point Law formally apologized to Rawlinson
for an uncharitable suspicion. He put it in writing so that
Rawlinson could show it to whom he wished.

Law is supposed to have become a pillar of Blackbourne's

congregation. We find him writing to Rawlinson about a Nonjurors' concern in 1734 and in 1753 he donated £10 to Thomas Deacon, via John Byrom, though this was probably a charitable act no longer indicative of ecclesiastical unity. We may presume that as the thirties wore on Law drifted away from the Nonjurors. They had little sympathy with mysticism and tended to be learned but essentially uncreative thinkers. At the same time Law valued the established Church more than they, and was creative and mystically inclined. Not only did he become a Nonjuror priest reluctantly but he refused to become a bishop, as Smith and Gandy especially wished.[3]

Law was well aware that there were theological problems of much greater import than those posed by the Nonjurors. The matter was put ironically but essentially by Thomas Deacon in a letter to Byrom. He had never been to Cambridge, and having only heard of it by tradition wonders if it really exists?[4] The publication in 1730 of Matthew Tindal's *Christianity as old as the Creation, or the Gospel a Republication of the Religion of Nature* brought the arguments of the Deists to a crown and precipitated Law's refutation.

Hooker had stated the Caroline position (in which Law was brought up) regarding the balancing of revelation and reason, when he asserted that:

All points of Christian doctrine are either demonstrable conclusions or demonstrative principles. Conclusions have strong . . . proofs as well in the school of Jesus Christ as elsewhere . . . the principles . . . have their evidence where they had their original, and as received from thence we adore them.[5]

It is easy to see how this system could suffer once men began to see that tradition was not what they took it to be and that reason offered the possibility of such assurance.

We have noticed already the main ways in which opposition to orthodoxy developed towards the end of the seventeenth century. Deism was one way in which men came to interpret religion. Lord Herbert gradually gained more and more disciples and sympathizers. At the beginning of the new century Samuel Clarke could distinguish four classes of Deist: those who

believed in an external creator of the world; those who admit
a divine providence in nature; those who admit providence
and believe in the moral perfection of God; those who add to
this a sense of man's duty to God and a future stage of rewards
and punishments.

Among Deists we find Blount emphasizing the merits of
heathen faiths and questioning the authenticity of Christ's
miracles; Toland, following Locke, arguing for a distinction
between knowledge of God's essence and attributes. We have
not knowledge of the former and knowledge of the latter is clear,
simple, and largely moral; Collins bitterly attacking the clergy
for priestcraft and doubting the value of miracles and prophecy
for establishing faith; Clarke also disclaiming knowledge of
God's essence and betraying a strain of scepticism in his
writing.

A debate centred on the question of analogy in religion.
Wallis had used the terms 'figurative', 'metaphorical', and
'analogous' indifferently. Peter Browne tried unsuccessfully to
distinguish divine analogy and divine metaphor. In a popular
book Jenkin stated that he could not comprehend the meaning
of words like 'person', 'begotten', and 'proceeding' in Trinitarian doctrine, but he believed them useful because they
kindled religious affections and predisposed men to accept the
gospel. Toland asked what value lay in believing a thing if an
account of its nature cannot be given? A number of writers
came to see that if a sharp distinction be made between substance and attributes, and the claim of knowledge is made for
attributes alone, substance may be dispensed with. Various
thinkers, including Locke, Browne, and Berkeley, used the
intuitive idea we have of ourselves to argue analogically for the
fact of God.[6]

Whilst no English genius was a Deist, the movement clearly
asked important questions—questions inevitable with the rise of
natural science and a developed respect for discursive reason.
When Bishop Butler declared in 1736, 'It has come . . . to be
taken for granted, by many persons, That Christianity is not
so much a subject of enquiry, but that it is now at length discovered to be fictitious',[7] he was expressing the popularity of
Deists' views among the reading public.

Matthew Tindal (1653?–1733) had already opposed High

Church views and in his 1730 book covertly rejected revelation in favour of a religion of reason. Tradition, he claimed, is too uncertain a foundation upon which to build religion. Traditions vary, but there is 'a clear and distinct light, that enlightens all men, and which, the moment they attend to it makes them perceive those eternal truths which are the foundation of all our knowledge'.[8] This light is reason. There is no need, for example to refer to . . . tradition in order to establish the importance of 'mutual benevolence'. It is necessary on the rational grounds that men must live together.[9] Likewise, reason shows the way to happiness. The happiness of beings consists in their perfection. The rational man is the most perfect and therefore the most happy. Rational inquiry into the action of God in the world shows that it lies in the fitness of things. This must be so for otherwise God would be an arbitrary Being. Revelation can add nothing to the religion of nature, which is perfect. By distorting it men have become guilty of all the cruelties and superstitions of the Church. Consider God's supposed punishment of people. As God is perfect, he is not injured by man's wrongdoing. He punishes us to help us not to sin. On no rational grounds can we believe in hell as a place of eternal punishment. As church order is a mutable matter, human discretion can decide it.

The Old Testament is not verbally inspired. The Song of Songs, for example, is only a love song. We cannot suppose that the Book of Revelation came from God. The uncertainty of the New Testament text must be accepted, as the work of Bentley and Clarke shows. The moral parts are the clearest, but reason must guide us even here as reflection on the practicality of the Sermon on the Mount indicates.

A fair example of his attitude to church tradition is his statement that the 'Creeds were the spare arms with which contending parties combated each other'.[10]

More than thirty authors, including Leland, Foster, and Conybeare, attacked Tindal. In 1731 Law published his *The Case of Reason*, which proved the most significant contribution to the debate until 1736 when Butler's *Analogy of Religion* was published.

In the Introduction Law gives the arguments he believes he must answer. Human reason, or natural light, is the only means of discerning God's will, revelation differs from reason only in the method of its communication, on any other basis God would be an arbitrary Being. Anything required in religion which reason does not dictate is gross superstition. Any external revelation given to some people must equally have been given to all people. He concludes the Introduction with the reminder that the railing accusations with which Tindal assails the clergy will not be answered. He will only add to reason the safe light of revelation.

Pride may be suggested by the inability to accept religious truth other than that indicated by reason. To succumb to pride is to ally oneself with the devils. A decent humility is required before the mystery of God. Even had we been innocent we could not have understood the will and nature of God. In the 'present state of *sin, ignorance,* and *misery*' it is more necessary that divine help and forgiveness should issue 'from some *incomprehensible depth* of divine goodness'.[11]

Opponents of revelation assume that God must be an arbitrary Being if he acts in any other way than the fitness of things require. Certainly many moral duties are apparent from the relation men bear to each other and to God. But this implies a conclusion the opposite of Tindal's. If the fitness of actions is founded on the nature of things and persons the rule of God's actions must often be incomprehensible to us. The fitness must be what God considers such and we 'can no more tell what is, or is not *infinitely wise* in God, than we can raise ourselves to a *state* of infinite wisdom'.[12] Indeed, were God an arbitrary Being he might act according to the fitness of things but because he is not arbitrary he acts consistently with his own superior wisdom.

Consider how problematical and mysterious reality is. We cannot understand God's providential ordering of things. But we must live and plan even though we cannot always understand. This means that we must have faith. If such is the case in this matter it is likely to be similar when we consider revelation.

Law refers to the mystery of the origin of the human soul and its relation to the body. Was the soul created with the body? Did it enter the body as a fallen spirit? Though unresolvable these questions have important bearings on morality. Again, what is the origin of sin and evil? We can find no rational answer. In fact, we can discover 'as large a bill of complaints against natural religion, and the mysteries of providence, as is here brought against revealed doctrines'.[13]

Because God is God and man is man, man is bound to encounter incomprehensibility when he speaks of God. To suppose that God must either propose arguments to our intelligence or act upon us as a seal upon wax is absurd. The inability of reason to deal with religious reality is illustrated by the paradox that man receives everything from God and yet he is morally responsible and exercises free will.

Religious discourse must make use of analogy. Regarding God's relation to the world, for example, we speak of his Fatherhood or Governorship. Such conceptions are imperfect. They

> are very plain and certain, as to the *reality* of their existence; and highly mysterious and inconceivable, as to the *manner* of their existence . . . that which is *mysterious* and *inconceivable* in them, is a just and solid foundation of that *profound humility, awful reverence, internal piety,* and *tremendous sense* of the divine Majesty, with which devout and pious persons think of God, and assist at the *offices* and *institutions* of religion'.[14]

We cannot rationally comprehend the effects of sin and the nature of the Atonement. Indeed 'we cannot take upon us to be *knowing,* and *philosophers,* in these matters, but by deserting our Reason, and giving ourselves up to *vision* and *imagination*'.[15]

The divine would be natural to us if we were able to apprehend it in its own nature. It is supernatural because of the disparity between God and man. The divine must assume forms appropriate to our understanding to communicate with us. Thus angels appear to men in corporeal form. Misunderstanding has resulted from pressing too rigorously words derived from a human context to explain the divine. Arguments for and against the Atonement often illustrate this point.

Tindal subjugates God to his effects. It is a mistake, for example, to say that the will of God is determined by the nature and reason of things. The verb 'to will' should be put in the active, and not in the passive mood. Further, God's omnipotence must include more than we can discern.

Similarly, we should not say that God's laws are founded on the eternal reason of things. It is God who is eternal. Everything else is dependent on him. Nor does this mean that God is arbitrary. Perfection of will must be ascribed to God along with every other perfection. Thus, 'his own will is wisdom, and his wisdom is his will. His goodness is arbitrary, and his arbitrariness is goodness.'[16]

Because of the disparity between God and man we cannot agree with Tindal that reason in God and man differ in degree but not in kind. The 'perfection which we call *reason* in God, has some degree of likeness to reason as it is in man, yet infinitely and beyond all conception different from it . . . our share of reason is so small . . . that we can scarce think or talk intelligibly of it, or so much as define our own faculties of reasoning'.[17]

Tindal made much of the scandal of particularity. God should have given a universal revelation, and not favoured the Jews. But we are faced with the 'incomprehensible' with this question. If there is a God he must foreknow everything. But self-consciousness proves our existence and free-will. Providence thus exceeds our capacity to understand. In any case a universal revelation would only have increased men's guilt. Persons unfit to receive would only reject it.

Law rejects the idea that if God's will is incomprehensible, we should have no means of judging it. We have some natural capacity of judging right of God. Thus, although we cannot judge why revelations are given, or the form in which they are given, we can judge the reason for receiving them as divine. Revelation must be judged by itself and not by external criteria. Miracles and prophecy are a sufficient proof of divine revelation. Whilst they cannot prove bad or false doctrines to be good and true, they prove 'that we ought to receive such doctrines, both as true and good, which we could not know to be true and good without such miracles'.[18] Nor can the validity of miracles be tested by the reasonableness of the doctrines revealed by them. Revelation and miracles are necessary because something had to be divulged that reasoning could never discover.

Reasoning is, of course, as natural and inevitable to man as seeing. The question between believer and unbeliever is not whether reason should be used, but how to use it well.

Christians oppose unbelievers, not because they *reason*, but because they reason *ill*. They receive revelation, not to suppress the natural power, but to give new and heavenly light to their reason; not to take away their right of judging for themselves, but to secure them from false judgements.[19]

As bigotry is weak reasoning, unbelievers are as prone to it as believers.

The value of reason is easily overstated. Social custom rather than any internal power usually determines our development. Among Hottentots we should become Hottentots. What reason asserts it first accepts as custom. Tindal confuses what we procure by education with natural reason. So called natural reason is usually a mixture of reason and custom. If natural religion is sufficient why cannot we name men who attained perfection in religious knowledge without revelation? The course of six thousand years argues against Tindal's central position. We can no more reason sufficiently about God than love our neighbours sufficiently. If Tindal is correct in asserting that men left the light of reason and succumbed to priestly falsehoods, what credit can be given to a light men so easily leave?

'Was our reason steady, and of one kind, there would be just the same steadiness and regularity in our tempers.'[20] But as foolish aversions and loves are as much the operation of reason as judgement is the act of reason ('right reason in morality, is nothing else but right love, and right aversion') what we call the blindness of the passions ought to be called the blindness of reason. If human loves and hates cannot be our standard, neither can reason.

According to Tindal it is by reason that we are distinguished from beasts. In this case imprudence and immorality are attributable to reason, for no beast, being without reason, can be either of these things.

In a passage with probable autobiographical overtones Law maintains that bodily spirits are engaged in reasoning, and the more closely we reason the more the spirits may be excited:

Sometimes the attention of the mind is so great, and has so engaged and called in all the animal spirits to its assistance, that the operations of our senses are suspended, and we neither

see, nor feel, till the attention of the mind has let the spirits
return to all the parts of the body.[21]

His conclusion is: if reason is the universal agent in natural
man we cannot assert its perfection because man is so imperfect.
Whilst religious assertions must be agreeable to right reason
human reason no more attains this than men the angelic condition. Right reason is attained only with difficulty. It is absurd to
maintain that men should be governed by natural reason alone.

In 1790 Burke could assert that Deism had been forgotten.
Together with the work of Hume from a different angle,
Englishmen look to Law's book and those of Berkeley (*Alciphron*
1732) and especially Butler (*The Analogy of Reason* 1736) as
largely determining its death.

Law's conception of reason is a little curious. His reference
to it is clearly transitional between the Augustan confidence in
the *Serious Call* and the later deprecations of the affective mystic.
Malebranche could term reason that faculty used in inquiries
concerning the natural world, and the reality that speaks to us
in prayerful solitude.[22] In this book Law seems to accept the
restriction on reason by Enlightenment thought to ratiocination. His point of departure must also be remembered. In
*The Fable of the Bees* he was arguing against one who flaunted
reason. Here he was arguing against one who idolized his
conception of it.

He has not forsaken Malebranche yet. His master was aware
of the need for revelation to supply the deficiencies of reason.[23]
But Law has probably been reading the fourteenth-century
German mystics with renewed attention. Super-rational truth
was all-important for them. Tauler was their spokesman when
he asserted that because of the Fall 'man has wounded himself
mortally with blindness in his reason'.[24]

What chiefly distinguishes Law from Tindal is Law's latent
mystical feeling. This has been well characterized by G. R.
Cragg: 'Law was a believer who felt deeply the majesty of God
and the mystery of life. Tindal was a scholar whose understanding of religion was abstract and academic.'[25]

Law anticipated some of Butler's arguments. Like Law, Butler
refused glib rationalism. Nature is obscure and perplexing.

This being so we should not be surprised that revealed religion presents difficulties. 'We are placed . . . in the middle of a scheme . . . every way incomprehensible', he concludes.[26] But Butler restricts himself more to ratiocination than Law. Where Law speaks of the necessity for vision and imagination, Butler is more content to speak of the probable truth of the Christian scheme on the supposition that 'there is a God'. There is an analogy between accepting truth about nature and revealed religion, despite obscurities in both.[27]

It is said that Tindal wrote a second volume answering his critics. It was never published because Bishop Gibson suppressed it. It seems that Law intended also returning to the theme. Indeed, the first editions of *The Case of Reason* bore the qualification, 'Part the First'.[28] Walton reckoned to have come across a hundred pages or so of the projected continuation. Fragments of what may have been this are still extant. In them Law questions whether the perfect religion need be given to all men at the beginning of time, and draws conclusions from the fact that 'The Life of Man is a progressive State of Wisdom'. He believes that God's nature and our duty to him are self-evident. He is as certain of God as of his own existence. The matter is too plain to be demonstrated. But he allows that belief in God is due to custom as well as reason. He considers, also, that the idea of eternity 'confound(s) the mind of man'.[29] That this volume was never completed was due to a change in Law's understanding of the human approach to God.

The value of Law's remarkable book lies in its appreciation that the difficulties confronting natural religion are as serious as those confronting revealed religion. He is also conscious of the danger of pressing the use of analogy until God is merely an ideal likeness of man. His willingness to use introspection and what he calls vision and imagination enables him to supplement reason in questions of philosophical theology. He believes in the direct apprehension of God, the use of analogy to give terms to this apprehension, and the use of reason and analogy further to establish the reality of God and belief that what is unknowable in God will not contradict what is communicable. Those who are willing to credit faculties other than observation and reason are likely to find Law convincing.

# 8

## LETTERS TO A LADY

A pastoral case with which Law was confronted in 1731–2 was that of an Anglican lady, personally troubled and feeling the attraction of the church of Rome. Though not intended for publication, the letters Law wrote to the lady are interesting in showing his power as a spiritual adviser and his literary fluency.[1]

A scrap of paper prefacing the original letters intimates that the lady was Miss Elizabeth Dodwell, daughter of the Nonjuror and sister of the clever pamphleteer of that name. Internal evidence and the judgement of Overton agree with this identification.[2] The same informant mentions that Miss Dodwell had been impressed with the visions of Jane Lead, the Philadelphian.

She seems to have written two letters before Law replied. She describes herself as a Christian believer, but she considers the Reformation 'mean', and private judgement unreliable. The unity of the Church is required and the Pope should be the focal point of this. Comparing Roman Catholics with Anglicans she thinks it odd that the king should be head of the Anglican church, and wrong that Anglicans have less regard for their religion and priests than have Roman Catholics for theirs. Roman Catholics often write the best books—she mentions à Kempis and Pascal—and they have more charity. She can understand (accept?) such doctrines as transubstantiation, purgatory, prayers for the dead, celibate priesthood, seven sacraments, fasts, and the denial of the worship of images and giving the laity the Scriptures. Difficult points, like the denial of Communion in both kinds and the use of a foreign language in worship may be resolvable by the authority of the Church. She is greatly troubled.

Her brother has rejected Christianity because of its lack

of authority and quarrels. The liberty of the press is a scandal. She has been in touch with a convent. Dr Hickes' *The Dignity of the Christian Priesthood* helped her to value Roman Catholics and Nonjurors. Law dates her letters 18.10.1728 and 17.8.1730.

His first reply is dated 25.5.1731. Someone had put her papers into his hands. He believes her attraction to Rome is caused really by her anxieties due to her brother.

We cannot ask the Church to prevent abuse in the press. It no more argues against the providence of God respecting the Church than his allowance of pagan tyranny in former times which resulted in apostasy.

Predestination and absolute decrees are not so plain in the Bible as she thinks. All that we can tell is that

> God has an eternal knowledge of, and exercises an eternal providence over all things that are; the justice, wisdom, and goodness of which, are not possible to be comprehended by creatures of our size, but are to be believed and adored.[3]

Miss Dodwell believes that if the Anglican church was a channel of God's grace, Anglicans would be more pious. If she lived in the pre-Reformation Church, she would have even more reason for scruple. The same might apply if she was a Roman Catholic now, at least they are no better than us. The defect in Christian ordinances is due to 'that liberty which we have of rendering them useless'.[4] Nor is it true that if Christians lived as they should we would not wish to leave the earth. If Christians lived as they ought we would wish for heaven even more than now, for the earth can never satisfy us. Life is a continual struggle against evil. There are enemies within and without and our corrupt nature needs 'fiery trials and purifications'.[5] But the Church assists society to secure what happiness is available. It is difficult to make a moral generalization about Christendom. There are surely proofs of piety in her own family? Might not such instances be extended?

In fact a 'blamable curiosity' attaches to her question. We may not ask why angels fell, why their state is irrecoverable, why God seems to treat our fall with more compassion than theirs, so we cannot measure providence or the depths of human or divine nature. We should meekly resign ourselves to an adorable providence.

G

He allows that the history of the Church is often not reassuring. But papal history can be as disturbing as Reformation history. A consideration of the work of the Convocation in England and the Council of Trent makes it difficult to decide who contributed most to the schism. But sins cannot be automatically transmitted to future generations. The 'means of Christian salvation are fully preserved both in the English and Romish communion'.[6] Only if we live in a schismatical spirit do we incur the guilt of that most dreadful sin, schism. A divided Church is not something to be happy about, of course. People in each section are educated in party zeal and learn to wrangle. Christians are exposed to the very passions Christ came to destroy. At the same time it may be that more people will be saved because in the providence of God history took the course it did. Roman Catholic leaders were made to remove various scandals only because reformers added their voices to those of saintly members of their own communion.

Dr Hickes' book certainly has merit, but his ideal description fits no earthly Church. If Nonjurors think the true Church is to be found only among them, they are more blamable than Roman Catholics. They are wrong if they try to found a Church distinct from that established, or if they think they exist in a greater state of purity. Either they accept the laws and doctrines of the established Church as theirs or they do not. If they do, then purity of the Church is theirs also. If they do not, they are new reformers without authority, and deserters of what they accuse the Reformers of deserting. Law would rather worship privately than with a Church which unchurched all other Christians.

She believes that Hickes' ideals would come nearer realization if we accepted the Pope as head of the Church. But the Early Church gave power to the Pope for the Church's good. It is conceivable, therefore, that the Church might remove that power for the Church's good. Again, if the Pope adds temporal power and tyranny to his spiritual power, must not princes protect their people from such tyranny? All the patriachates were established only after a lapse of time. There is nothing divine in their office. Living in different days we must establish different governmental forms for the Church.

It is true that Roman Catholic writers have written books

indicating the inspiration of God in their work. This leads to the conclusion, 'I trust to be received by him [God] as truly of the same communion with all his saints, as if I had been a member of every particular church in which any of them lived'.[7]

He ends with the hope that God will prevent her deception by any error he might have written and the assurance of his prayers on her behalf.

Miss Dodwell's reply is dated 17 June 1731. She says that Law has given a better account of her mind than she herself could have done. She is tormented thinking about the destiny of her brother and believes Law's writing too harsh. She almost refused to read *Christian Perfection* because some said 'that it was full of Impossibilities such as must frighten some, and harden others'. Perhaps the doctrine of universalism is true. A letter from Francis Lee to her father commends it. He said that Origen believed it.

Law replied on 9 November 1731. He assures her of his prayers for her. He had three or four conversations with Lee and found him learned and pious, but he 'seemed to be very notional, and much exposed to every new way of reasoning, that came into his mind'. For a while he was a Philadelphian and they cannot be praised. They 'pretend to immediate communications with God and the spiritual world'. These pretensions are founded on 'nothing'. Angels are members of a higher order than humans and we cannot penetrate their secrets. Law read various plausible accounts of the Philadelphians' experiences but found that they contradicted each other. Such experiences appeal to us because of our ignorance.

We can only turn to God as penitents. Man was turned out of Paradise into a cursed world so that he might purify his soul for its 'return to God'.[8] When we consider how poorly philosophers have talked about God and religion and compare with this the depth of wisdom disclosed in Scripture without any aid 'from human parts, or human learning', we discern the true fountain of religious knowledge and those best qualified to partake of it.

Origen was one of the first to trouble the world by fancies bred from his own erudition. Despite his mortified life and vast knowledge Law would be pleased to leave his company to learn his religion with a poor mechanic of whom he read, who was governed by this spirit: 'I am nothing, I have nothing, I am worth nothing: I desire nothing, but to love, adore, praise, and obey God, in everything, and for everything'.[9] Knowledge can trap us. Law only wants the knowledge that Christian virtue and the love of God will give him.

> These virtues fill the mind with more light and knowledge of God, than all the libraries of human learning. . . . They are the keys of Divine Knowledge . . . they make us friends of God . . . they are, as it were, so many inward eyes of the soul, always receiving a sufficiency of light from God.[10]

We cannot know whether all things will be restored, determine the full meaning of hell, or know why there is so much disorder in the world. Whilst learning and reason have their place in religion, 'Religion never entered into the fallen world that way (through reason), by condescending to explain all the difficulties . . . so it is against reason to think, that it must now, or at any other time, be supported in that manner'.[11] Christian lives, not new arguments, will root out infidelity. The fall of Adam and Eve seems to have been occasioned by an innocent desire for knowledge not suitable for them. We sin, likewise, by curiosity respecting knowledge higher than that revealed to us.

The tenor of Scripture and the 'constant general belief of the Church' do not favour belief in universalism. Until God casts fresh light upon the subject we must resign our friends and ourselves to God knowing that his goodness far exceeds our own.

Law does not wish to lessen the affection she feels towards her brother. But she must know that sometimes we must choose between God and man. The love of God must curb natural love and broaden it so that we learn to love all men. We must not dwell upon the possible destiny of our loved ones nor renounce God because of the melancholy destiny that might be theirs.

Miss Dodwell replied on 10 December 1731. Her brother had been taunting her about her Christian profession. He had said that some used the cloak of Christianity to give expression to their 'ill-nature' (a reference to Law?). But she concludes, 'Your Prayers, for Us, give me the greatest Satisfaction imaginable, which I earnestly beg the Continuance of.'

On 29 May 1732 Law answered his correspondent. Respecting her fears for her brother he reminds her that she is enjoined by God, a greater authority than any Church, to be humble and resigned. Reason, scripture, and all the Churches agree on this. He sees no point in her words concerning the comforts of the Church of Rome.

The Bible is the best devotional book. After that, à Kempis' *Imitation*. She may wish to confine herself to the Bible and Law singles out Christ's discourses as specially valuable.

Her real trouble is her restless, inquisitive spirit. The antidote is resignation to God. The more confidence we give him, the more will experience confirm that confidence. 'You have no more reason to fear distraction than I have. Your *danger is my danger, and my security is yours*. When I consider my own weakness, how often my mind is affected and discomposed with trifles, I might justly apprehend, that if I was left to myself, very common misfortunes might put me besides myself.' God's ominpotent goodness preserves him.

Law's last letter is dated 16 September 1732. She seems to have found peace of mind partly through Law's advice and prayers. It seems that she had received a proposal to marry and she asks Law's advice. He counsels that if the gentleman 'is a friend to all your virtues and ready to join with you in a Course of Piety, I think it to be a very providential call from your present trial'. He will hear of no acknowledgement for his labours. The obligations have been mutual and he will be pleased to be of service to her at any future time.

Law emerges from these pastoral letters as an apt, if somewhat harsh, adviser. It is interesting to note the value Miss Dodwell put upon his prayers for her and the fact that, despite Law's celibacy and rigorism, he can appreciate marriage, penetrate to the psychological core of the problem, and even end gallantly to a woman who doubtless deserved such attention.

He remains at the transitional stage theologically. He heeds what Bible, Church, and reason determine in commending doctrine, but his approval of learning is perfunctory and the weight of his approval is upon piety, spiritual apprehension, and good living. He seems to have recognized the great importance of the Fall and he will later enlarge that recognition. In view of his later opinions we should notice his knowledgeable and cool assessment of the Philadelphians' enthusiasm. But he will later prize the writings of Francis Lee. These letters show how far he had come from the position of the *Serious Call* wherein he states that reason is our universal law.[12] It is likely, also, that he has grown more charitable on the question of church membership. Although Anglicans and Roman Catholics are alone mentioned, he recognizes the work of human ill-will in schism and the possibility of being above church divisions in worship and love.

# 9

## LAW'S PROSE

Law's distinction as a stylist is not disputed. We have noted some of those who have admired his prose.[1] We may consider briefly certain important features of his style since these help to elucidate his character and developing views.

Throughout his literary career Law fulfilled the maxims of Cicero that literature must teach, delight, and move. Certain changes accompanied his absorption in Boehme so that we can conveniently distinguish an earlier and a later style.

In the first period clarity and force predominate. Clarity was to be expected of an Augustan writer. This was the Age of Reason. Mathematical proof was the type of all proof. Even as late as his letter to Miss Dodwell Law could say that if Christians concentrated on good living 'Christianity would be more than mathematically demonstrated to common-sense'.[2] The dry symbols of a mathematical proof, with a close argument proceeding necessarily to a conclusion affected the sensibility of Augustan men, including Law. He refers often to reason, common sense and occasionally to mathematics. Many of his books are constructed in whole or part as arguments. This is the clue perhaps to the 'continuous' nature of his prose noted by Maurice's friend.[3]

The force with which he wrote is partly characteristic of his age. Men had shown the universe to be orderly and established regard for civil order. Men were proud to be English, as Newton and Locke were fellow-countrymen, and England was a rising European power. But there is extra force in Law's work different from anything in Addison or even Johnson. He was by nature forceful and this was augmented by religious conviction.

He quotes little from other sources. The chief literary source moulding his prose was of course the Bible. He must have known most of it by heart and he continually ruminated its

message. Quotations and reminiscences from the Bible are
common in Law. Consider this random passage:

> We must fear, and *watch, and pray*, like Men that are always
> in Danger of *eternal Death*, and we must believe and hope,
> labour and aspire, like Christians, that are called to *fight the
> good Fight of Faith, and lay hold on eternal life*.[4]

Of these forty-four words seventeen are biblical (and italicized).
In addition words like 'believe', 'hope', 'labour', 'Danger', and
'called' are probably derived from the Bible. His occasional
divergence from the Authorized Version is probably due to
his preference for the Greek text.

Despite his intimacy with the Book of Common Prayer there
are few direct quotations from it,[5] but as the Prayer Book
makes constant use of biblical words, muted reference to it is
more likely than we might suppose.

His reading of the mystics influences some phrases. He writes
of 'seraphic love', 'friends of God', and the overflowing love of
God, all of which he must have encountered among the mystics.[6]

Law probably quoted little from others because of his creative
ability as a writer and because he was a religious essayist rather
than an academic scholar. It is also true that the revulsion
against the 'scholastic' writing of the seventeenth century,
together with the rise of the coffee-house as a meeting ground
for educated men, meant that witty, unbulky, well-argued
volumes were at a premium.

His style is direct and almost conversational. He hopes he
has 'hit upon' the true state of perfection.[7] Important words
like 'reason' and 'perfection' are never precisely defined.
Enumerated points do not always seem essential. Such features
emphasize the unacademic quality of Law's writing but not
imprecision in the mind of the author. He told Byrom that he
would not learn shorthand because he could write faster than
he could think.[8] As Law must have been a quick thinker, he
must be referring to the care with which he wrote.

He uses italics liberally and arbitrarily. Consider this almost
random passage:

> You go to hear a Play: I tell you, that you go to hear
> *Ribaldry* and *Profaneness*; that you entertain your Mind with

extravagant *Thoughts*, wild *Rants*, *blasphemous Speeches*, *wanton amours*, *profane jests*, and *impure Passions*. You may as well ask me, Where is the Sin of *Swearing* and *Lying*? For it is not only a Sin against this or that particular Text of Scripture, but it is a Sin against the *whole Nature* and Spirit of our Religion.[9]

No eighteenth-century author known to the writer uses italics as frequently as Law. In this passage seventeen out of ninety words are italicized. Nor is his method of italicizing fully rational. If the adjectives preceding the nouns 'Speeches . . . Passions' merit emphasis, so do 'extravagant . . . wild'. If 'whole Nature' is to be italicized, so should 'Spirit' be.

This literary unbalance suggests a personal root. It is corroborated by the violence with which he can write about the importance of rigorism. His own life cultivated humanist virtues more than his writing would lead us to expect. Match Law's style with the remarks of T. S. Eliot on Lancelot Andrewes:

The most conspicuous qualities of his style are three: ordonnance, or arrangement and structure, precision in the use of words, and relevant intensity. . . . Intellect and sensibility were in harmony; hence arose the peculiar qualities of his style.[10]

Law's unbalance was partly congenital and partly due to cultural factors. It accounts in some measure for the possibility of eccentric features developing in his thought.

His literary cartoons in *Christian Perfection* and especially in the *Serious Call* are most successful. He was aware of course that Plato used myths and that the Bible used parables to point truths difficult for the reason to absorb. Gibbon mentions the work of La Bruyère.[11] But the most obvious source is the *Spectator*. Steele's portraits of Sir Roger de Coverley and his circle were meant to be morally educative and were successful with the leisured classes whom Law himself wished to influence.

Without such cartoons his readers might have grown bored. As illustrative of moral truth they were able to prove by example what argument limped to show. Law was aware of this. Of his foolish characters he wrote:

If you are only told in the gross, of the folly and madness of a life devoted to the world, it makes little or no impression on you; but if you are shown how such people live every day . . . this would be an affecting sight . . . and are therefore nowhere more proper than in books of devotion.[12]

An additional reason prompted his portraits of ideal Christians like *Eusebia* and *Ouranius*. He blamed the misdirection of *Matilda*'s life upon the corrupt times that gave her no models.[13] He supplies imaginatively what was to be encountered only rarely in life.

He omits physical features from these portraits. Steele and La Bruyère make good use of such qualities to enforce deeper points. Might not Law have made us disapprove of *Succus* all the more if he had drawn our attention to his fat belly and bulging face?[14] Platonism and rigorism seem to have diverted Law from concentration on the physical. Even so he succeeds, so that O. Elton can say that 'Law sometimes reminds us of Newman in his power of transfixing'.[15]

Gibbon remarked upon the flavour given to Law's writing by his gifts of satire and wit. Here again he is a child of his time. We need only mention such names as Pope, Swift, Steele, and Gibbon to recall the outcrop of satire the age produced. According to B. Willey the root of this satire lay in the disparity felt by cultivated men between Christian and humanist ideals and the commercial and low realities of life apparent in the eighteenth century.[16] The disparity between the ideal and the actual certainly tormented Law. With Gibbon satire often sneers. With Swift it can hate. With Law it is rarely far from humour. Elton remarks justly, 'the foe of the stage has some of the gifts of the comedian. The figures are often drawn with a kind of good temper, and Law does not frown until he comes to the application.'[17]

His bad or ridiculous characters are more alive than his good ones. Caroline Spurgeon traced the reason for this to the fact that Law valued mundane life so little. One good person therefore resembles another: a good doctor is acceptable to God because he is good, not because he is a doctor.[18] The influence of Platonism is again at work.

The appearance of *The Spirit of Prayer* (1749–50) signified the transformation in Law's style that had been developing for years. Advance in holiness and the discovery of a satisfying myth to express his beliefs brought new integration and charity to his character. These are reflected in his writing. Elton comments:

> He discovers a gift for soaring eloquence that keeps at a steady height. He is very copious, and his reiteration of image and symbol produces a kind of dazzling obscurity . . . The effect can sometimes be majestic: a word we use charily at all times, and of eighteenth-century writers very seldom.[19]

In a similar vein Caroline Spurgeon observed:

> There is a tolerance, a tender charm, an imaginative quality and a melody of rhythm rarely to be found in the early work. The sentences are longer and move at a different measure.[20]

Such qualities emerge in an arbitrarily chosen passage from *The Spirit of Love*:

> And did not the supernatural Light stream forth its Blessings into this World, through the *Materiality* of the Sun, all outward Nature would be full of the *Horrors* of Hell. And hence are all the mysteries and Wonders of Light, in this material System, so astonishingly great and unsearchable; it is because the *natural Light* of this World is nothing else but the Power and Mystery of the *supernatural Light*, breaking forth, and opening itself, according to its Omnipotence, in all the various Forms of elementary Darkness which constitute this temporary World.[21]

The rhythm is slower now as it lifts a more numinous vision. Obscure phrases like 'supernatural Light' are repeated, especially if they suggest the numinous. Analogies and reminiscences from nature—water, sunlight and the opening of buds—give wings to his thought, for in a particular way Law came to think that nature revealed God. Intuitive impressionism takes the place of logic and praise the place of force in his style. The majesty of Love that he visualizes and somehow saw melts his satire and thin clarity into deep love and the sense of the beauty of God.

Whatever the truth or falsehood of Boehme's vision, it brought that kind of assurance to Law which resulted in deeper personal integration and sanctification and the release of the springs of poetry and imagination. Of course truth can be communicated by myth as well as by rational discourse. It is therefore not surprising that an orthodox Christian and English scholar, appreciative of Norse and other myths, should write thus of the *Appeal* :

> I . . . like it as well as any religious work I have ever read. The *prose* of the *Serious Call* has here been melted away and the book is saturated with delight and the sense of wonder; one of those rare works which make you say of Christianity, 'Here is the very thing you like in poetry and the romances, but this time it's true.'[22]

Law wrote no more primarily for literary effect in the second than in the first stage of his career. Primarily he remained an apologist, an evangelist and a pastor. He wrote to Thomas Langcake during the second stage:

> It is for the sake of this *spirit of prayer*, that I have endeavoured to set so many points of religion in such a view, as must dispose the reader to give up all he inherits from his fallen father, to be *all hunger and thirst after God*.[23]

It is likely that he only wrote after 1740 when he felt divinely compelled to do so. He came to rely more and more on divine guidance with time, and there is a warmth and rhythmic quality about his later work suggesting that it welled up as he wrote in a spirit of prayer. The gap of nine years between the publication of *Trapp* and *The Spirit of Prayer* thus finds a more complete explanation than that provided by Hobhouse, who only drew attention to Law moving house, learning German, and becoming more absorbed in Boehme.

Having mentioned the misfortune of Boehme's system not appearing in one book he improved the situation by writing the *Appeal*, in which his appropriation of that system is set down. In *The Spirit of Prayer*, *The Spirit of Love* and *The Way to Divine Knowledge* he drew out particular aspects of the system and showed how his thought had matured in certain aspects. The writing in this second stage is superior to that of the first, as its thought is deeper. The exception is the *Dialogue on Justification* (1760), which Law wrote hurriedly, with interruptions and when he was old. That the *Address* (1761) shows some flatness and diffuseness may suggest a criticism of the eventual effects of affective mysticism on the personality or only point to the decrepitude of old age.

On four separate occasions in this second period Law employed the dialogue form of writing. It was often used by contemporary writers as the dialogues of Berkeley and Hume suggest. Its traditional value had been shown by Plato. Possibly Boehme's use of the method in *Of true repentance* and *Dialogues on the Supernatural Life* influenced him most. Law's mastery is wanting here. His characters are somewhat lifeless and usually ploys to enable the person representing Law to state the truth.

It is a pity that Law never translated Boehme. The reason he gave for not having done so was that he had 'never yet been enough moved to enter upon them'. He believed that Elliston and Sparrow's translation showed much piety and ability but that it is

> *too much loaded with words*, and in many places the *sense is mistaken*. A new translator of J.B. is not to have it in intention to make his author more intelligible by softening or refining his language. His style is what it is, strange and uncommon; not because he wanted learning and skill in words, but because what he saw and conceived was quite new and strange.

Law would let Boehme speak in his own way, add notes to guard against misapprehensions, indicate the most important books and by prefaces and introductions guide the reader to the true use of the writings.[24]

Three important conclusions follow from this brief discussion. First, Law was a child of his time much influenced by the cultural currents of the day. Second, he was possessed of a certain vehemence and instability. Third, Boehme brought him new life and peace.

# 10

## JACOB BOEHME

So deeply affected were John and Charles Wesley by Law's two devotional treatises that they were prepared to walk from Oxford to Putney to consult Law. John's first visit was in 1732.

Their friendship continued until the breach in 1738, John venerating Law and Law respecting John. We find John beginning to read the *Theologica Germanica* in July 1732, probably on Law's advice. He was with Law frequently; at 9.15 a.m. in November 1733, for example, when he records, 'with Mr Law, not understood all he said'. He corresponded with Law in June 1734 concerning a student friend who agreed with Law's method in religion (including Lenten observances and faithful attendance at the Eucharist) but refused to practise it. In November 1734 he was with Law for three hours.[1] That their conversation went deep and manifested Law's capacity as a spiritual director emerges from two sayings that Wesley later recalled:

> I see where your mistake lies. You would have a philosophical religion; but there can be no such thing. Religion is the most plain, simple thing in the world. It is only, 'We love him, because he first loved us.' So far as you add philosophy to religion, just so far you spoil it.
>
> . . . . . . . . . . . . . . . . . . . . . .
>
> Sir you are troubled because you do not understand how God is dealing with you. Perhaps if you did, it would not so well answer his design. He is teaching you to trust Him farther than you can see him.[2]

It is difficult to think of Welsey being clay even in Law's hands. In 1756 he recalled his opinion of Wesley at this time:

> I was once a kind of Oracle with Mr Wesley. I never suspected any Thing bad of him, or ever discovered any Kind, or

Degree of Falseness, or Hypocrisy in him. But during all the Time of his Intimacy with me, I judged him to be much under the Power of his *own Spirit*.[3]

The direction of Law's thought and the impression he could make on people is suggested by the interview which another Oxford Methodist, Benjamin Ingham, had with him in 1735. Ingham related 'He talked about man's fall, and the one thing necessary', and concludes, 'He is a divine man.'[4]

John Walker wrote to Law asking his advice concerning the work of Madame Bourignon. Law replied in January 1735. He did not want to dissuade him from reading her writings; he also read her with great admiration, despite certain dangerous passages. Perhaps her claims respecting inspiration can be substantiated, her books do 'have something strangely awakening in them'. But if he meets anything reason and Scripture cannot account for, he passes it over as not touching the substance of religion. He cannot judge her for 'I am myself a stranger to, and utterly unworthy of that divine illumination which she pretends to'. If she does not lead Walker into a disregard for the external institutions of religion she may prove a good instructor.

On the question of the renunciation of the world Law says that it is a condition of our baptism. But the phrase means the rejection of what is evil; complete renunciation would end society, and this is not intended. Life is a means of penitence and we should seek employment so that we can exercise humility, charity and penitence. A man may renounce his trade in order to devote more time to religious exercises but 'he that renounces humble, charitable, and painful labour that he may advance in devotion, seems to mistake the point, and to renounce the very best preservative of true devotion'.[5]

Byrom visited Law at Putney that summer and Law seems to have been disturbed by his uncritical acceptance of Madame Bourignon. As they walked in the garden, Law questioned whether she did not mix her own spirit with inspiration as Luther did. He mentioned her statement that she was the only Christian and that the death of Christ was needless (which death was 'the very foundation of all Christianity'), and her belief concerning the end of the world. Tauler had all the good to be found in her and yet was 'the humblest man alive'.

Begging Byrom's pardon for his freedom, he said it was absurd to call Ruysbroek the greatest mystical writer. Every age since the time of Christ had produced mystical writers. He mentions Suso.

> The bottom of all was that this world is a prison into which we were fallen, that we had nothing to do but to get out of it, that we had no misery but what was in it, that to be freed from it was all that we wanted, that this was the true foundation of all . . . that the philosophers Epictetus, Socrates, had, by the grace of God and their own search, observed that this world could not be what God made it . . . there was a necessity for every one to feel the torment of sin, that it was necessary for them to die in this manner and to descend into hell with Christ, and so to rise again with him; that everyone must pass through this fiery trial in this world or another.

On the question of reading devotional books he advised that we must 'fall in with grace' when we find ourselves touched. Otherwise we miss the point of devotional reading. When called upon to suffer we should abandon ourselves to God and rejoice Gloriâ Patri. Justice was done to God by our suffering. Law believed that there was music in the phrases of the Lord's Prayer.[6]

A student of Boehme might have spoken as Law did, but there is kinship among all Christian mystics and particular affinity among some. The man who relished the fourteenth-century German mystics was well prepared for Boehme, and the lover of such French writers as Madame Guyon and Madame Bourignon was prepared to accept much of Boehme's practical teaching.

He encountered Boehme about this time. He told the Moravian, Francis Okely, not long before his death, that he first came across Boehme's name in the *Fides et Ratio* of Pierre Poiret (1646–1719). Soon afterwards he obtained accidentally one of Boehme's best books.

> When I first began to read him, he put me into a *perfect sweat*. But as I discerned sound truths, and glimmerings of a deep ground and sense, even in the passages not then clearly intelligible to me; and found in myself a strong incentive to

*dig* in these writings, I followed the impulse with continual aspirations and prayer to God for his help and divine illumination, if that I was called to understand them. By patiently reading in this manner again and again, and from time to time, passing over any little objections and difficulties that stood in my way for the moment, I perceived that my heart felt well, and my understanding kept gradually opening; till at length I discovered the wonderful treasure there was hid in this field.[7]

We may proceed to a brief account of Boehme's life and teaching in order to understand Law's appreciation of him and profound indebtedness to him.

Jacob Boehme (called Behmen in eighteenth-century England) was born in 1575 in German Silesia. He was the son of solid, possibly well-to-do, parents. His ancestors were German and his father was a farmer. He was one of eight children and received a pious Lutheran upbringing. Though troubled by ill-health he proved a good pupil. On leaving school he became an apprentice cobbler and undertook journeyman's travels which broadened his horizon. In Upper Lusatia he found considerable religious and social conflict and as a consequence his own faith was challenged and he came to dislike religious squabbling. He was a close student of the Bible and attended church regularly. Eventually, he settled in Gorlitz, a lively town where many of the cross-currents of the age met. He became a cobbler and in 1599 he married. Family life was happy and his wife bore him four children.

He came under the influence of the town's pastor, Martin Moller. Moller was devout and scholarly, translating patristic literature and leaving references in his literary remains to Tauler, Augustine, Bernard of Clairvaux, the Victorines, Ruysbroeck, Suso, and à Kempis. Though a Lutheran, his theological emphasis lay upon regeneration rather than upon justification. Stoudt believes that 'Martin Moller was the first and perhaps the dominant influence on Jacob Boehme'.[8]

Though legend has embellished the fact, Boehme seems to have had a shattering spiritual experience in 1600. He had been very melancholy and troubled. He remained faithful to God and reconciliation came:

H

What kind of spiritual triumph it was I can neither write nor speak; it can only be compared with that where life is born in the midst of death, and is like the resurrection of the dead.[9]

In the course of this fifteen minutes' experience he believed that he

> saw and knew the Being of all beings, the ground and the unground; the birth of the holy Trinity; the source and origin of this world and all creatures in divine Wisdom . . . I saw three worlds in myself, 1. the divine, angelical, or paradisaical; . . . 2. the dark world . . . 3. the external, visible world . . . and I saw and knew the whole Being in evil and in good, how one originates in the other . . . so that I not only greatly wondered but also rejoiced.[10]

Boehme seems to have been troubled by the clash of Protestant and Catholic belief, the impact of Renaissance thought upon orthodoxy, and the mystery of evil. In his report we notice the crude strength of his writing, the influence of Bible and Luther on his mode of expression and his sense of the ineffable. We must also agree with Stoudt that the experience was 'gnostic in the sense that from it he gained what was for him new knowledge'.[11] Boehme believed that he did not climb up into the Godhead, the Godhead climbed up into him.[12] As Stoudt claims, this is the mystical heart of Lutheranism, but we need not agree that in Boehme's experience the old mystical hierarchy of states of being had been cast aside.[13] Traditional ascetical features are present in Boehme's life, Moller was profoundly indebted to Catholic thought, that thought has always asserted the initiative of God, certain impurities mingle with Boehme's experience and interpretation and Law was permeated with the traditional schemes, yet relished Boehme.

He believed that God had given him a message for mankind. He committed his thoughts to paper and a friend published them. They fell into the hands of Moller's successor at Gorlitz, Gregory Richter, whose rationalistic theology and poor piety were in sharp contrast to the teaching of Moller. By the instrumentality of this vicious man Boehme was banished from Gorlitz.

The offending book was the *Aurora*. In its pages we discover the influence of Moller, Platonism, Neoplatonism, and the

Renaissance humanism of the Silesian humanists. Mention of the Seven Qualities of nature suggests the early influence of the Jewish Cabbala. Readers of G. G. Scholem's *Major Trends in Jewish Mysticism* will notice frequent affinities between that mysticism and the thought of Boehme. In both we find ideas of emanation, the Fall meaning materialization, frequent allusions to fire, the paradox of thesis and antithesis used of God. Scholem calls special attention to 'Boehme's doctrine of the origins of evil, which created such a stir, indeed bears all the traits of Kabbalistic thought'.[14]

There followed a period of literary inactivity during which Boehme read much, meditated, and exchanged views. He associated with a group of scholars interested in alchemy, Schwenkfeldianism, and the Renaissance Platonism proclaimed by Reuchlin and Paracelsus. Stoudt believes that Boehme was 'well and perhaps deeply read in contemporary scientific and theological literature'.[15] In 1619 he seems to have had a second illumination.

With the publication of *Forty Questions* the concepts of Wisdom and the Unground make their appearance. Schopenhauer and Stoudt trace eastern influence here. Perhaps Boehme's cosmopolitan friend, Balthazar Walther, was the source. We do not know, of course, what teaching he may have encountered as a member of a secret religious society. Peuckert considers that the members studied St Paul, the *Theologia Germanica*, Tauler, à Kempis, Weigel, Arndt, and the Schwenkfelders. The publication of *Signatura Rerum* exhibits the strong influence of alchemy.

The devotional tracts gathered together in *The Way to Christ* and *Of Christ's Testaments* show the deep influence of the Bible, Luther and Lutheranism, Schwenkfeld, and Weigel. Alchemical terms virtually disappear. In *Of Predestination* and *Mysterium Magnum* he achieved his greatest writing.

Boehme had been allowed to return to Gorlitz on the understanding that he would publish no more books. Nevertheless his writings circulated in manuscript form. In 1624 some rich friends published his devotional tracts. Richter was stirred to irrational fury. Boehme defended himself with dignity but was forced to leave the city. On his deathbed in the same year he confessed his acceptance of Lutheran principles. Just before

6 a.m. on the morning of his death he asked his son Tobias to open the door because he could hear the strains of sweet music. At about 6 a.m. he gasped, 'Now I go hence to Paradise', and died.[16]

The specific account of Boehme's thought must be short so as not to expand this volume intolerably. The reader is asked to remember that Boehme's understanding developed with the years and that his expression is not always lucid.

Writing of the theogonistic process he asks that only the devout and sympathetic will consider his work. Human words can only hint at the divine reality.

At the basis of everything is the Unground or Abyss. It is a stillness in which nothing has developed. Will is manifested. It fashions a mirror in which to see itself. This Mirror is called sometimes God's visibility, the eternal Wisdom or the Maiden. The Mirror and the Will are so thrilled at seeing reflected the potential glories of God and heaven that they desire its actuality. Eternal Nature is roused as it lies in God and comes forth as the medium through which the imagined realities become actual. The form-giving energy is the Seven Natural Properties or Forms. Three compose the dark ternary and three the light ternary. The middle Property is Fire or the Lightning Flash. The First Property is Desire. It is harsh and hard, what Martensen calls 'Contraction'. The Second Property is movement, what Martensen calls 'Expansion'. The Third Property is born out of the conflict of the first two. It is Anguish, called by Martensen 'Rotation'. Nature in this tortured state longs for freedom. The Fourth Property, or Lightning Flash, gives freedom by turning the dark ternary into a light ternary. Its first touch causes shock and terror. This is inevitable as the first contact between Nature and Spirit, between what is truly God and what is not.

With the conquest by transfiguration of the dark ternary or Fire-Principle begins the light or good ternary. The Fifth Property is Wisdom or 'true love-fire'.[17] It moulds the harsh elements in nature into ripeness and gentleness. The Sixth Property is intelligible sound, by means of which the undifferentiated divine powers become differentiated and audible. 'The Seventh Principle is the corporeal comprehension of the other qualities. It is called *"Essential Wisdom"* or the *"Body of*

*God*".'[18] The image God beheld first in the Mirror is realized through the action of this Property.

The Properties do not act successively, nor are they separate entities. In eternity they act simultaneously. Nor does Boehme intend to say that evil is in God. 'In God all the spirits triumph as one spirit.'[19] Evil arises through separation.

The Trinity expresses itself through Eternal Nature. As the eternal Will is lord over the Fire-Principle God exists as Father. As the eternal Will is bearer of the Light-Principle God exists as the Son. The Son softens the anger of the Father into compassion. The Spirit goes forth from the Father and Son as lord over the united Principles of Fire and Light. Thus there are three will-centres in the one Person of God. Eternal Nature, the Seventh Property, can be understood as the Glory of God; that which exists as an infinite periphery to him.

The divine motive for the creation of life is love and pleasure. He creates, out of himself, the world as an outbirth of Eternal Nature, by means of Eternal Wisdom. Having existed from eternity as a possibility it becomes fact. He recognizes that there are deep questions here that the human mind cannot penetrate and he declares that God would have us children, not lords!

Creation can be thought of as a number of circles. The first circle comprises the angelic world. Michael, Lucifer and Uriel are the archangels, each having a kingdom and a host of angels. Lucifer did not continue as an angel of light. Temptation came through the Fourth Property where the higher and lower ternary meet. Instead of exclusively adoring God he fixed his imagination on himself, he came to envy the Son of God and to perceive the fiery foundation of the created world. He fancied that he could become God. The Fire-Principle burnt up within him and his light was quenched. Hell and the principle of the wrath of God became manifest. Thus Lucifer fell and fell of his own free-will.

He drew his Nature-world with him. God in his mercy set in a reaction. He submerged the whole under water and began a new creation. Lucifer's kingdom was this world, and the first chapters of Genesis record the later actions of this drama.

Man is a microcosm of the universe. The soul descends from the dark Fire-Principle and points to the Father. The spirit descends from the Light-Principle and points to the Son. The body descends from this world of the senses. In Adam the Light-Principle held the other qualities in strict subordination. He understood the speech of God and angels. As the visible world was illumined by the invisible, his body resembled that of Christ after the resurrection.

The world into which he was born was unstable and God intended that he should be the instrument of raising it to its former glory. But he shared the instability of his environment and it was necessary that he should be tempted so that he might attain stability and blessedness. He allowed himself to be excited by the devil into lust for the world. He fell, becoming earthly and finding the divine image in him growing pale. One effect of the fall, which happened gradually, was that Adam, originally androgynous, was separated into two persons, male and female. Because Adam's opposition to God was indirect he could, unlike Lucifer, be saved.

Before the Fall the present four elements of fire, water, air, and earth were one element. In place of the present discord there was harmony and only with the Fall did the hard material appearance of the world occur.

History is important because it is the scene of redemption. Christ became man in order to save man. He is the Second Adam. But his significance is cosmic, through him all things that can be redeemed, will be. To facilitate the birth of Jesus, the Son and the heavenly Virgin Wisdom united with Mary. Thus Jesus possessed the essence of Mary, the essence of the Word and the essence of the heavenly Virgin. The conception and birth were without sin and by them Mary herself was made perfect because the heavenly Virgin penetrated her essences.

Like Adam Christ was essentially androgynous. Outwardly he was a male, fighting evil. But he compasses both sexes showing, for instance, infinite self-devotion and obedience.

His main work was that of Atonement. Love quenched wrath. In the 'Process of Christ' different manifestations of wrath were successively overcome by his love. To conquer the principle from within he had to surrender himself to death. On the Cross he was tried to the uttermost, but once more love conquered every temptation to self-will erupting from the Fire-Principle and the principle of this world within him.

He rose from the grave in a paradisiacal body, his earthly body having been absorbed into it. The resurrection demonstrated the true lordship of Christ. When he ascended to the right hand of the Father he passed to the inward basis of the visible world.

On the day of Pentecost the Holy Spirit was poured into men, so that the history of Christ might become our history. Men could enter into the process of Christ. In promoting such regeneration the work of the Church, especially the preaching of the Word and the administration of the sacraments, is vital. But regeneration is not automatic in the church-goer. An 'historic faith' is useless. The beginning and end of everything is the new birth. He criticizes denominational Christianity, which often gives the appearance of Babel with so many mutually condemning voices and merely letter-learned Christianity.

In baptism a new 'tincture' is added to the individual, but faith must be added for this tincture to unfold. Faith is not just assent, it is the strong desire for Christ, a reaching after him. Christ himself starts the right movement of our wills and when we respond, he gives us himself. Much the same theory underlies his eucharistic theology.

Boehme writes often and well about the life of grace. He frequently categorizes the root sins as pride, covetousness, envy, and wrath. Prayer is the Christian's great aid. He draws often parallels between our difficulties and Christ's experience in the wilderness.

Though a soul may repent in this life, death seals our destiny. The quality of life attained here is determinative. We are bound either for heaven with God or hell with the devil.[20]

We have omitted to mention certain features of Boehme's thought—such as his use of alchemical and theosophical terms, his interest in the mystical significance of names and numbers, and his speculations about ghosts—because of their subsidiary importance, Law's neglect of them in his published works, and considerations of space.

There were English admirers of Boehme before the time of Law. His manuscripts became known after $c$. 1630. R. Whitaker wrote a short biography in 1644. Between 1645–62 the Anglicans Sparrow, Ellistone, Blunden, and Hotham translated them. Charles I admired Boehme's work and he may have financed the translation. T. Whyte and E. Taylor acknowledged their debt to him and Puritans such as Francis Rous, William Dell, John Saltmarsh, and Morgan Lloyd had ideas reminiscent of Boehme. J. Webster, T. Tryon, and of the Cambridge Platonists, at least Henry More, read him, as did the Ranters. George Fox imbibed ideas from an environment permeated with Boehme's influence. Milton, Sir Thomas Browne, and Muggleton may have read him, and Thomas and Henry Vaughan probably did. J. Pordage, Mrs Lead and the Philadelphians, Dr Francis Lee, and Andreas Freher and his associates were disciples in some fashion. John Byrom read Boehme before Law and was content to turn works of Law suffused with Boehme's influence into verse. It is interesting to note that Byrom acknowledged to Mr Kirkhall that he did not understand such books as those written by Eugenius Philalethes, when he visited him in May 1735. Such was the pseudonym of Thomas Vaughan. We are left with the unanswered question whether Byrom and Law had been puzzled by any of Boehme's admirers before meeting the master himself.[21]

It is difficult to know whether Sir Isaac Newton knew, and if so to what extent he was indebted to, the writings of Boehme. The researches of S. Hobhouse and H. McLachlan have suggested that there is no direct evidence of any influence.[22] This view has been challenged by S. Hutin. He believes that hermetic and theosophical treatises by Newton may exist and that he may have had an alchemical laboratory at Trinity College, Cambridge. But he was probably less dependent on Boehme than Law states.[23] We must wait for further information on this subject. Whilst Law may have been wrong in maintaining the tradition of the link between Newton and Boehme, it is worth remembering that he was naturally shrewd and had good connections with Cambridge University.

Boehme has never had many disciples. Few would want to advance his value beyond that ascribed to him by Henry More: 'Honest Jacob is wholesome at the bottom, though a philosopher, but at random.'[24] Why did Law, who assessed the worth of Madame Guyon, Madame Bourignon, Swedenborg, and various enthusiasts so circumspectly, succumb to his influence?[25]

There was some intellectual affinity between them. Both loved the Bible and believed that sound theology unfolded the biblical message. Both appreciated such authors as à Kempis, Tauler, Suso, the writer of the *Theologia Germanica*, and Ruysbroeck. They share a Neoplatonic strain. Gnosticism and the Cabbala were common influences. If Law read these (we cannot be definite that he read the Cabbala) only after encountering Boehme, he was evidently the kind of person to receive their message sympathetically.

Boehme was a powerful thinker and mystic. His odd expression and ideas make him obscure in any century but especially to the commonsense mentality of the eighteenth century. Further his language is large poetic, we cannot apply to him the strict rules of Scholasticism or empiricist philosophy. Most men of the Enlightenment would agree with Warburton:

> *Jacob Boehme*, delivering to us . . . a heap of unmeaning, or . . . unintelligible words . . . if indeed, this *Wisdom* did come from above, it hath so degenerated on its way down, as to be ever unfit to return.[26]

But such a view evaluates Boehme according to mistaken presuppositions. Coleridge, writing from the different presuppositions of the Romantic Age, was able to declare Boehme to have been a stupendous person. With education and knowledge to have corrected his delusions he might have ranked with Plato.[27] It is to Law's credit that he was able to penetrate Boehme's secrets and appreciate his brilliance.

As a mystic of the affective type he stressed the inadequacy of discursive reason in divine things. As reporting a vision rather than promulgating a doctrine his thought is non-, or semi-conceptualist in expression. He dwelt on the prime importance of the new birth. All this appealed to Law. He was prepared to consider the claim that revelation occurred in the seventeenth century, because it might be the divine answer to the loss of primitive enthusiasm and the intellectual problems raised by new knowledge. He accepted Boehme's distinction between *Verstand* (intuitive reason) and *Vernunft* (discursive reason) and the credit Boehme gave to *Verstand* in theology. The difficulty here, of course, is that the individual may mistake feeling for inspiration.[28] Without questioning the inspiration of the Bible he believed that revelation was less propositional than the manifestation of ineffable reality.

As a Christian Gnostic Boehme was more tormented by the problem of evil than that of sin. Enlightenment doubts of Christianity often centred on this question. Law may well have thought that Boehme addressed himself to this ancient problem with more penetration than orthodox theologians.

In common with most men of his day Law had an immense respect for Sir Isaac Newton. Newton made the idea of light important in cultured discussion and directed men's imagination to the cosmic framework of the physical universe. Contemporary theology was more concerned with morals than with mysticism and had little interest in the cosmic setting of belief. Boehme offered Law a theology that made admirable use of the idea of light and was profoundly cosmic in interest (the teaching of Malebranche and the popular idea of the Chain of Being also prepared him to hope for this). In addition Law believed, on the affirmation of a trusted friend, that Newton had made large abstracts from the works of Boehme and that he had looked for the philosopher's tincture partly in accordance with Boehme's recipe. Together with his nephew he had set up furnaces to further his investigations. Newton's ideas concerning attraction and the first three laws of nature were proved most deeply by Boehme with his conception of the First Three Properties of Eternal Nature and their derivation in temporal outbirth.[29]

The need to discover a credible framework for belief had probably become urgent for Law. We can see the Caroline tradition fall into decay as we progress through his writings. Because of this the *Serious Call* is less than lucid. At the same time he was disappointed in the Nonjurors and questioned their tenets. The empirical approach to reality esteemed by the Enlightenment mind, which finds perfect expression in the early memorandum of Bishop Berkeley: 'to be eternally banishing Metaphysics, etc., and recalling Men to Common Sense',[30] was impatient with tradition and desirous of proof. Law began his literary career using reason as a knife. He found the knife striking his own vitals. Deism had challenged him as much as he had challenged it. *Humanus* in *The Way to Divine Knowledge* seems to reflect Law's own experience. He says that he will not try to show from reason and antiquity the need for general and special revelation. The Deist can stand his ground in any battle concerning creeds, doctrines and the 'History of Facts'. 'I . . . have been twenty Years in this Dust of Debate. I had frequently a consciousness rising up within me, that the Debate was equally vain on both Sides.'[31] In some such state as this he met Boehme. He discovered a new cosmology and confirmation of the use of *Verstand* appropriately to prove religious truth.

Theosophy was represented throughout Europe at this time.[32] Religious minds, alienated from tradition, became prone to exaggeration. The point is elucidated by T. S. Eliot in reference to William Blake, who sometimes reminds us of Law. He says, about

> Blake's supernatural territories, as about the supposed ideas that dwell there, we cannot help commenting on a certain meanness of culture. They illustrate the crankiness, the eccentricity, which frequently affects writers outside the Latin traditions . . . they are not essential to Blake's inspiration. Blake was endowed with capacity for considerable understanding of human nature, with a remarkable and original use of language and the music of language, and a gift of hallucinated vision. Had these been controlled by a respect for impersonal reason, for common sense, for the objectivity of science, it had been better for him. What his genius required, and what it sadly lacked, was a framework of accepted ideas which would have prevented him from indulging in a philosophy of his own.[33]

These words can be applied to Law. What is remarkable in his case is the fact that Law agreed with much of what Eliot says. His suspicion of fanciful writers has already been noted. Consider his opinion of Marsay, a curious French mystic, influenced by Boehme:

> I much admire this author, where he only treats of the nature, progress and perfection of the spiritual life. But . . . he is a very fanciful writer; mixing ungrounded notions and flights with that part of religion which should be freest of them. Spirituality itself is such a contrariety both to learned and

to unlearned human nature, that nothing whimsical or conjectural should be connected with it. This gives Rationalists too great an opportunity of exploding it all as chimerical and makes even people well-inclined to it, to be distrustful of it . . . whereas, if the true spirituality of the Christian life was kept within its own bounds, supported only by Scripture doctrines, and plain appearances of nature and experience, human reason would be strangely at a loss to know how to expose it. I could almost wish we had no spiritual books but those wrote by Catholics.[34]

Law has stated the difficulties inherent in speculation with great justness. With respect to his later theology we must conclude that the line dividing sense from nonsense is thin and that there is much that is suggestive and persuasive in Boehme. This latter point is significant because, with an emphasis upon introversion and truth shining in its own light, the believer is prone to confuse objective with subjective fact. Feuerbach and Coleridge considered Boehme's metaphysics to be an esoteric psychology.[35] Tillich believed the Seven Properties in man to anticipate the divine/demonic structure felt by Romantics such as Schelling, and Freud's idea of the unconscious and the conscious.[36]

# 11

## CONTROVERSY WITH THE QUAKERS

Edward Gibbon came down from Cambridge in 1734. He journeyed to Paris and after a year returned to England for marriage and a settled existence. Though Law's formal employment with the Gibbons therefore ended in 1734, he remained in the household until 1738 or 1739; Mr Gibbon senior died in 1737. There is silent testimony here, not only to the munificence of the old merchant, but to Law's personality as being in some sense domestically pleasing.

Edward Gibbon married Judith Porten in June 1736. Their son, Edward, the future historian, was born the following year. Law officiated at the wedding in the church of St Christopher-le-Stocks, as he had done two years previously for a relative of Gibbon. The occasion must have been satisfying for Law, not only because the bridegroom had been his pupil, but because he seems to have reconciled the elder Gibbon to the prospect of the marriage.

In the autumn of 1736 Byrom asked Law's help respecting a young friend of his, Fanny Henshaw. Fanny was a pious Christian on the point of changing her denominational allegiance from Anglicanism to the Society of Friends. In a document called the *Case* Fanny set out her troubled state of mind. After reading this Law agreed to correspond with her.

We may summarize the *Case* as follows.[1] God declared his will to Fanny eighteen months ago. She must obey his will to be Christ's disciple. She must lay aside the foolish amusements of the world so that God's word might take root in her heart. In rejecting the world and applying herself to the Bible she found it often opened at John 4. She was advised by a neighbouring Quaker to resign herself to God if she was worried about her sister's illness and to apply herself to the Bible if she was concerned about herself.

A secret impulse showed her that to be Christ's disciple she must be reborn. Though affected by the sincerity of Friends she noticed that they did not permit the sacraments of baptism or the Lord's Supper. A voice answered her that if she obeyed God's will she would find that his flesh is meat and his blood drink; that he does not dwell in temples made by hand; that the Bible teaches that obedience is better than sacrifice. The voice seemed to intimate that she should become a Friend. But the Anglican Church was the Church of her youth and friends might misunderstand her change of allegiance. A voice seemed to answer her that she must obey almighty God. Continuing fretfully and in prayer she found formal prayers hindering her.

She was invited to hear a visiting Quaker woman preacher. She refused to go but was troubled by her decision. Her distress was evident and the local clergyman tried to convince her of the groundlessness of her opinions. But she could not deny her experience and hopes to become faithful to God's will.

In response to this *Case* Law composed six letters to Fanny between November and Christmas 1736, intended to dissuade her from her intended action. Fanny read three of them and before Law finished his sixth letter she had crossed her Rubicon.

The present-day respect accorded to Friends was not general in the seventeenth and eighteenth centuries. Charles Leslie had been an early critic of the Society. He was a distinguished writer and Nonjuror and his work must have been known by Law. If he missed the good, he fastened on the unfortunate and bad aspects of the new movement. In his *Snake in the Grass* (1697) we find him quoting Friends who believe that the soul is a part of God; that sinless perfection is possible in this life; that immediate revelation is equal to what the Bible teaches; that the doctrine of the Trinity need not be believed as it does not appear in the Bible; that inspiration could be accompanied by quaking and blowing. Fox called himself 'the son of God', and writing to Cromwell mentions 'dirty priests'.[2] Macaulay's doubts about William Penn are well known,[3] and John Woolman seems to have been an exception even in comparison with George Fox, who, for all his genius and strength of character was opinionated and prejudiced.[4] According to the Quaker scholars, Rufus Jones and Stephen Hobhouse, eighteenth-century Friends were often worldly and infected by Quietism.[5]

In his first publication Law had classed Friends with Ranters, Muggletonians, and Fifth-Monarchy Men as fanatics outside the pale of the Church.[6] In *Christian Perfection* he mentions their error in neglecting the sacraments.[7] We should not be surprised that his response to Fanny is to dissuade.

His first letter begins with a quotation from her *Case*. She said that God declared he would accept her if she would lay aside the foolish amusements of the world. Does she mean that certain thoughts came into her head? that she heard a voice? If so, how was she sure it was God's voice? She must have known that Quakers speak of immediate inspiration and perhaps she desired to be inspired. He wonders what her relations with Quakers have been and he would like to have known more about her early life.

She thought it remarkable that her Bible kept opening at John 4 (which contains the Friends' favourite text about God being a Spirit). Law suggests that she is 'upon the watch for things extraordinary'.[8] God does not open a book for us. Coincidence suggested a false significance because she knew how Friends valued the chapter. He believes that a Roman Catholic priest, finding Fanny young, imaginative, tender, and desiring to serve God, would have persuaded her to become a Roman Catholic. Had this happened she would in any case have been free from the 'natural disorders' Quakers tend to engender and filled with humility and faith.

As Popery prevails against sense it recommends self-denial and faith, gaining an entrance by us closing our eyes. Quakerism prevails against the deliberations of Christ, the Bible, tradition, reason, and the counsel of the saints. It gains an entrance by exciting the soul and body. Lowly institutions can be ignored by those who expect supernatural happenings. He counsels patience. 'Haste, impetuosity, and eagerness of mind are not from the Spirit of God.'[9] Being inwardly divided she mistakes good and bad. In the fervent exposition of the theme that the Church is the refuge for distressed souls he quotes the Te Deum.

Law begins his second letter by commending her desire to forsake the world and be reborn. Had she joined with this godly desire the request to be relieved of self-will, the new birth would be proceeding in her. She might as well forsake the Bible as forsake outward ordinances. The outward word and

sacrament were only ordained for the sake of the new birth.
'Every mystery of our redemption is more or less signifyed,
represented, and offered to us by the Holy Sacraments of
Baptism and the Lord's Supper.'[10] Furthermore, the more we
are reborn the more we must love what Christ said, did, and
appointed. To despise the sacraments only means that we are
born of ourselves.

The message of John 4 that God is a Spirit has not been
specially appropriated by the Quakers. They have a human
society full of distinctions invented by fancy.

The poor woman in the Gospel believed she would be healed
if she could only touch the hem of Christ's garment. He commended her faith despite her use of an outward thing. Pride
afflicts the Quaker no less than the Pharisees. The Pharisees
were proud of their good works and the Quakers, by their
neglect of Christ's command, are proud of their bad works.
It is easy to be deceived. He counsels *humility and contrition*.[11]

Law's third letter is missing and only the two final paragraphs
of the fourth letter remain. He urges humility and the willingness to be crucified for Christ's sake, despite the natural wish
for more dramatic and speedy effects.

The fifth letter begins with Fanny's claim that she heard
God's voice saying that obedience is better than sacrifice.
Though words of Scripture were involved this is no proof of
divine utterance. The devil quoted Scripture when he tempted
Christ in the wilderness. Auditions should be tested 'by the end
and design that was intended' by the words.[12]

Biblical words intend now what they intended at first. We
cannot believe that David wished for the rejection of outward
institutions because Solomon, who succeeded David, built a
temple in accordance with God's will. It is useless and possibly
indicative of pride to quote Paul's words at his conversion as
applicable to herself. In any case after his conversion he had
hands laid upon him and was baptized. Again Jesus was
baptized by John. If Jesus was not too high to receive John's
baptism, is Fanny too high to receive that of Jesus?

Her unrest may be due partly to her progress towards a
more spiritual form of prayer. But this should not lead to the
overthrow of outward forms. Even if she were called to such
intimacy with God that her soul became the instrument of the

Holy Spirit 'not only outward forms of prayer, the hymns and psalms of the Church, but all the actions and occurrences of life become harmonious to it'.[13]

She must see that 'meer nature' is at work in her difficulties.[14] A sign of this was the guilt resulting from her refusal to hear a woman preacher. She felt guilt at not listening to what the Apostle absolutely forbids, and no guilt when she realized her need of the new birth. He ends with the assurance that he has 'not the smallest spark of enmity towards the persons of any one sect in the world'.[15]

Law's final letter lists all the sacrifices Fanny wishes to make for God and which gain his approval. She wishes to be humble and loving and to renounce the world. Hobhouse doubts if Law can really have meant that she wished to renounce the 'ordinary allowed employments of life'. He thinks that Law intended to have written here, 'diversions'. But Law rarely wrote loosely, he had already stated to Mr Walker that ordinary employments might be sacrificed for God, and he approved of the spirit of monasticism which developed this principle.[16] In addition he would commend the spirit that left the ordering of the Church and State to God who is Governor of both. With such good desires she cannot want to be a Quaker. Almost every page of the New Testament presupposes an outward Church with outward authority and ministers. Such outward offices and ministry were settled in the Apostles' days when revelations and miracles were common. In those same days when there was so much liberty in prophesying women were forbidden to preach. Here the letter is interrupted . . . Fanny had become a Quaker!

We learn from a letter that he wrote to Byrom on 17 December 1736 that he saw 'M. Guion at the bottom' of her unrest and that he intended referring to this. He intimates that he wants his letters returned, which suggests that his interest in the Friends was greater than the mere counselling of Fanny Henshaw.[17]

Certain drafts against Quakers suggest that Law intended publishing as part of his *Demonstration* a refutation of Friends.[18] He probably withdrew the piece because he decided on a more detailed criticism. His absorption in Boehme and change in theological view meant that he came to value the Friends and no longer wished to refute them.

I

The first draft begins with charging the Quakers with inconsistency. They reject outward ordinances but are as bound by the ordinances of their sect as are church members by the institutions of Christ.

The foundation text of Quakerism is that 'God is a Spirit and they who worship him must worship him in spirit and truth'.[19] The affirmation of the text was as true in the time of Moses as when Christ taught his disciples outward prayer. We find the Jews instituting outward rites and Paul declaring 'he is a Jew which is one inwardly' (Rom. 2.28). The Jews never rejected outward rites under pretence of the spirituality of the gospel. Like the Pharisees the Quakers have a religion of outward ordinances. The former delighted to observe them, the latter to forsake them.

In the second draft he maintains:

> The spirituality of the Gospel above the Law consists in the mystery of godliness, Jesus Christ was hid under the letter of the Law, and therefore it is more spiritual than the Law or is the very spirit of the Law, because it has revealed that which the letter of the Law pointed at'.[20]

The spirituality of the Gospel cannot consist in the rejection of outward ordinances for the body and blood of Christ on the Cross is as much an outward thing as the body and blood of Christ on the altar. Similarly, St Paul says that the forgiveness of sins is dependent on Christ's resurrection. (1 Cor. 15.17). In fact, 'The outward institutions of the Gospel and the outward Christ must stand and fall together.'[21] Further, if we say that a spiritual Gospel cannot have outward institutions we must say that it cannot have outward rules of life. 'The truly spiritual man is he that sees God in all things, and sees all things in God. . . . Every outward thing has the nature of a sacrament to him.'[22]

In the last fragments Law considers the question of water-baptism. He has especially in mind the teaching of Robert Barclay (1648–90), whose *Apology for the True Christian Divinity* (1676–8) had established itself as an important verbal exposition of Friends' belief.

Barclay says there is only the baptism of Spirit and fire. John's baptism was a figure of this. Law replies that Jesus

commanded the disciples to baptize all nations (Matt. 28.19–20).
Barclay, referring to this passage, asked how we know that
water-baptism is intended? We know it in the same way that
we know that the preaching to all nations referred to in the text
is an outward preaching. Further, baptism has a determinate
meaning in Scripture. Because of this meaning we can refer to
other baptisms—those of affliction and fire for example. St
John's allusions to the baptism of the Holy Ghost and fire
refers to the descent of the Holy Ghost. Christ had promised the
disciples that they would be baptized with the Holy Ghost.
When Peter visited Cornelius, the Holy Ghost fell on them as at
the beginning. That such a baptism was distinct from water-
baptism is plain from Peter's words that water-baptism could
not be refused to those who had accepted the Holy Spirit.

The Church's water-baptism differs from that of John in
that it joins believers to Christ as John's joined people to him.

He dismisses the appeal to the Epistle to the Hebrews where
it is stated that shadows must be dispelled now that the Gospel
has come. The same Epistle requires water-baptism (10.21–2).

Barclay believed that water is ineffectual spiritually. Law
imagines a prince promising benefits to captives if they will
undergo baptism. It would be absurd to say that water is of
no more use in this instance than for washing. The application
is obvious.

We note in these encounters how Law remains a High
Churchman and agile disputant. There is much psychological
penetration of Fanny's position but little regard to spare her
present pain. As against Barclay's false spiritualizing of religion
Law defends outward institutions most justly, believing with
Suso that the man who sees the inward in the outward as well
as in the inward, sees more deeply than the man who only sees
the inward in the inward. A fundamental idea of Malebranche
is put to good use in his assertion that we should be able to see
all things in God. We are also reminded how wide was Law's
engagement with the religious problems of his day.

The insensitivity he could show in personal relations was
felt often by Byrom. Doubtless sad at the unsuccessful outcome
of his endeavours with Fanny, he had to endure as Law's first
words when they were in private after the affair: 'Well, have
you made any more Quakers?'

# 12

## THE 'DEMONSTRATION'

A prayer written for personal use sometime after Law fell under the spell of Boehme has been preserved. It is headed: '*A Prayer*, for the destruction of the evil, bestial, and serpentine properties of the old Adam, and the quickening of the divine Spirit of the Second Adam, in the soul.' Despite the change in phraseology the content of the prayer resembles those previously quoted. It expresses profound penitence and a petition for the Holy Ghost. It might have been written any time after 1735.[1]

Byrom visited Law at Putney several times in the spring of 1737. Conscious of Byrom's appreciation of Madame Bourignon and Madame Guyon and the dangers that might come from addiction, he referred to them dismissively. They wrote too much and were inclined to delusion. He expressed belief that the world would be reformed but those fit to do it had not yet appeared. Opposers of the Quakers gave them the advantage for they seemed to be writing against the Spirit. After a good beginning the Quakers had become a subtle and worldly people. He commended Tauler, Ruysbroeck, à Kempis, 'the old Roman Catholic writers' Hermas and Dionysius, and he may have especially commended Macarius. He believed of Boehme that 'it was by force that he writ', but it was a pity that his vision was not contained in one book.[2]

Two undated fragments in Walton continue Law's comments on mystics. Of Brother Lawrence he said, 'he was a living example of the divine life, and did not, like most of the rudimental, formalist divines, and scholastic mystics, divide and subdivide it into various invented rules and gradations; which he condemned'. He referred to Gregory of Lopez as a 'highly divine soul', though he did not wish to commend his outward mode of life. In this fragment Law gives his own statement of the progressive stages of human life. In our return to God we

118

must pass through nature, law, the state of Christ come in the flesh and the state of Christ come in the Spirit.[3]

In 1735 a book, probably written by Benjamin Hoadly, was published called, *A Plain Account of the Nature and End of the Sacrament of the Lord's Supper.* It caused a sensation. Overton lists twenty-one writings that it called forth. Whiston and Leslie made their contribution and Waterland had it partly in mind when he wrote his great exposition, *A Review of the Doctrine of the Eucharist* (1737). He gives the reason for the disturbance caused by the book when he states that 'his scheme is nothing else but the doctrine of the Sacrament socinianized'.[4]

The author believed that the words of Christ and the Apostles guide us to the true meaning of the Eucharist. 'It is of small importance to know what writers since New Testament times have written about it or what people by their own authority may teach.'[5]

The meaning of the words of institution become apparent if we remember that Christ blessed God rather than the bread. St Luke and St Paul teach us that the rite is in remembrance of Christ. It is a figurative rite in commemoration of the New Covenant. There can be no eucharistic sacrifice as Christ was sacrificed on Calvary.

Prolonged self-examination is not required before we partake of the Lord's Supper. All worthy partakers need is a 'sincere and serious remembrance of Christ, as . . . Lord and Master'.[6]

There is no Real Presence in the rite. John 6 is not a reference to it. Spiritual gifts are given immediately by God. Christ annexed the gift of the Holy Spirit to prayer.

The sacrament is a memorial whereby Christians acknowledge Christ as their master and themselves as his disciples. By doing this in an assembly they profess themselves to be members of that fellowship; namely, the Church.

This was not a book to please William Law. In 1737 appeared his, *A Demonstration of the Errors of a Plain Account, etc.* As evidence of his concern for the Church he commends it especially to 'the younger clergy'. As evidence of his conviction of the harm done by the rationalistic spirit he says that those allying themselves with the author will become blind to 'the most important Parts of the Gospel'.[7]

Law enumerates the principles on which the book proceeds: the bare words of Christ and the Apostles teach us the truth of the sacrament; only the rules applied to common speaking are appropriate to these words; no other approach is possible; knowledge of the sacrament depends on information resulting from this examination. If these principles prove false the author's argument falls to the ground.

To these principles Law turns. He asks how we are to apply the rules of common speaking to the words of institution, since Christ's words and action are unique? Interpreting Christ's words by human standards reduces their significance to our poor level. The author is really in the position of the disciples before the descent of the Holy Spirit. Divine enlightenment is required for the Eucharist to be understood.

The outward form and matter of the sacrament are given by the words of institution but not the nature, end, and effect of it. Now, either the sacrament has some relation to other doctrines of Scripture or it has not. If it has not it cannot be said to be in agreement with other parts of Scripture. If it has, then it must be understood only in relation to other doctrines of Scripture. The Apostles did not understand the rite merely from the words of institution because the doctrines and mysteries to be confessed by them needed the '*Light* which brought the Apostles and the Church after them into a true and full Knowledge of the *fundamental* Articles of the Christian Faith'.[8]

Law refers to the '*poor literal* Exactness' of the author's theological method.[9] The group of which he is a member is like the ancient Jews, suffering from blindness and hardness of heart. As Christ perceived the Pharisees to stand on the outside of the Law, so this author stands on the outside of the Gospel. St Paul says that the letter kills and the Spirit gives life. Those faithful to the letter are '*speculative* Christians, *Idealists*, *Critics*, and *Grammarians*'. But 'Scripture, interpreted not by *Lexicons* and *Dictionaries*, but by *Doctrines* revealed by God, and by an *inward Teaching* and *Unction* of the Holy Ghost, is that Spirit which giveth Life'.[10] Christ himself said that his words are spirit and life (John 6.63). As such they cannot be interpreted by the common rules of speaking. He told them also that he had many things yet to teach them that they could not immediately bear. They had to await the '*Death, Resurrection,* and *Ascension,* and the *coming* of the Holy Ghost'.[11] The truths signified by the words of institution then became apparent.

It is extreme to say that the sacrament is a positive institution and that it is not therefore a duty apparent to us from the nature of the thing. The means employed are positive but not what is done by these means. The end of the sacrament is to remember, acknowledge and profess Christ to be our Saviour. This is a natural duty arising from the relation between him and us.

The sacrament has two distinct equal parts. In the first are the words, 'This is my Body . . . This is my Blood . . .' in which we 'confess Christ to be the *Atonement* and *Satisfaction* for our Sins'.[12] The second part is the eating Christ's body and drinking his blood in which he 'is to be owned and received as a *Principle of Life* to us'.[13] The sacrament is no bare remembering of Christ. Our faith is exercised by our believing Christ to be the atonement for sin and a principle of life in us, and by the fact that these truths are 'made *certain* and *confirmed* in us, by taking the Bread and Wine to be the true *Signification* of them'.[14] In the action of the Eucharist remembering is an '*Act of Faith*', a faith which can '*see*, or hear, or *understand*, or *do* that which is done in the Sacrament'.[15]

Law traces the author's attenuated theology to a socinian root. Unable to affirm the Godhead of Christ, he must be either not a Christian writer or one whose profession refutes his writing.

Scripture tells us that Christ must be formed in us; that we must put on Christ; that we must progress in the new birth in Christ. These phrases suggest the reality of which the Eucharist is the appointed outward signification. Similarly it is absurd to ask whether John 6 refers to the sacrament, the sacrament refers to it.

The sacrament is an

> *Object* of your *Devotion*, that is to raise, exercise, and inflame every holy Ardour of your Soul that tends to God. It is an *Abstract*, or *Sum* of all the Mysteries that have been revealed concerning our Saviour, from the first Promise of a *Seed of the Woman* to bruise the *Serpent's Head*, to the Day of Pentecost.[16]

All the names by which it is called are useful except for the contention they arouse. Each tells us something, but not everything, about the rite. Thus 'the Help of all of them is wanted'.[17]

It is a quibble to say that we can only remember an absent person. Christ is unique. Many texts illuminate the statement that he is the same yesterday, today, and forever. So his atonement did not just occur on Calvary. It began 'with the *Lamb that was slain from the Foundation of the World*; for he was the Lamb of God slain in all their *Types* and Sacrifices through every Age, till be became the *real* expiatory Sacrifice on the Cross for the Sins of the World'.[18] Types and prefigurations alone ended with that event. He rose from the grave with power over death and as Royal Priest over the Church so that his Atonement has been continually augmented. He supports this statement with quotations from Hebrews (e.g., 7.24, 25; 9.24).

He develops the theme to which he will often now refer: Christ the Second Adam. It is the foundation of natural goodness and revealed religion. Everyone fell when Adam fell for we were all 'in the loins of Adam'. But Adam and his posterity were put in a state of redemption by the general pardon and the promise of a seed of the woman that would bruise the serpent's head. No longer need reason trouble us with the thought of the destiny of Adam's children being hard to bear. So ravishing does Law find the vision conjured up before his eyes that he exults, 'I know not how to content myself with bare arguments'.[19]

God's pardon is not merely external. It is the pardon of one 'who is the *Centre* of that which is most *Central* in us, the Life of our Life, the Spirit of our Spirit'.[20] Since 'his Words are Power, and what he speaks he acts' God's declaration of pardon was 'the *real Communication* of something to *Adam*, which made him *capable* of enjoying God as his *Good*'.[21] If we resist the innate '*Spark* of Life . . . *Attraction* to God' within us our destruction will be our own doing. According to how we respond to the inward Spark when the carcase of flesh and blood drops off we will fall into hell or the fullness of God.

Infidelity cuts deeper than we might think. We cannot exchange the light of the Gospel for the light of reason. Christ cannot be divided. He is 'the same in the *Heart* that he is in the *Gospel*'.[22] He was incarnate to make the light of the mind which we received from him effectual for our salvation. John stressed this when he said that Christ was the light that enlightens every man (1.9).

The general light to which Law refers is not the light of reason. He wishes men as much good of reason as of the sun, but those who worship reason are as idolatrous as those who worship the sun. Reason is no more use for promoting salvation than a discourse on Food is useful to the hungry. He lays it down that 'Men may have the *Good* of Religion much assisted and secured . . . by the right Use of Reason, though Reason has not the *Good* of Religion in it.'[23]

The light to which Law refers must not be confused with reason as that word signifies a manner 'of viewing the Relations of the Ideas of Things, and drawing Consequences from them'.[24] The light of the mind is '*Goodness* itself'. Ratiocination 'is only the *Activity* of the Mind upon its own *Images* and *Ideas* . . . it has nothing of the Nature of the Images that it views, nor gets the Nature of them, because it views them'.[25] A needle touched by a lodestone, if it is endowed with the faculty of reason, could frame many theories about its attraction towards the lodestone. Such theories would be distinct from the attraction itself. This analogy is imperfect because all things come from God and have something of God in them. Indeed, 'There is nothing in the Universe but Magnetism, and the Impediments of it.'[26] The truth of this remark becomes apparent when we suffer a shock and 'the secret Power of the Soul' awakens.[27]

Properly understood natural religion is not the religion of reason but the heart made ready for the Gospel. Infidelity is really '*Insensibility* of Heart'.[28] Thus we are bidden to read our own hearts for 'The Gospel is *within* you, and you are its *Evidence*'.[29] The central truths of the Gospel only draw out what is inscribed there. Learned books avail little.

This Inner Light is part of revealed religion. It enables us to hear God's word rather than to dispense with it. It is preventing grace, going before us and not being dependent on our activity. Recognizing this we cannot accept the Calvinist doctrine of election and reprobation.

Scripture often says that spiritual truths are spiritually discerned. But this no more means that the unreasonable part of us is addressed than does the admission that the natural world does not directly address our reason. The external world addresses our senses and reason makes use of the images of sense.

> It is the *Sensibility* of the Soul that must receive what this World can communicate to it; it is the *Sensibility* of the Soul that must receive what God can communicate to it. Reason may follow after in either Case, and view through its own Glass what is done, but it can do no more.[30]

Though Samuel Wesley went too far in claiming that Law's *Demonstration* proved Hoadly an atheist, he successfully defended traditional Christian teaching on the Eucharist. Jeremy Taylor (much influenced by the Roman Catholic, Ludolphus of Saxony) says 'As it is a Commemoration and Representation of Christ's death, so it is a Commemorative Sacrifice. As we receive the symbols and the mystery, so it is a Sacrament.'[31] These are the points specially emphasized by Law. As usual he develops them in his own way and there is the usual tendency to reject academic jargon and to be content with a minimum adequate statement. Like the High Churchmen before him he stresses that remembering at the Eucharist is no bare activity but commemoration.[32] More than them he seems to have penetrated towards the biblical idea of memory 'making present' the thing remembered. It is worth noticing that the philosophy of substance and accidents, which had been used by many Caroline churchmen to express the mystery of the Real Presence, had fallen into discredit in Law's day. It had consequently become difficult to resolve the meaning of Christ's union with the elements in the Eucharist. Neither Boehme and other mystics nor contemporary writers helped Law much here and this is probably one reason why he came progressively to believe in a figurative doctrine of the sacraments. By contrast he has a ready vocabulary to express Christ's union with the soul, so that this belief remains strong and his profound sense of the immanence of God is not frustrated.

Cardinal thoughts of Boehme make their appearance in this work. The importance of the Inner Light and the inadequacy of ratiocination in theology, the drama of the Fall, and redemption beginning with Adam and continuing through the Process of Christ to that of sanctification in the believer, are themes we will meet continually. They represent a development of, rather than a break with, his previous teaching.[33] We have noticed his emphasis upon the Fall, the importance of the new birth and his praise of intuition as against discursive reason. The enthusiasm with which he develops the new understanding is interesting. It witnesses to the solutions he found to the problems posed to orthodoxy by Enlightenment thought.

Law's careful formulation of the relation of Inner Light to reason is not merely an individual effort. The contrast was a favourite theme with the affective mystics of the fourteenth-century German school.[34] He must also have pondered *Fides et Ratio*, the book edited by Pierre Poiret (1646–1719) and written partly by W. F. von Metternich. Poiret was well known to Law as an interpreter of mystics and he mentioned him to friends.

We may summarize here the section in which the principles of Locke are criticized. Boehme is singled out for praise as a religious teacher. Locke's idea that reason is superior to faith is repudiated in an essay of 474 sections. Faith is described as an intuition which brings the soul into direct touch with God. Reason is concerned with only the dry bones of dogma. It is called 'that crafty reason, the most pestilential offspring of the serpent'. Reason 'is . . . solely adapted to the creature, wholly unfit for divine things'. Divine activity is described as 'magical'. There is a fund in the soul where God darts his Light. The Kingdom of God is thus a spark in all men.[35]

We may compare briefly Law's treatment of this subject with that accorded by Daniel Waterland in *A Review of the Doctrine of the Eucharist, as laid down in Scripture and Antiquity* (1737). Waterland treats the subject in the light of Scripture and right reason with such help as tradition, the scene of Providence, is able to give. Scripture alone is 'our compleat *Rule of faith and Manners*'.[36] It is not just a positive duty as God bears his part in it. He deprecates the 'Socinian Way' for it 'excludes God'.[37] He interprets John 6 to mean feeding on the benefits of Christ's Passion, that is, pardon and grace. The Early Fathers saw no special reference to the Eucharist here as outward signs are not mentioned.[38] He accepts the idea of the Real Presence:

> The elements of bread and wine in the Eucharist . . . are, after Consecration, called by the names of what they are

pledges of, and are ordained to convey . . they are, though not literally, yet in just construction and certain effect (standing in Divine promise, and Divine acceptance) . . . The Body and Blood of Christ to all worthy receivers.[39]

Chapter 10 is called, 'Of the sanctifying grace of the Holy Spirit conferred in the Eucharist.' In chapter 11 he emphasizes the federal nature of the rite. It is a means of renewing the covenant entered into at baptism because a vital communion between God and man is made in the Eucharist; drinking blood or wine is used by various nations as a means of ratifying covenants; Christ says it is a covenant; Paul notices the analogy between the Eucharist and the sacrifices of Jews and Gentiles, which were federal rites.

Law's general method of theologizing is similar to Waterland but he appropriates especially certain parts of Christian tradition, that is, that favourable to Boehme's teaching. He is thus vulnerable to the charge of eccentricity, but he is also enabled to make certain penetrating points, such as that of the mercy of God to humanity from the beginning. Law is delightfully free from academic jargon.

# 13

## THE BREACH BETWEEN
## LAW AND WESLEY

In December 1733 there appeared in *Fog's Journal* a letter deprecating the activity of Oxford Methodists. The anonymous reply to this was made by a gentleman living near Oxford who had inquired personally into the activity of these enthusiasts. It has been suggested that the gentleman was William Law. This is most unlikely. The correspondent states that he was unacquainted with the Methodists when the request was made that he should investigate their activities.[1] But the Wesley brothers visited Law first in the summer of 1732. Furthermore, the writer's style lacks Law's distinctive features.

We have noticed how Law was helping the Wesley brothers in a more significant fashion. This pastoral relationship came to an end in 1735 when the Wesleys responded to General Oglethorpe's request for assistance in religious work among colonists and natives in America.

During his sojourn in America new influences came to John Wesley. The heroic, pious spirit of the Moravians challenged him. He discovered that they united Reformation and Pietist principles; that they believed in the propitiatory theory of the Atonement; that they attached particular importance to the doctrine of justification by faith, sanctification as a separate theological category, the sense of assurance, fellowship, and religion as a felt experience. At the same time Law's method in religion was not helping him much. He seemed to teach that sanctification led to justification. But rigorous endeavour did not seem to make Wesley more fit for God. By November 1736 he decided that the mystics had almost made shipwreck of his faith. Mystics for him were those 'who slight any of the means of grace'. Molinos, Tauler, and the author of *Theologia Germanica* provided examples. He drew up a scheme of their teaching and sent it to Samuel Wesley for comment.[2]

He returned to England in February 1738, a disappointed and disturbed man. The Moravian, Peter Bohler, told him that faith must be accompanied by 'Dominion over sin, and constant Peace from a sense of forgiveness'. This news amazed Wesley and seemed a new gospel. Recourse to Scripture and the testimony of Bohler's friends convinced him that Bohler spoke truth.[3] Already convinced intellectually of the Evangelical method in religion between 5 and 7 March he attended a Moravian meeting in London on 24 May.[4] As someone was reading from the Preface to Luther's Commentary on Romans, the part describing the change God works in the heart through faith, 'I felt my heart strangely warmed. I felt I did trust in Christ, Christ alone for salvation: And an assurance was given me, that he had taken away *my* sins, even *mine*, and saved *me* from the law of sin and death.'[5]

Just before and after this crucial day a sequence of letters passed between Law and Wesley. Before considering them, however, it will be helpful to consider the characters and form of belief of the correspondents.

The reader has already an impression of Law. He has exceptional intellectual and artistic gifts and is personally formidable. He is not gregarious and his friends seem only to have had a subservient relation to him.[6] He can be stubborn and eccentric. There is much of the introvert about him. Jung's characterization of the introvert might have been written with Law partly in mind. He is subjective and tends to exclude views other than his own. He is easily, and sometimes falsely, charged with egocentricity. His incomplete relation with the external world means that he can receive 'overwhelming impressions' from it. He can believe objects to possess magical powers. Intensity rather than extensity is his aim. He is not convivial. As he tends to identify his views with himself, he can make venomous retorts to criticism. He has often a vague dread of the other sex. He may become a mystic seer or an artistic crank. If the latter, the sublime, whimsical, and banal mingle in his work.[7]

Law's testiness may be accounted for partly by his practice of the mortified, celibate, and impecunious life. Despite the inadequacy of the material the question can also be posed: How sexually normal was he? The human body seems to have been

something of an offence to Law. Jeremy Taylor's treatment of
mortification and the body was much more moderate than
Law's. Although a High Churchman like Taylor and a Nonjuror like Bishop Collier could be twice married, Law remained
single and lived in close proximity to two women without
difficulty. He advocated a celibate priesthood and praised
virginity. In the *Serious Call* there are portraits of parent–child
relationships but none of married happiness. With some justification John Wesley accused Law (1738) of 'extreme roughness,
and morose and sour behaviour, at least on many occasions'.[8]
He eventually teaches that the fleshly part of human beings and
their division into sexes are due to sin.

None of these points need presuppose a homosexual streak
in Law. His introverted character, rigorism, mortification,
developed piety, and love of Boehme might account for excessive
features in his life and work; but we must add to these his
friendship with Thomas Langcake.

All we know of this elusive man is that he was a London bank
clerk and that he became a disciple of Law. His letters suggest
that he was a sincere Christian with undistinguished talents.
He probably came into relation with Law in about 1750. Law
refers to him as 'Son of my Love', which suggests that Langcake
came to faith or the radical deepening of faith by Law's
instrumentality.[9]

While Langcake always refers to Law with deep respect Law
employs surprisingly affectionate and loving terms. They are
present in the letters of Law edited by Ward and Langcake
and published with Law's consent.[10] His unpublished correspondence is more fulsome. He intimates to Ward, 'I like everything my Langcake does, and have no corner of my heart that
I would conceal from him.'[11] In the same year (1757) he writes
to Langcake, 'The friendly salutation of this house waits upon
my best beloved friend—Je vous porte dans mon *coeur*'.[12] In a
letter of 1760 we find, 'End all your letters to me as I do this,
with only adding my name—Your name is compliment enough
for me.'[13] The two most intimate records are these:

I kiss you with the lips of my heart.
If this begins with saying, "I am glad to see you', You must
understand it without considering it as a strong figure of

speech, for before I set your name on the top of this page, you did more than stand in my sight. If you take this to be a little frantic, you must grant me the benefit of the old saying, *Amare it insanire idem est.*[14]

This relationship had not been developed by personal encounters. Langcake wrote to Henry Brook in 1776 that it was through correspondence rather than by meeting that his friendship had been maintained. Nothing occurred in conversation that might not have been said to other disciples.[15]

The word 'friend' occurs often in Law's later works, and it is true that his heart was easily kindled by examples of piety. In an early letter to Langcake (1750) he stated that to live in God was to live in love and that this was all he wished for himself and others. People of Langcake's spirit kindle in him 'every holy affection of honour and esteem'.[16] Accordingly we find him writing to Byrom 'Mon cher ami . . . Yours most affectionately'. To George Ward he writes, 'friend—whom I heartily love and embrace as a living member of the body of Christ'.[18]

We know that St Francis of Assisi enjoyed a holy love with St Clare, as did St Francis de Sales with Mère de Chantal. He intimated to Mère de Chantal that they had 'become one only spirit'.[19] But Law's love was directed towards a man. It seems at least possible that, unknowingly, Law had a homosexual strain in his nature. If so, his earlier tendency to asperity can be readily understood.

Wesley is quite a different person. He was sufficiently formidable for the agnostic historian, J. H. Plumb, to describe him as 'one of the greatest [men] known to modern times'.[20] Much of Wesley's life is documented. He was intensely active, becoming the champion and chief formative influence on the Evangelical Revival. This revival started a new Church, radiated round the world, and proved an important social force in England for over a hundred years.

Beginning in 1738 Wesley travelled 225,000 miles, mainly on horseback, in all kinds of weather, communicating with friendly and hostile people. He preached over 40,000 sermons, often in the open-air and several a day, to crowds that could number 20,000. One collected edition of his writings runs to fourteen volumes and about 7000 pages. In addition he condensed and published the writings of many others. His organization of, and care for, the swelling ranks of the Methodists was meticulous and time-consuming. A wiry 5 ft 3 ins. tall and with piercing eyes, he was the most portrayed man of his day. Horace Walpole recorded his impression of the elderly Wesley preaching. He was 'lean . . . His hair smoothly combed. . . . Wondrous clean, but as evidently an actor as Garrick.'[21]

He had a trained and practical intelligence. Although much of his reading was done in early life he had read widely in the eclectic fashion of the eighteenth century. References to the classics, philosophy, science, and literature are scattered across his *Journal* and *Letters*. He could 'tear[ing] the heart out of a book'.[22] He knew Latin, Greek, French, German, and some Spanish and Italian. He was interested in medicine and electricity. Dr Johnson commented instructively, 'John Wesley's conversation is good but he is never at leisure. He is always obliged to go at a certain hour.'[23]

His practical bias meant that he tended to be undiscriminating in his judgements. Despite its volume there is little creative thought in his writing. Occasionally impressive, it is more often dull. Words like 'useful', 'practical' and 'business' are frequently found. Dates and times (even at his conversion!) are important matters. He is more like a politician or second-rate scientist than a theologian. After a study of his English a Methodist scholar concludes, 'The absence of any reference to humour . . . is due simply to the fact that Wesley himself is very deficient in this quality . . . not an innovator nor an original thinker . . . nor even a visionary. He is not imaginative.'[24] Knox mentions his treatment of Calvinism. The problem of predestination has tormented the greatest minds of the Church. Wesley considered it for a fortnight and spent the remaining forty-odd years of his life confidently arguing against it.[25] He dismisses Voltaire as a 'creature' and believes that his literary style betrays the meanness and poverty of the French language.[26]

All this amounts to saying that there is much of the extrovert about Wesley. Jung says of this psychological type: '*Interest* and *attention* follow objective happenings and, primarily, those of the immediate environment.' He can be so caught up in objects that he sacrifices the subject. Jung instances the business man engrossed in expanding his trade.[27]

K

Despite his energy and idealism we do notice in Wesley a tendency to overbear and to judge situations from his own standpoint. We can be struck by both his humility and his ability to rationalize inconvenient matters. He was, for example, indiscreet in his efforts to marry and eventually he married the wrong woman. His clumsiness in the affair of Sophy Hopkey is generally allowed. Notwithstanding her unsuitability he wanted to marry her. Then he decided against her and she married another man. We then hear that Wesley publicly repelled her from the Eucharist because he believed she showed lack of devotion. In the ensuing disturbance, which led to public action, Wesley returned to England. But his record of the affair shows no penetration into the feelings of others. He can even justify himself by speaking of shaking the dust of Georgia off his feet.[28]

The same characteristic emerges in his high-handed action in ordaining men. Whilst insisting that he and all Methodists remain Anglican, he performed an action in rebellion against the fundamental principles of that Church. Charles Wesley tried in vain to dissuade him. A year after his ordination the dilatoriness of Parliament was overcome and the bishop whom Anglicans wanted to be ordained was ordained. Apart from the usual justifications Wesley relied theologically on the identification of bishops and presbyters in the Early Church, made by Stillingfleet and King. But this thesis was much controverted and King eventually changed his mind and became an Anglican.[29]

Such inconsistencies mark Wesley's appeal to authority that Knox suggests that his real authority was 'his own interpretation of the Bible'.[30]

Charles Wesley's *Journal* gives a clear example of Wesley's obstinacy and insensitivity in human relationships.

We sang, and fell into a dispute whether conversion was gradual or instantaneous. My brother was very positive for the latter, and very shocking; mentioned some late instances of gross sinners believing in a moment. I was much offended at his worse than unedifying discourse. Mrs Delamotte left us abruptly. I stayed, and insisted, that a man need not know when he first had faith. His obstinacy in favouring the

contrary opinion drove me at last out of the room. Mr
Broughton was only not as scandalised as myself.[31]

It is not surprising that an introvert and an extrovert should
clash nor that an introvert's religion tended to the Catholic
and monastic form and an extrovert's to the Evangelical and
activist. Disagreement between the subjects of this chapter was
all the more likely because both were formidable and masterful.
In addition Law had a natural suspicion of feelings in religion,
but these had become important for the Wesleys. Charles was
surprised that when he brought Thomas Bray, a recent convert
to Methodism, to see Law he 'resolved all his feelings into fits,
or natural affections'.[32] This suspicion stemmed less from
Enlightenment fear of 'enthusiasm' than from the deep
Catholic understanding of the human heart. In this instance it
is noteworthy that Law resolves Bray's feelings, but not his
religion, into natural affections.

That a breach was developing between the Wesleys and Law
is apparent from the record of a conversation between Charles
and Law in 1737. In August Charles talked much about his
spiritual state with Law. The sum of Law's advice was, 'Renounce yourself; and be not impatient'. A week later he was
with Law again and plied him with questions relating to
commentaries on the Scripture, the destiny of the unconverted,
and correspondence with someone. Law's answers were short
and negative. To the question, should Charles write to him?
he responded, 'Nothing I can speak or write, will do you any
good.'[33]

Green finds the picture of Law 'unpleasant'. To do so is
surely to forget that Charles is recording only a summary of the
proceeding, that he records it from his own point of view and
that Law's aim in his answers is to teach the ardent, impatient
young man resignation!

It is doubtful if the Wesleys understood the mystics they so
easily condemned. In July 1737 Charles brought John's letter
against the mystics to Byrom, together with Samuel Wesley's
reply. Byrom reckoned the views 'very ill understood'. John's
definition of the mystics as those who neglect reason and the
means of grace is countered by Byrom asserting that he learnt
the value of the means of grace from the mystics. He found

Charles obstinate in not allowing the trifling nature of his objection that the *Serious Call* recognizes no divine command to public worship. Byrom believed that Charles had met someone who did not like Law and that Law may have given the brothers good strong advice that they had misinterpreted.[34]

In conversation with Byrom John Wesley approved a Moravian's definition of Tauler as a 'spiritual deist'. Byrom believed that in speaking about saving faith Wesley and his friends were too concerned about certain words, the meaning of which could be otherwise expressed. Stonehouse was present on this occasion. He later admitted to Byrom that he thought Wesley's views of the mystics 'outrageous'. Byrom believed that the mystics often spoke of saving faith as Wesley did.[35] It is possible, in fact, to chart Wesley's spiritual progress according to the mystical ladder of ascent along which Law was guiding him. His religious vows of 1725 thus correspond to the rung of awakening. The years leading to 1738 correspond to the rung of purgation by discipline. The 1738 experience corresponds to the rung of illumination or vision.[36]

Wesley saw matters differently and we are led accordingly to the tense, abrupt letters of May 1738. The first is dated 14 May 1738. The abrupt style indicates the spiritual travail of the writer and the constant allusions to Scripture suggest the thoughts deeply preoccupying him. He writes in obedience to what he considers the call of God. He had desired to learn the first elements of the gospel from Law. 'If you are born of God, you will approve of the design. . . . If not, I shall grieve for you.' For two years in particular he has been preaching and trying to practise the advice of Law's ethical treatises. But the law, though excellent, is 'too high for man'. Nor did the means of grace help. He could not conquer sin. A holy man told him to strip himself of his own works and believe in Christ, faith and salvation being God's free gifts.

Why did not Law advise him thus? If he thought Wesley not ripe for such advice he was misconceiving the foundation. He was mistaken if he thought Wesley already had saving faith. Perhaps the true reason was 'that you had it not yourself'. Indeed Wesley's 'man of God' had recently had an interview with Law and found that whenever he spoke of faith Law was silent and then spoke of mystical matters. He 'saw his state at once'. In his judgement it was a serious one.

Wesley asks if Law's 'extreme roughness, and morose and sour behaviour, at least on many occasions' could be the fruit of living faith in Christ?

Law's reply is dated 19 May 1738. His somewhat aloof and ironic style suggest his offence at Wesley's letter. He remarks upon Wesley's claim to inspiration and reiterates, with a contrary intent, Law's designation of his friend as a divine man. He will not pursue the matter of Wesley's inability to preach the substance of the practical treatises, but he will defend the advice he gave him. In the *Imitation*, which Wesley had translated and Law had recommended for meditation he will find the true, fundamental Christian reaching. He had recommended also the *Theologia Germanica*. 'If that book does not plainly lead you to Jesus Christ, I am content to know as little of Christianity as you are pleased to believe.'

As Wesley had made himself a judge of Law's heart he will know that his recently published *Demonstration* is governed by the principles of dependence on Christ and the need to shoulder the Cross to follow him. 'If you are for separating the doctrine of the cross from faith in Christ, or following him, you have numbers on your side, but not me.'

Wesley must remember that changing expressions about faith is not the same as changing faith.

> The head can as easily amuse itself with a living and justifying faith in the blood of Jesus, as with any other notion; and the heart, which you suppose to be a place of security, as being the seat of self-love, is more deceitful than the head.

Law's silence with Bohler (the divine man) was 'in approbation of what he said'. He doubts if he introduced mystical matters but if he did, 'Is not faith in Jesus Christ the very sum and substance of what is meant by mystical religion?'

Wesley replied on 20 May 1738. The corrections to his first draft show that he prepared the letter carefully. He concentrates on the central question: was he advised to seek faith in the blood of Christ?

Law advised the use of the books mentioned. In the *Theologia*

*Germanica* he remembers something about Christ our Pattern, but nothing express about Christ our Atonement (the first draft is less qualified: 'finds' replaces 'remember' and 'express' is omitted). The maxims governing the *Demonstration* may imply, but they do not express, the fact that Christ is our propitiation through faith in his blood. Law is chargeable with Wesley's late dilemma. He had never helped him to find the answer.

Conscious, perhaps, that he might have been too outspoken, he ends, 'I ask pardon, sir, if I had said anything disrespectful' (the original draft omits 'disrespectful' and adds 'inconsistent with the obligation I owe you and the Respect I bear your Character').[37]

Law answered on 30 May, six days after Wesley's evangelical experience. Without the least disregard for Wesley or his letter he replies only to remove misunderstanding respecting those present at the interview with Bohler. (In fact Wesley had written about the report of the interview to himself, not Bohler's interview with Law.)[38]

But he defends himself again. He gave Wesley the *Theologia Germanica*, not because he was learning the rudiments of Christianity in preparation for baptism, but because he was a clergyman who had made profession of divinity, and read many good books, and 'because you seemed to me to be of a very inquisitive nature and much inclined to meditation'.

It is only a dispute over words to argue whether the *Demonstration* implied or expressed belief in the propitiatory sacrifice of Christ.

Wesley had brushed aside parts of Law's previous letter. But this is odd, as these were replies to points in Wesley's first letter reputedly written under divine direction. He believed Wesley's real intention referred not to the Atonement but to a dislike of himself and a willingness to communicate Bohler's adverse view of him. He was offended that the pleasant interview he had had with Bohler should have led to such an unpleasant recollection of it by Bohler when he told Wesley of it.

He ends by roundly asking who made him Wesley's teacher? He might as well blame the bishop and the Church for defects in his knowledge. He bids Wesley be at peace with him.

We proceed to the interpretation of this correspondence. The defects in Law's character at this time have been mentioned often and have been illustrated in the present work. Special attention to the character of Wesley's shortcomings has been given because of the tendency of commentators to neglect these and find Law much the more culpable of the two.[39] This is specially clear in the writings of Green and Baker who survey the present controversy. They also favour very much Wesley's version of Christianity.[40]

Wesley's first letter betrays the disturbed condition of one wrestling with mighty spiritual facts. He interprets these facts according to the tradition of evangelical Christianity. At the same time he presumes to identify this tradition with real Christianity. He openly questions whether Law is a Christian and gives to Bohler and himself a quasi-divine status in certain opinions.

As Wesley had not seen Law since 1735 and had come to question Law's version of Christianity, his writing to him at this juncture reveals his past debt to him. But why did Wesley *write*? Putney had been accessible to him for some time. Friends of his had visited Law. The name of his past mentor must often have been included in conversations and thought. It is also common knowledge that letters can be misunderstood, especially with the type of communication Wesley wished to impart. The lucidity of both letters and the care with which at least the second was prepared means that he was not too distraught to be responsible. It seems that the insensitivity of the extrovert and his penchant for judging matters from his own standpoint were at work.

Nor can we exculpate Wesley for identifying Christianity with his own version of it. Two hundred years of debate since this time suggests that Christian validity is to be found within both the Protestant and the Catholic traditions, that the traditions sometimes say the same things in different ways, and that they need each other. Law's method was Catholic and Anglican, somewhat unbalanced by rigorism and affective mysticism. It is imperfect but not wrong.

There is presumption in Wesley's questioning of Law's Christian life. The reader of this book must have received sufficient assurance to refuse Baker's judgement that Law only passed from νόμος (law) to χάρις (grace) as he came under the influence of Boehme.[41] But even if this was the case we must

notice that Boehme's idea of Christianity was not that of
Wesley's and that apart from speculative matters he had much
in common with the teachers Law followed and which he
recommended to Wesley.

It is likely that if Wesley had held to the religious method
advocated by Law he would have gained the peace he sought.
Knox believes that when he was in America he was at the
parting of the ways. His inner scruples were a darkness through
which God was leading him. Law had already said that God
was teaching him to trust him further than he could see him. But
the Moravians urged him along another path. He resolved the
crisis by giving his allegiance to them. He might have chosen
otherwise. Knox quotes references indicating Wesley's longing
for solitude and the life of the recluse (this had been noted by
Law). He was even tempted to become a Roman Catholic. Nor
did the 1738 experience relieve him from doubt and darkness,
despite Bohler's promises. It is also significant that in later life
he praised mortification, sacraments, ascetical and mystical
writers. Wesley was never a simple Protestant. Workman
recognizes the affinity between Methodism and mysticism and
between Wesley and St Francis of Assisi. R. Davies believes
that Methodism stands between the Anglican church and the
Quakers.[42]

The privileged authority Wesley gives to Bohler and himself
is misplaced. It is a trifle breathtaking to read Wesley's
comment that in the interview Bohler had with Law he 'saw his
state at once'. Bohler was twenty-five at the time and his
religious views suggest more enthusiasm than maturity. Law
was about fifty-two; a tested Christian, remarkably gifted, a
spiritual director and justly famed Christian author. Wesley's
later admission that Law was a Christian is the best comment on
his present words.

Law must have been startled and hurt to receive Wesley's
missive. In reply his dignity, restraint, and literary skill are
everywhere evident. He defends his position and makes the
crucial distinction respecting religious language and spiritual
reality. His humility in the interview with Bohler is inadvertently suggested. His limitation lies in not gauging sufficiently the
spiritual travail of his correspondent. Because of the rudeness
of the letter and the limitations Law had probably noticed in

Bohler and others with whom Wesley was now mixing, perhaps this was too much to ask of him. But he is too aloof and in old age would have written differently.

Wesley's second letter adds nothing to the interpretation except his realization that he might have been too outspoken. It is interesting that the letter he sent abbreviated his salutation to Law.

Law's second letter adds nothing to the interpretation either, except his belief that Wesley's theological objections must have a personal root. The passion and directness with which Wesley wrote, his recent drift away from Law, which may not have been only theological,[43] and his reservations about the theology Wesley believed gave him reasons for this. It is possible also that the introvert's tendency to confuse criticisms of opinions with personal criticisms is at work.

As a general remark it is obvious that the tone of the correspondence was set by Wesley. Law's response was at least commendable. It is worth comparing his relation with Charles to see how well he could react to those whose views differed from his own. From the influence of Law he had come under that of the Moravians and Luther. He underwent an evangelical conversion. Visiting Law a year later he recounted his experience, denominated Law his John the Baptist to bring him to faith (a deep criticism really), and was doubtless enthusiastic in manner. Law responded to Wesley's testimony with the words, 'Then I am far below you (if you are right), not worthy to bear your shoes.'[44] There is something notable about the humility and generosity of Law who was prepared to be deferential and open-minded towards one who quite possibly confused nature and supernature in his account of the victory and realization of the Holy Spirit in his life.

# 14

## 'CHRISTIAN REGENERATION'

Law's association with the Gibbon household came to a natural end with the death of old Mr Gibbon and Edward's marriage. Towards the end of 1738 or early in the New Year Law moved to lodgings near Somerset Gardens, London.

In 1739 he published *The Grounds and Reasons of Christian Regeneration, or, The New Birth, Offered to the Consideration of Christians and Deists*. He always treasured this small book and wished he could send it to all parts of the kingdom.[1] The influence of Boehme is pervasive, extending even to the numbering of paragraphs, a habit which became usual. There is a new warmth in his writing now. In the Introduction he speaks of Deists and unbelievers having 'a great Share of my compassionate Affections'. He has an 'impatient Longing' to see them partake of faith. His confidence in the value of Boehme to answer objections to faith is clear from the assertion that those who read without '*Prejudice and Aversion*' will be touched.

Man is made in the image of God. In his unfallen state each member of the Trinity brought forth 'their *own Nature* in a *creaturely Manner*'.[2] Man stood in open enjoyment of the Kingdom of God. The grossness and enmity of this present world were hidden from him for 'Paradise was *over* all'. Even the nakedness of our first parents was hidden by 'their *paradisaical* Glory'.[3] In paradise man saw with a divine light shining forth from the kingdom of God. This light was broken at the Fall, when he was left with the firmamental light of this world.

The death man suffered at the Fall was the loss of the generation of the Son and the proceeding of the Holy Ghost within him. He lost the birth which was the brightness of his soul's glory, and that Spirit which was 'its *amiable Life*'.[4] As all life is fire his soul became an immortal 'dark *Fire*-breath' and without repentance it will remain such. This is the case with devils.[5]

Profligate persons do not perceive the full misery of their position because the blood carries the cheering light of the sun to the soul and partly allays its true pain. Even so, '*frequent* and *strong* Intimations' of our real condition occur to us 'in the *inmost* Ground' of our souls.[6]

The reasonableness of self-denial follows. The world is a hospital. We are sick people wanting to be healed 'and made fit to *leave* it".[7]

Scripture confirms this sequence of thoughts. Man was created in Paradise with a life suitable to it. Sin brought sorrow and death to him. Before he ate of the Tree of the Knowledge of Good and Evil he did not know them. Discontented with his happy superiority, and aided by the devil, he longed to look into the secret working power of outward nature. God's command that he should not eat of the Tree can be interpreted as: Keep in Paradise and do not fall into the outward world. When man ate the fruit it was as if he said: I desire to come under the influence of stars and elements. Man's free choice and not God's anger brought his calamity.

Consideration of redemption also shows how the Fall must have occurred. As Moses only knew obscurely the meaning of redemption it is fitting that he should not know the whole truth respecting the Fall. After the Incarnation it became clear that redemption meant receiving Christ's life. 'The Nature and Greatness of our Redemption, must show the Nature and Greatness of our Fall.' There is a necessary correspondence here which only the prejudiced can deny.[8] In telling us that we must be re-born from above the New Testament is telling us also what birth we have lost. St Peter reinforces this truth when he says that we must be '*born again of an incorruptible Seed by the Word*'. In calling the Holy Ghost the Sanctifier we state that actions performed without his inspiration are unholy. There is a suggestion here that once he always inspired our actions, and that the relationship with him has been broken.

The rite of Baptism signifies these great truths. We are baptized in the name of the Trinity and thus made living images of it. In the sacrament we seek and obtain the new birth.

Experience is also confirmatory. We know that virtue becomes man. Thus the mind testifies to the perfection of our first state.

The fallen soul is made up of the following combined elements: a restless selfishness, a restless envy, a restless pride and a restless anger or wrath. The evil spirits live inevitably in the same elements; because of this they have great power with fallen souls.

Repentance is but a kind of '*Table-Talk*' until we see the deformity of our inward nature and are frightened by it. There must be some kind of 'Earthquake' within us before we become sensible of our state of death and desirous of a Saviour.[9] Even our apparent virtues need to be made genuine. When the fire of the soul is sprinkled with the blood of the Lamb, its fire becomes the fire of light, and its strength becomes the strength of love, and it becomes able to take its place among the '*Flames of Love*, that wait about the Throne of God'.[10]

Law reminds his readers that religion and morality can keep them from true spirituality. These and the delights, comforts and cares of the world keep us from true faith.

> *True Faith* . . . is a Faith of *Love*, a Faith of *Hunger*, a Faith of *Thirst*, a Faith of *Certainty* and firm *Assurance*, that in Love and Longing, and Hunger, and Thirst, and full Assurance, *will lay hold* on Christ, as its loving, assured, certain and infallible Saviour and Atonement.[11]

Scripture uses a variety of phrases to describe regeneration: our being in Christ, Christ being in us, our putting on Christ, our eating his flesh and drinking his blood, his being our atonement, justification and righteousness, our life coming from him as branches from the vine.

Calvinist doctrines must not mislead us. It is wrong to think that God is so full of wrath that only the blood of his Son could satisfy his vengeance. Nor has he rejected a large part of the human race to manifest his glory and justice. God is love and the Christian religion 'is nothing else but an *open, full* Manifestation of his *universal* Love towards *all* Mankind'.[12] The only wrath is that of our own natures and God gave his Son to appease that. When we speak of God's wrath what we mean is the misery that follows departure from him. As for our final destiny, 'No Creature will be finally lost, but what *Infinite Love* cannot save.'[13] But there is no security in infidelity. At death we might find that our soul is an imperishable fire that cannot be saved, and God may not be able to save a soul in any other way than that proposed by the Gospel.

The Christian religion stands upon the two great pillars of 'the Greatness of our *Fall*, and the Greatness of our *Redemption*'.[14] Only when a man is awake to these things will his repentance cease to be superficial. The majority of Christians are content with 'the *History* of Scripture-Doctrines' and the outward forms of religion. But these are useless where the central truth is not 'livingly felt in the Heart'.[15]

We were chosen for salvation before the foundation of the world. The decree was repeated when Adam fell. He was admitted into the terms of Christian salvation and all mankind, being in his loins, were admitted into the same covenant of grace, 'The *Bruiser* of the Serpent' given to Adam was no mere verbal promise, but Christ himself. What was given to Adam is given to his posterity. At the Incarnation the one salvation was fully declared.

Regeneration requires faith and repentance, themselves the fruit of God planting a seed of life in us. By acts of faith and repentance the soul grows. We should not separate faith and works in the new-born man. 'Its Faith is its Works, and its Works are its Faith'.[16] The new man is unable to sin and sees everything with new eyes. The old man is the rational man, a poet perhaps, or historian. We must distinguish the two and remember that 'the *Life* of the one, is the *Death* of the other'![17]

There is no obligation to know and feel the advancement of our state. Such inquiry can be dangerous. There is no harm in people thinking they are in a worse state than they are. Regeneration is ensured by fidelity to the doctrines, life and death of Jesus Christ. Inquiry can make people seek certain effects when they should be directed to the cause that produces them.

God saves souls in different ways. Some may be given a sense of assurance. If so it should be received as a sign of the soul's need of it. Someone with this gift should not 'call peremptorily upon others' to seek it and condemn those who are resigned without it. To do so is to be a busybody.[18]

We know that we are regenerated in the same way that we know that we are alive. The soul is the subject of the old, as of the new, nature. In addition there are the outward fruits of each nature. As 'the outward World is but a *Glass*, or *Representation* of the inward 'we must expect the same variety in the spiritual as in the physical world. To be angry with those whose *attrait* is different from ours is to be guilty of sin.

He imagines a person of strong complexion demanding of others if they have the witness of the Spirit? If they can name the time and place when they received forgiveness? If they have an absolute assurance of salvation? Who is the kind of person who will fall in with these demands? Not the humble, for they do not want to add something of themselves to the Gospel they believe. Not the resigned, for it would contradict their state to seek such assurance. Not those touched by a pure and perfect love of God. Such a love seeks no self-comfort.

The young will fall in with these demands. They are inexperienced and long for the strength of conviction promised them. Restless self-lovers will respond, for in this way they will find rest. Those of a sanguine, tender and imaginative complexion will respond. They receive impressions vividly and would transform imaginations into certainties. Those who believe in election and reprobation would respond for the sense of assurance would relieve them of the fear of reprobation. Hypocrites would respond for they would be pleased to enter a religion where they could pass immediately for saints. Feelings have their place but they are not holiness, 'they are God's gracious *Allurements*, and *Calls* to seek after Holiness and spiritual Perfection'.[19]

This is the first book in which Law fully submits to Boehme's teaching. But his submission involves appropriation as well. He never copies his master so much as absorbs his vision and writes individually. The somewhat chaotic vision of Boehme is reduced to order and certain central themes receive proper elucidation. Evidence of this can be found in what Law writes about the Trinity, the nature of God as Love with the correlative concern about man's final destiny, the paramount need for regeneration and the symbolical relation between the visible and the invisible worlds. Where Boehme could seem often to enjoy speculation it is noteworthy that Law speculates only to draw out practical truths. His concern about non-believers is one reason why he employs Boehme's teaching.

Continuity persists between his past and present writing. The central importance of the Fall and regeneration, reference to the Bible, reason and experience, rejection of the world and a rigorist ethic are marks of this. His references to baptism is consonant with his previous convictions but this is a point on which his thoughts will change. Boehme was a Lutheran and the theology of the *Three Letters* would scarcely admit him into intimacy with God. The same applies to the theology of the Eucharist and the Church.

His words about assurance probably had a more local inspiration. Surely, he has the Wesleys, Whitefield (who was a Calvinist), Bohler, the Moravians, and the Methodists in mind. John Wesley is probably specially thought of when he writes of those with strong complexions, persons peremptorily calling on others and busybodies. But the reference could include Whitefield, Bohler, and others.

In view of Law's words on this point it is interesting to note Wesley's changing ideas on assurance. The 1745 Conference confirmed his previous teaching that all Christians must have a sense of God's pardon for salvation. In 1747 he writes to Charles that this sense is the common privilege of Christians. In 1756 he allows that a justified man may have no sense of assurance. This became his general view although he believed that such a sense distinguished a son from a servant of God.[20]

Law's position on this matter seems mature. Various Fathers spoke of the invisible testimony Christians have but they did not prejudge the issue of Judgement Day. The Council of Trent pronounced an anathema on those holding a sense of assurance to be essential to faith. The Westminster Confession decided that assurance was possible but not essential. Law would easily have agreed with the muted comments of Hooker and the *Homilies*.[21]

At about this time Law was beginning to make the respectful acquaintance of a number of Quakers. Byrom informs us that he borrowed some manuscripts of Andreas Freher, a devoted interpreter of Boehme, from the Quaker, Joseph Clutton.[22] Correspondence passed between Law, staying at or near the Three Nuns, adjacent to Whitehall, and a Quaker, Roger Shackleton. In January 1740 Shackleton recommended various

Quaker books to Law, and offered to lend him Fox's *Journal* and
Sewell's *History of the Quakers*. As Law had not read Fox when
he wrote against Trapp it seems that although he came to
appreciate Friends he felt no special need to examine their
form of religion yet.[23]

He must have been pleased to have lighted upon the manuscripts and drawings of Freher (1649–1728). Freher was born
in Nürnberg and came to London before the turn of the century. He was a disciple of Boehme and reduced his vision to an
ordered presentation, believing his contradictions to be superficial.

We may summarize a few of these manuscripts to indicate the
nature of writings to which Law turned often.

When we say God is before or without Eternal Nature we are
using images drawn from creaturely experience, for there is no
sequence in eternity. The phrase means that God is the root
from which Eternal Nature comes.

The generation of the Trinity may be described as follows:

> The first groundless will generateth in itself a grounded
> comprehensible will, co-eternal indeed to the first will, and
> having nevertheless in a sense, an eternal beginning. Which
> *second grounded will is the first will's eternal something, or essentially
> and perceptibility*, through which the first will goeth out, and
> introduceth itself into an eternal contemplation of itself,
> which outgoing is the *Third*, and is a moving life of the first
> and second.

He commends Boehme's use of the relation between heat, light
and air in combustion to indicate the mystery of the Trinity.

There is a 'mutual permeation' of all Seven Properties as of
the members of the Trinity. He calls the First Property 'astringency'.

Souls pre-existed as 'ideas in the divine intellect'.

There is a typological relation between Adam and Christ.
Adam was forty days in Paradise until he slept, then forty days
with Eve. Christ was forty days in the wilderness, and so-
journed forty days with the disciples between the Resurrection
and the Ascension. These parallels extend to small particulars.
He explains the fact of our being in the loins of Adam thus: 'we
all, when yet in the loins of Adam, have been nothing, lying in

one only chaos, without all distinction from each other'.

Phrases like 'anger-fire', 'wrath-fire', and 'love-fire', describe present conditions in the world. The verb 'to break' indicates the force of certain worldly happenings. He uses alchemical terms and considers the nature of male and female semen and dreams.

It is a cardinal fact that 'no eye can see beyond its own sphere'. Reason 'hath for its own proper and adequate object only the transitory things of this world, and even them also, since the Fall, but in part, and great obscurity'. We live and move and have our being in God, as Scripture says, and thus we see all things in God. The unregenerate cannot understand this.

At the Incarnation Christ assumed fallen human nature.

During the Last Supper the elements of bread and wine entered the bodies of the disciples. But Christ's words, 'take, eat, etc.', 'came forth from Christ's eternal or inward body, and was surrounded with heavenly flesh and blood: this the soul took, and put on as a new body'.

Regeneration, pardon of sins, justification, sanctification, and redemption are not sharply to be distinguished. They are 'so many different denominations of one and the same principal thing'.

'In Christ is no distinction between a priest and a layman, but all that are appointed with his Spirit are priests.' As congregations do not understand this, however, laymen should not celebrate the Eucharist.

Respecting the 'soul's introversion' he believes that eventually 'the soul is made wholly God-like (dei-formis)'. In the advanced stages of introversion he believes that a person can stop his breath for about two hours. But introversion can be easily hindered. If noticed, even the closing of the eyes can break it.[24]

With much of this teaching Law agreed, as it simply repeated what Boehme said in a systematic manner. Freher helped Law to understand Boehme and no doubt his diagrams summarizing Boehme's system also proved helpful. Phrases of his like 'anger-fire', derived from Boehme, passed into Law's vocabulary. But Law happily discriminated against the use of alchemical terms and speculations regarding dreams, semen and the like. Only gradually did he come to share Freher's and

Boehme's position respecting the sacraments and the priesthood. He is fully in accord with what they say about the office of reason, the fact that we can see no more deeply than the organ of vision permits, and the importance of not distinguishing too sharply the key words in the redemptive process.

Byrom has left us records of various conversations he had with Law in and about Somerset Gardens in the late summer of 1739. They spoke about the Pretender and Law related certain things in his favour. He lent Byrom various manuscripts indicating his interest in apocryphal Christian literature, frequently of a Gnostic type, including *The Gospel According to the Arabians*, *The Apocalypse of the Virgin Mary*, *The Doctrine of the Apoc. According to the Tradition of the A-r-r-s*, *The Glorious Message of the Prince of Peace*, *Mislemiria*, and *The Acts of James*. Law and Byrom believed that the Apocrypha might contain good things, though uncanonical. He even estimated that 'the first Christians had probably the very truths of J. Behmen''. Law states that Dionysius the Areopagite was the author of the works ascribed to him. He could not assent to the idea of the Virgin being without sin as it was not 'apostolical doctrine'. He believed that educated people often had the defect of their learning and illustrated this by reference to Fénelon. But he believed the doctrine of pure love. Love and interest were different things. He reckoned Byrom had 'incontinence' in theological matters(!) but was so pleased with him that he hoped that when 'our king came' Byrom would take holy orders.

Intermixed with these fascinating speculations were references to the Methodists. Law mentions the '*Weekly Miscellany*' of what he had heard. Whitefield had shown spleen against the clergy; Charles Wesley was going to Mr Bray to touch his spiritual pride; before writing to Law John Wesley had gone hastily to Mr Stonehouse to save him from Law, who was bringing him over to faith without works; Whitefield's sanctimoniousness amused Law but had exasperated Hutton; Law had been wrongly accused of railing against Whitefield.[25]

In a significant but not unexpected valuation Law says that Byrom was more easily wrought upon than himself and that 'his (Law's) strings were more hard'.

Such conversation, obscure sometimes in meaning, reminds us of Law's interest in, and knowledge of, Christian antiquity,

and of the positive regard he had for some apocryphal literature. Although there was convincing evidence to the contrary
we are not surprised that he wanted to grant primitive origin
to Dionysius the Areopagite. It seems that he still regarded the
Stuarts as the rightful kings of England. Law's detached but
amused regard for the Methodists can hardly be criticized.
Whimsicality and emotionalism clung to the movement and
their method in religion was not only not that of Law; indeed
certain Methodists disliked him. John Wesley's belief that Law
valued faith at the expense of works is, of course, without
foundation.

# 15

## DR TRAPP AND 'THE APPEAL'

In 1740 Law published two pieces against Dr Joseph Trapp. This was perhaps inevitable since Trapp was 'a very incarnation of eighteenth-century feeling'.[1]

He was born in 1679, educated at Oxford, ordained, and elected the University's first Professor of Poetry in 1708. As a High Churchman he acted as Sacheverell's manager in his trial in 1709. He opposed Hoadly in the Bangorian controversy, but mainly from the political side. He became chaplain to Bolingbroke and was active in Tory affairs. He published works on the Trinity and against Whitefield. He translated Virgil, wrote a tragedy, and translated *Paradise Lost* into Latin verse.

He strongly denounced the Methodists in pulpit and book. Published sermons on the theme were called *The Nature, Folly, Sin, and Danger of being Righteous Overmuch*. He allows that one cannot properly be too righteous and that the age is little enough righteous, but he opposes 'Certain modern enthusiasts'. He contends for the Aristotelian mean. 'To be righteous overmuch is to place much religion (where there is really none, but the contrary) in extraordinaries, in new inventions.'

Law and the Methodists are guilty of such enthusiasm. When Law's practical treatises were published he prophesied 'they would do harm . . . shortly afterwards up sprung the Methodists'. The *Christian Perfection* will make Christians too scrupulous and enable the wicked to say that Christianity is not practical or rational. The world can be enjoyed in part. Christ attended feasts and entertainments. He turned water into wine for the sake of pleasure. Some of Christ's rules were obligatory only for the first Christians and hyperbole is found in the Sermon on the Mount. Pomp and vanity are inevitable in this world. Belief in the Inner Light and talk of the Spirit of God reminds one of the fanaticism of the seventeenth century. Such Quakerism should be shunned.[2]

Vituperation is to be found in the pages of Trapp and in some of the replies to his attacks. Typically, Law's *An Earnest and Serious Answer to Dr Trapp's Discourse, etc.* is forceful but never loveless or abusive. At the very outset he says that controversy easily seems 'unkind' and that only the danger of Trapp's words to Christian souls put his pen into his hand.[3]

Trapp was wrong to base his remarks on the text from Ecclesiastes (7, 16) as these words are put by the author into the mouth of a fool or infidel. Trapp nowhere defines the piety about which he writes so much. As the piety of two thirds of the devout in the land is unreformed, his discourse is likely only to prevent amendment.

To allow that the Holy Spirit operates on us but that his working is as indistinguishable as that of our minds is to advocate '*inward Insensibility*', whereas Scripture is full of 'Proof of these inward Senses'.[4] It refers also to hardness of heart, which may be overcome by a broken and contrite heart.

It is true that error can emerge by abstaining from things indifferent and making other indifferent things matters of duty. But Trapp uses this principle wrongly. We can abstain from indifferent things on a higher principle. Thus St Paul avers, "All things are lawful to me, but all things are not expedient' (1 Cor. 6.12). He practised the precept when he refused to burden the Church financially while working as a preacher. Modern clergymen, for whom gain counts for much, could learn from Paul and edify the world.

Some may conclude from Trapp's advice that indifferent things are no concern to the church. But by the proper or improper use of eating, sleeping, dressing, resting, working, and money some live up to, and some die to, the gospel.

Law proceeds to a brief account of the nature of Christianity so that the reader can judge the issue between Trapp and himself. (From now on the reader can assume that Law uses the framework of Boehme's thought; our expositions often can be curtailed.)

The visible universe stands in the place where Lucifer and his angels had their kingdom before they fell. It is right that they remain in the place of their sin; God would not introduce them here to tempt man; as the universe has to pass through a purifying fire it cannot be in its first created state. It is polluted.

The Bible indicates the sequence of events. Having brought their kingdom into ruin 'Darkness was upon the Face of the Deep'. God made the present universe from 'the *Materials* of their ruined angelical Kingdom'.[5]

Man came on the scene on the sixth day of creation. He came as lord to discover and manifest the wonders of the world and to bring forth a holy offspring to fill the places of the fallen angels. After this the last purifying fire was to raise Paradise to the state of creation before Lucifer's fall.

Adam had a glorious angelical body, such as we will have after the resurrection. The resurrection takes away *'Sin,* and *Death,* and *Earth'* and reveals the first created body which it was Christ's aim to restore. His resurrection appearances indicate what this is.

Had Adam been content to eat only from the Tree of Life and live by the Word of God, he would have been established as 'an eternal Angel, or Divine Man',[6] but 'his imagination wandered after the secrets of this outward World, after the Fruit and Knowledge of such Good and Evil, as wrought an entire Change in his Nature. For *everything* must have the Nature of that which it chooses for its *Food*.'[7] He got what he desired and fell from glory into earthly life.

Bereft of divine life God, in his mercy, breathed a spark of that life into Adam 'in the Declaration of a *Serpent-Treader*'.[8] At this point Christ began to enter human nature. This process came to a culmination in the Incarnation, Death, and Resurrection of Christ and the offering to us of a birth from himself and the Holy Spirit.

The need for mortification and devotion to God emerge from such considerations. Learned men (such as Waterland) may speak of baptism as a federal rite and others allow the ordinances of religion to polish their manners. But the death-blow to the old man comes only through the new birth. Religious opinions and modes of worship 'stand on the *Outside* of Religion'.[9] Mortification 'can have *no Excess* till [it] . . . hinder[s] the *Purification* of the Soul',[10] and our measure of charity must be that of the New Testament.

Trapp's account of Jesus' visit to the marriage feast at Cana

strikes Law as 'horrid'.[11] The water miraculously affected by
Jesus was not made alcoholic but given heavenly properties
such as would allay the heat of the guests. In the same way he
augmented the spittle that gave sight to the blind man. Nor did
Jesus approve the feast. He came to it as to other unholy places,
seeking the lost.

John the Baptist was a 'severe Master of Mortification'—a
point often made now by Law. He was also the preparer of the
Kingdom of God.

It is true that St Paul recommended widows to care first for
their dependants, but this advice was given to widows alone.
The New Testament abounds in sayings that a family will never
be ruined by the charity of its father. He considers an imaginary
rich bishop of Winchester (in fact, Hoadly) so helping the
needy of his diocese that his own family were treated frugally.
One son could become a carpenter like Christ, another a tent-
maker like Paul. He bequeaths £20 a year to them to be used
only in cases of need, otherwise the money should be distributed
to the poor. If at the same time the bishop has cultivated the
spiritual discernment of his family, they will bless his memory.
Such a bishop would not only not ruin his family but he would
also bid fair to end infidelity in his diocese.

He expostulates with the clergy, numbering himself in their
ranks. At a time when the light of religion is almost quenched
they must remember that they are called by God to be chief
instruments to preserve the world from corruption.

To ask whether we are to expect ordinary or extraordinary
assistance from the Holy Ghost is like asking whether a minister
should be an ordinarily or extraordinarily good man. Nor do we
need the assistance of the Holy Ghost less now that religion has
been established and learning increased in the world. Prosperity
and learning need as much sanctification as persecution and
distress. God 'is an *all-speaking, all-working, all-illuminating*
Essence'.[12] Let the clergy therefore, among their books, be most
attentive to the book of the heart, and let the Bible be
approached with love and humility uppermost.

He rejects Trapp's assertion that *Christian Perfection* condemns
all trade and secular pursuits. Law quotes from the two practical treatises to show that he maintained their value. Nor did he
condemn riches; he showed rather the happiness that follows

their wise deployment. Nor did he assert that a Christian could make no use of a law-court. We live under government and the safeguarding of property is the first value of law. But a Christian may refuse to use the court out of considerations of spiritual advancement.

He concludes that he has taught New Testament doctrine as well as that of 'the most eminent Saints through all Ages of the Church'; Thomas à Kempis and Jeremy Taylor for example.

Law's *An Appeal to all that Doubt, or Disbelieve the Truths of the Gospel, whether they be Deists, Arians, Socinians, or Nominal Christians* was also published in 1740. The title indicates his continuing interest in contemporary questions, and the contents justify the common opinion of its literary and theological eminence.

He begins by disputing the doctrine of creation *ex nihilo*. Scripture says, 'Good breathed into Man (*Spiraculum Vitarum*) the Breath of Lives, and Man became a Living Soul'.[13] The soul came from God, not from nothing. What was breathed into man was the light, life, and Spirit of God. The making of man in the image and likeness of God means that man had a beginning and being out of God. St Paul teaches the same truth when he says that in God we live, and move and have our being (Acts 17.24. Law often uses this text now).

Reason is offended by the idea of creation *ex nihilo* no less than Scripture. A thing can no more be created out of nothing, than by nothing. As every creature is nature formed into a particular form it is contradictory to think of one not having been formed out of nature. Nor is it a part of God's omnipotence to make a thing to be without having any one quality of being in it.

Our thinking and willing never began to be; they are eternal. It is 'as possible for Thought *in General* to begin to be, as for that which thinks in a particular Creature to begin to be of a *Thinking* Nature: therefore the Soul, which is a *Thinking, Willing* Being is come forth, or created *out of* That which hath *Willed* and *Thought* in God, from all Eternity'.[14] The created soul is a creature of time, but the soul's essences were formed into the creature in a state of distinction from God, but are nevertheless from God and had been with him from all eternity.

Hence the *'uncontrollable Freeedom'* of thought and will. As God is self-existent so they have *'Self-motion,* and *Self-direction'*.[15]

Had we been brought into being out of nothing we should have nothing of God in us. If we have something of God in us we cannot have been created out of nothing.

We desire eternal life and this desire testifies to our eternal origin. As a line can reach no further back than the point from which it arose, so we, who look into eternity are assured that we rose from thence.

We shrink from the thought of 'falling into Nothing'. Had we arisen from nothing we would desire to return to our origin. Being would be a burden to us. Thus the divine nature of the soul, 'which the *Schools* prove with so much Difficulty' is seen as a self-evident truth of nature.[16]

The soul is obviously immortal. It can be no part of God's omnipotence to annihilate something that inevitably bears his eternity.

The present world, with its mixture of good and evil, can be no more reckoned the first creation of God than a sick man. St Paul teaches that it descended from the spiritual world (Rom. 1.20). As every outside presupposes an inside, everything on earth results from *'something* that was in Heaven'. As heaven is the glorious outbirth of the one God in Trinity, so Temporal Nature is a *'gross Out-birth'* of Eternal Nature.[17]

God is the universal All. He has all qualities to infinite perfection. The creature is limited and finite. So qualities that in God are radiant may turn to evil in man. Evil, in the natural and moral world lies in the creature *'dividing* and *separating* itself from something which God had given to be in Union with it'.[18] Thus wrath in the soul and poison in the body are not only the same reality, they are evil only because separated from other qualities.

'Attraction, Astringency, or Desire' are the ground of every creature. What is necessarily existent in the creature must be in God. Creaturely desires are only *'Emanations'* from the 'Divine Desire'. Such divine desire can also be postulated from the fact that nothing could come into existence but by the desire of God. Such desire 'is justly considered as God the *Father'*.[19]

The eternal will of the Father is to generate the Son, whence proceeds the Holy Ghost. We find the same functioning in the creature. This is why Scripture says that the Father is the Creator, the Son the Regenerator and the Holy Ghost the Sanctifier. We are baptized in the triune name to teach us that we do not have the Son and Spirit by nature. Through this sacrament we are born again of the Son and the Spirit.[20]

Such an account of Adam's fall does proper justice to Genesis. Explanations treating the Fall as the loss of some moral perfection or acuteness of rational power are fictions and denials of Genesis. Only the present account, for example, enables us to see that Adam died on the day of his transgression, and did so by the loss of his first life. The opening of his eyes when he fell means that they were previously shut to the life, light and spirit of this world. His wish to hide himself meant that some great change had been wrought in his body.

Scripture and reason agree that unfallen Adam must have had a body differing from our present one. Scripture says that flesh and blood cannot enter the Kingdom of God. Reason supports Scripture in the view that Adam was created immortal and that his body must therefore have differed from ours, which is made from the four elements that bring strife and destruction.

The triune God seeks to raise the fallen race of men. The Father draws us to himself. In this process an anguishing, kindling fire begins within us. The Son enters the soul as the Regenerator. The Holy Spirit is the Sanctifier because he finishes the work begun by the other members of the Trinity. In the same way he is 'the *Finisher* of the Triune Life of God'.[21]

The discovery of some scholars (Augustine, Aquinas, etc.?) of three properties in the body and soul bearing likeness to the Trinity is not important. There must be a generation of the thing itself for there to be a true likeness. 'That which is a Life from the Deity, must have a Life of the Trinity in it.'[22] He believes that a harmony exists between God, nature and creature that must charm a rational man. We can represent his thoughts in tabular form:

| GOD | MAN | WORLD |
|---|---|---|
| Father | Desire (Father) | Desire (Fire) |
| Son | Son (derived) | Light (Light) |
| Spirit | Spirit (derived) | Spirit (Air) |

We may conclude from this that:

> Revealed Religion is nothing else but a Revelation of the *Mysteries*, of Nature, for God cannot reveal, or require any Thing by a spoken or written Word, but that which he reveals and requires by *Nature*; for *Nature* is his great *Book* of Revelation, and he that can only read its Capital Letters, will have found so many Demonstrations of the Truth of the written Revelation of God.[23]

Christian salvation is the one salvation possible in nature. Life and death in angel, man, and the lower creation is identical. Consider the flint. Its fire is imprisoned and it seems to be dead. But if a steel is struck against it we realize that 'every Particle of the Flint consists of this *compacted Fire*'.[24]

From this standpoint he feels able to accuse the Deists of believing in an arbitrary God. God is no prince rewarding men according to their services. He only wants such a life to be raised in us that will enable us to enter heaven.

Deists are also mistaken in treating different religions as similar. As well assume that any substance will extinguish fire. Indeed 'the particular *Doctrines, Institutions, Mysteries,* and *Ordinances* of a revealed Religion that comes from the God of Nature, must have their *Reason, Foundation,* and Necessity in Nature; and then your renouncing such a revealed Religion, is renouncing *all* that the God of Nature can do to save You'.[25]

Outward morality yields no salvation. It has only the life of this world in it. By contrast the person who loves to see a crucifix because in his heart he embraces Christ 'does an Action ... needless in itself, which yet by the Spirit from whence it proceeds, *reaches* Heaven, and *helps* to kindle the heavenly Life in the soul'.[26] Nor is there any partiality in calling on the name of Christ. As there is no partiality in God the goodness in the call of any man will be heard by God. Further, impure religion using any name will be discounted by God, and as Jesus Christ is the power of God at work in men's hearts using his name is only to discover the right vocabulary for prayer.

He proceeds to the subject of Temporal and Eternal Nature. Temporal creatures come from Temporal Nature and eternal beings from Eternal Nature. They are the strata from which particular beings are made.

Because there is eternity there can be time. Because there is infinity there can be the finite. From this we can argue the necessity of Eternal Nature because we observe Temporal Nature. It is also apparent that Nature stands between the creature and God.

Everything is either God, nature, or creature and these last two are a manifestation of God. Nothing began to be; every supposed beginning is only the achievement of a new state. Thus time did not begin to be. 'Duration, which always was, began to be measured by the Earth's turning round.'[27]

Temporal Nature is a gross out-birth of Eternal Nature. But the degrading of Eternal Nature cannot have been due to God's direct action. We locate the process in the Fall of angels. When Jude says the devils left their former habitation he meant they left their former nature. By God's interposition the effect of the fallen angels was limited and hope dawned for the world. Such a solution to the problem of evil gives Law great satisfaction.

Everything that is disagreeable has its root in hell. All that is delightful is heaven breaking through the veil of this world. 'The *Serenity* of the Air, the *Fineness* of Seasons, the *Joy* of Light, the *Melody* of Sounds, the *Beauty* of Colours, the *Fragrancy* of Smells, the *Splendour* of precious Stones' are examples of this.[28] As we have the 'Height and Depth of Eternity' in us so we respond to these different manifestations and choose heaven or hell.

Everything being an out-birth from eternity, as we separate off gross features from temporal facts we can understand their eternal state. Thus fire, light and air are the Trinity in its lowest manifestation. Fire generates light and air proceeds from both. The tri-unity of the Godhead, in which they are rooted, decides their unity and division.

Another example lies in the fact that 'The Elements of this World stand in great *Strife* and *Contrariety*, and yet in great Desire of *mixing* and *uniting* with each other; and hence arises both the *Life* and *Death* of all Temporal Things.'[29] As union can only be desired because once it has been, the elements must have been first united. Each of the four elements has something of the others in it. At the consummation the four will coalesce into one.

In Eternal Nature materiality is the garment with which

light is clothed. It differs from light by being 'the *Holder* and *Displayer* of all its Colours, Powers and Virtues'.[30] On earth materiality is dense and dark for it is separated from the united power of fire and light. But sunshine shows us that the earth's deadness can be revivified by the united power of fire and light. Its success is temporary because it has only temporary power.

Scripture supports this line of thought. At the end of time fire will dissolve everything. Thus created things will return to their unfallen state. Experience agrees. We call love divine because it brings unity where there was division. An intimation of our first glorious state can also be found in people's predilection for precious stones and the adornment of their persons.

Eternal Nature or the Kingdom of Heaven stands in a threefold life. It is the manifestation of the Father in fire, the Son in light and the Holy Spirit in spirit. Through this beatific visibility the 'incomprehensible Trinity *eternally* break[s] *forth*, and manifest[s] itself in a boundless Height and Depth of blissful Wonders'.[31] As God can only act according to the capacities of nature it is not surprising that after the Fall he came to have strange names that 'could not *belong* to God in himself'.[32] To those who have lost all of God but fire he is called a consuming fire. In himself he is overflowing Love. If we say that the dark fire living in the unregenerate comes from the Father, no theological error is involved. It is from the Father, but not of the Father. Its nature has been spoiled.

Fire is also an appropriate word to describe the soul. Fire is presupposed in Scripture wherever life, light and love are mentioned. Writers often refer to the divine nature and created spirits as fire. In a rare footnote Law calls attention to the use of the word by Dionysius in his *Celestial Hierarchies*. In its spiritual nature fire is working desire. It is 'its *own Kindler*'.[33]

As matter is a compaction of the materiality of the Kingdom of Heaven, spiritual properties are present everywhere in the materiality of this world. Thus the whole creation groans, as St Paul says, and this groaning is the desire of gross materiality to return to its heavenly condition. This desire will be fulfilled by means of the last Conflagration.

Law moves to a consideration of the true grounds of the gospel. The Socinians are wrong to think they safeguard the dignity of God by holding that he could have redeemed man

without the Incarnation. We must recover what we have lost
to be saved, and that is the birth of the Son of God within us.
The Bible records how this can be.

Christ's death was no penal sacrifice to satisfy God's *'just
Indignation'*.[34] For salvation to be possible, what Adam did must
be undone. The Old Testament sacrificial system showed that the
old sinful life must be given up, literally, poured out. That the
image of the Trinity might be regained by man Christ was born.

> God, according to the riches of his Love, raised a Man out of
> the Loins of *Adam*, in whose mysterious Person, the *whole
> Humanity*, and the *Word* of God was personally united. In
> this Union of the Divine and human Nature lies the *Founda-
> tion* and *Possibility* of our Recovery.[35]

As Christ is the life of God in all men he was perfectly fitted to
be the Second Adam, a common Father to men as Adam had
been. He had all humanity in himself, as it was before and after
the Fall. In 'his inward Man the *Perfection* of the first *Adam*, and
in his outward the *Weakness* and *Mortality* of the fallen Nature'.[36]
Thus all Christ's actions did not end with himself but became
ours as we derive life from him. Each stage of life Christ passed
through had to be successfully accomplished for salvation to
become possible. The Incarnation was necessary because his
action had to be done in and to fallen human nature to be
effective. His terror, confronted with death, 'was his Entrance
into the *last, eternal Terrors* of the lost Soul': that into which
men would naturally fall at death.[37]

The process of Christ must be understood as a whole, the
various parts *'jointly* qualifying' him as our Redeemer.[38]

A function of this saving act is to reclothe us with the celestial
flesh and blood which we lost at the Fall. Christ had a heavenly
humanity veiled beneath the humanity he received from Mary.
Such Johannine texts as, 'I am not of this world' indicate this
truth. From this humanity 'our heavenly, immortal Flesh and
Blood is *generated* and *formed* in us'.[39]

We receive Christ's heavenly body and blood in the Eucharist
provided it has become rooted in us at the new birth.

Appended to the *Appeal* is a short tract entitled *Some Anim-
adversions upon Dr Trapp's Late Reply*. The reply was, of course,

to Law's previous publication. He reckoned that such was the abusiveness of two-thirds of Trapp's work that this much must be left unanswered if he is to write as a serious Christian. An indication of Law's ability to respond Christianly to unjust personal attacks is found in his remark that he will not have a *'personal Contention* with any Man whatever'. He will leave Trapp to enjoy the triumph of his wrath against him.[40]

Trapp stated that at the marriage feast Christ turned water into wine, and did so in virtue of his creative power. Law replies that the wine was made out of water and not out of nothing. Ordinary wine comes from grapes corrupted by the Fall; that which Jesus made escaped the curse. We cannot believe that the purpose of the miracle was to increase wine for the guests, since only a cup was skimmed off from the vessels and this alone had become wine. The rest remained water in order to reinforce the miraculous impression.

Though Trapp resisted Law's strictures on the clergy, he notes that Trapp neither shows that the words of Paul used were misapplied, nor that the clergy fulfilled them. What is required of the clergy is renunciation and the new birth. Men may have 'preached and *prophesied* in the Name of Christ, in the Streets and Fields', but without these things they work in vain.[41]

Learning is insufficient qualification for the ministry. Learned men hold every error. Consider the recriminations of Protestants and Catholics.

The fact that many clergy have families cannot excuse indulgence. Indeed he must 'object a little' at the idea of married clergy. Neither Scripture nor Antiquity says a clergy-man must marry. The duties of office cannot therefore be mitigated on grounds of domestic affairs. The Reformation permitted married clergy as "an Allowance granted to Weak-ness'. As dons must be celibate to devote themselves to study, so should clergy be celibate to devote themselves to ministering to the congregation. *'Virginity,* or *Celibacy,* when entered into from a Principle of *divine* Love, from a Heart burning with the Desire of living *wholly* and *solely* to God, is a State that gives Wings to all our Endeavours.' A priest dedicated to the service of the altar must wish to present to God body, soul, and spirit 'in the utmost Degree of Purity'. Indeed, a primitive Christian 'must needs be much more shocked at Reverend Doctors in Sacerdotal Robes, *making Love* to Women, than at seeing a *Monk* in his Cell, *kissing* a wooden Crucifix'.[42]

John the Baptist was chaste and mortified. Christ constantly preached the need for mortification and said that virginity was for those who were able to choose it for the kingdom of God's sake (Matt. 19.12). We must consider St Paul discouraging clerical wedlock for he recommended the chaste and the unmarried as being able to devote themselves best to God's work. The twenty-seventh Apostolical Canon of the Church ruled that none above the office of singer and reader should be able to marry. Since a married man is as fit to become a priest as one who has a trade, we must distinguish those who are married before ordination from those who marry afterwards. He mentions the early apologists glorying in the number of virgins as proof of the divinity of Christianity, and quotes again the passage of Eusebius in the *Serious Call* where the celibates appear in the higher order of Christians.

Trapp wonders if George Fox could have outdone Law's sentiments. Though he has not read his books Law would be as glad to find truth there as in the pages of the Fathers. Though perverse divisions have lessened the means of salvation among the sects, their members may reach the journey's end like pilgrims with one leg.

Selfishness and partiality are the worst evils church divisions have caused. The partial orthodoxy of each is taken for total orthodoxy. Bossuet and Stillingfleet advocated the virtues of their Churches because they were born in them. But bring together a Catholic and a Protestant with 'the *Piety* of an Apostle, and the *impartial Love* of the first Christians, in the first Church at Jerusalem' and they would discover union in half-an-hour and write their deed of union on half a sheet of paper.[43]

There is a Catholic spirit different from the orthodoxy of particular churches. It is bred from mortification and the love of God. Truth is itself divided by the division of the Church. The true Catholic must have 'more of Truth, and less of Error, than is hedged in by any divided Part'. We must like the truth even if Ignatius Loyola or John Bunyan brings it to light, and dislike error even though Dr Trapp or George Fox (is Law thinking of Quaker sacramental teaching?) perpetrate it. Apart from the errors of the Church of Rome, saints like Bernard, Teresa, Francis de Sales and others shed great lustre. We cannot blame the Roman church particularly for its worst fault of persecution, since Protestants have also condemned toleration.

Trapp stated that Law offered no proof for his rigorist treatment of clerical families. Law answers that his proof lay in his exposition of the point. He adds words of St Clement, St Barnabas, and Justin Martyr to show that Christians once had all things in common and generously helped each other. He mentions such saints as Polycarp, Hilary, and Basil. In a learned note and footnote he enumerates the decisions of councils to the Council of Trent which support his position. He quotes for support the French Roman Catholic historian, Dupin.

The total condemnation of enthusiasm misleads. The life of every intelligent creature consists in will, imagination, and desire. As every such creature is its own self-mover, it can inflame itself with shadows or realities as it likes. 'And *this kindling* of the Will, Imagination, and Desire, when raised into a *ruling Degree* of Life, is . . . Enthusiasm.'[44] Thus all men are enthusiasts, scholars and field preachers, as well as those agreeing with Law. True from false enthusiasm is distinguished by its heavenly or earthly origin. Attention to the Inner Light and the institutions of the Church guide us appropriately.

Trapp believed that Boehme, Pordage, and Mrs Lead gave Law his peculiar notions and that he tried to pass off their ideas as his. Law replies that he knows little (but enough) of the views of the latter two and that he omitted mention of Boehme's name because of the prejudice against it. Newton knew Boehme's value. His concept of planetary motion was drawn from Boehme's idea of the Three Principles. He made extracts from Boehme's works and was impressed by the significance he gave to the number seven.

But Law's real court of appeal was Scripture. Further, had Trapp been conversant with mysticism, he would have realized that Law was indebted to many mystical writers. 'Doctrines of Religion I have none, but what the Scriptures and *first-rate* Saints of the Church are my Vouchers for.'[45] Boehme had nothing new to add to religion and his name cannot be classed

M

with those of the biblical writers. But the inscrutable mystery
in religion and nature was opened to him, and the peculiarity of
his style and the depth of his thought are what they should be,
fitted for those who want, and are qualified, to read him. He is
specially useful to combat the twofold idolatry of the day, that
of speculative opposition to the Gospel, and the nominal
Christianity founded on the acceptance of the bare letter of the
Bible. If the New Testament could not be proved by miracles
we say that the '*internal Characters*' of the text convince. We prove
Boehme similarly. 'Conversion of the Heart to God in the
reading' indicates the truth.[46]

These works of 1740 indicate that Law remains a High Churchman, but is more liberal than when he wrote the *Three Letters*.
Though he appropriates the method oddly, giving more credit
to mystical writers than other theologians, he is still concerned
with Scripture, tradition, and reason. Despite his strictures on
reason the *Appeal* shows how deeply Law wished to reconcile
Christianity and science and formulate a philosophy unifying
revelation and reason. He retains belief in the Catholic ordering
of the Church and the sacraments, though he expresses a
simpler, more liberal belief than previously. He believes that
Antiquity was the time when the Faith was most purely practised and his views on celibacy indicate how he was prepared
to correct Anglicanism by Antiquity. The Caroline divines
defended clerical marriage against Roman Catholic theologians, and no Caroline or Jacobean divine opposed clerical
marriage on principle. Hall was aware of the inadequate
theological basis for compulsory celibacy, but he, Hooker,
Thorndike, Herbert and others believed that as the world has
come into the Church, it is wise to admit clerical marriage.[47]
Law's constantly ambiguous feelings about the world being
now in the Church emerge plainly on this subject.
    Together with the quality of his praise of Boehme we should
note his statement that mystics may be grouped together and
that Boehme is only the most excellent of these, his teaching
being to some extent found in them. Of course he is right. All
Christian mystics stress the importance of conversion, sanctification, mortification and the accessibility of God. These and
other points that are also Boehme's, or upon which he im-

proved, can be found in the mystics Law loved. Assertions not inconsistent with Law's idea of emanation can be found in *The Book of the Poor in Spirit.* [48] The inadequacy of discursive reason in spiritual matters and the presence of the self-authenticating Divine voice in the human heart were commonly taught. [49] These same teachers recognize the priority of the new birth and value the sacraments to augment it. [50] The imagery of light and fire is often found. [51] This list of mystics, and points where suggestions of Boehme's teaching can be found, could be greatly extended. A brief review of some of Law's favourite writers indicates, however, the justness of his claim, though the omission of Boehme's bizarre elements is eloquent.

Confirmation of these elements came in part from the Gnostic and Apocryphal tracts he was reading so busily. These seemed specially important coming from antiquity. *The Book of John the Evangelist* relates how the devil fell through pride and that this meant the taking of light from him. The *Gospel of Bartholomew* states that the devil (unfallen) was 'fire of fire', and that he and his legion were cast down to the earth when they fell. *The Apostolic History of Abdias* relates that the devil has fiery eyes and breathes flame. *The Apocalypse of Peter* describes the dissolution of all things in fire at the end of the world and the coming in brightness of God and his angels in judgement. *The Acts of Peter* refers to Jesus as light, and light shines from him; it also sees the Atonement in terms of conversion and sacrifice because of the example of Christ. *The Acts of John* discourages marriage. [52] All these works purported to declare mysteries closed to natural reason and given to favoured persons. The examples quoted show only some of the opinions congenial to Law's recent thought that he must have found in these curious documents.

More orthodox theologians of antiquity could sometimes lend support. The Cappadocian Fathers, for example, painted unfallen Adam in glorious colours. Gregory of Nyssa even wrote about Adam as the Archetypal Man, perfect and without sex differentiation, comprising within himself all possible men and women. Foreseeing that he would fall, God divided him into a man and a woman. [53] Irenaeus' Atonement doctrine included the notion of Christ as the Second Adam recapitulating in a victorious manner those actions in which Adam had failed. According to Irenaeus Adam contained in himself his

descendants and Christ recapitulated in himself the whole
sequence of humanity.[54]

We cannot spend time evaluating fully Law's belief concerning the profanity of the times.[55] But as the question bears on the
development of our subject a few points can be made. Any age
must have seemed wayward to a rigorist like Law. But a special
laxity is discernible in eighteenth-century religion, consequent
upon dismay at the interminable religious quarrels of the
seventeenth century and the new this-worldly view and reliance
upon discursive reason emerging at the end of that century.
W. B. Stevens is a more typical clergyman than Wesley. His
*Journal* reveals him going to the races, playing cards for money,
preaching a sermon by Bishop Wilson, making frivolous remarks
about worship and preaching, being fond of cheese, Shakespeare, and the classics, dancing and taking pleasure in two
women 'whose conversation delights in allusive obscenity'. He
was also concerned about the truth of Christianity, opposed
the slave-trade, preached an anti-Calvinist sermon in the
presence of Calvinists, and was complimented by the local
gentry on his '*comfortable* and *useful*' sermons.[56] The deepest
criticism of Stevens would be that there is no flame in his life.
Thus he is unable to overcome the frustrations of schoolmaster-
ing and love.

A reductionist form of Christianity with an emphasis on
sanctified common sense in daily life was thus usual. This could
degenerate into place-seeking, plurality, and drunkenness
among the clergy, and the mere form of Christianity among the
laity. But more can be said about the age than this. Law and
the Methodists were products of the time. Devotional books
sold well and J. W. Legg indicates that concern for prayer and
worship was common. Bishops Berkeley and Butler were
thinkers of the first order. Religious zeal founded the Society for
the Reformation of Manners (1692), the Society for Promoting Christian Knowledge (1698) and the Society for the
Propagation of the Gospel (1701). Most clergy had to reconcile
themselves to genteel poverty and insecurity of tenure. Until
after Law's death most earned annually between £30 and £40.
The diary of Robert Meeke shows the mid-point between
worldliness and heroic devotion that many clergy probably
practised. As vicar of Slaithwaite, Yorkshire, from 1685 until

1724 he could count on £24 4 a year and survived because he was single, and had simple habits and some private means. He founded a school in the parish, bequeathed a parcel of land to it, and helped to redeem the chapel. In 1718 he received £200 from Queen Anne's Bounty to augment the living. After his death part of his library was sold and the proceeds given to the poor, the rest preserved for the resident minister. The editor of the diary believes Meeke to have been intelligent, kind and always ready to serve.[57]

We may conclude that Law's strictures had point, but that he failed to give the credit possible. His inability to make room for humanist virtues limits the value of his picture of an Apostolic Bishop of Winchester. Money and social position enabled a youth to cultivate the mind and reach an influential post, whilst poverty or impecunity might coarsen or frustrate the just ambitions of his children.[58]

Commentators have asked if Law realized that Hoadly was the contemporary Bishop of Winchester. Surely he did. Law never wrote irresponsibly and to have made imaginary strictures that could be mistakenly applied to a living person would have been very irresponsible when we remember that Hoadly's position was well known and certainly known to Law. Winchester was, of course, a rich see and Hoadly was far from being an apostolic man!

His references to field-preachers and the like show his continuing concern with Wesley and the Methodists.

# 16

## LIFE AT KING'S CLIFFE

Law continued to compose prayers for personal use. Walton has preserved one that comes from the Boehme-period of his life. It is 'A Prayer, for the destruction of the evil, bestial and serpentine properties of the old Adam, in the soul'.[1] He calls himself a 'poor, miserable, helpless creature', and asks God to break down the evil within him, to 'shake and awaken the inmost depth and centre of his soul', and to give him humility and love to be 'the stringed instrument, sound, and harmony of thy Holy Spirit'. Though he dwells more now on the Atonement as an inward reality and upon the Holy Spirit, this prayer reminds us how much of personal piety remained constant throughout Law's life.

He moved from London to King's Cliffe in 1740 and remained until his death. The house to which he moved was called King John's House, and lay near the church and parsonage. It had belonged to Law's father.[2] It is an ancient foundation and may have been rebuilt by King John and used by him on hunting expeditions. It is surrounded by a pleasant garden and a close of pasture belonged to it. A benefit of his move was the proximity of his brother, George, who lived at King's Cliffe, employed as a kind of bailiff for the Earl of Westmorland.

Law's removal was no retirement from life. Attitude rather than vicinity decides that. In any case friends and relations lived near, correspondents and visitors communicated, and Hester Gibbon and Mrs Hutcheson figured in his plans from the beginning.[3]

We have already met Hester. In the London house of her father she had come under the influence of Law and seems to have accepted the ideal of virginity in the name of Christ. Mrs Hutcheson was evidently willing to fulfil her late husband's request and lead a retired life under Law's direction. He was engaged as 'chaplain, instructor, and almoner' to the ladies and in 1743 they moved to a house found for them by Law at Thrapstone, ten miles from King's Cliffe,[4] but in 1744 they joined Law. Bad weather made passage between the villages difficult and Thrapstone proved too small for the charitable enterprises the ladies envisaged. Law's house was adapted for them (including the handsome Adam fireplace? Was the less rigorist influence of the ladies involved in the choice of this?). They remained at King's Cliffe until their decease, Mrs Hutcheson dying in 1781 and Hester in 1790.

The dominant purpose of Law's move was to set up a holy household and to live according to the principles of the *Serious Call*, with devotion and charity as the twin pillars of existence. Monasteries in England had been officially suppressed in 1540, but the value of the retired, celibate life given to prayer, good works, and possibly to learning, had been upheld by such Caroline divines as Andrewes, Thorndike, and Bramhall. Experiments had been undertaken. Bishop Ken supervised an Anglican Sisterhood at Naish. Nicholas Ferrar was responsible for a Community at Little Gidding. Recommendations for such houses were made by the Nonjuror, Robert Nelson, who, in his list of charitable works lacking in England included 'places of religious retirement for the devout'.[5] Mary Astell (1668–1731), the close friend of Lady Elizabeth Hastings (who embodied the ideal in her life, and corresponded with, and was much admired by, Law) wrote a *Serious Proposal to Ladies* (1694), suggesting the establishment of a Protestant Nunnery 'being not only a retreat from the world . . . but likewise an institution and previous discipline to fit us to do the greatest good in it'. There were to be no permanent vows and the establishment was to be run on Anglican lines.[6]

Law must have known about the thoughts and enterprises of some of these worthies, not to mention the development of monasticism in the early centuries. We can trace with some confidence the likelihood that he knew of the life and work of Nicholas Ferrar. Little Gidding lies only fifteen to twenty miles from King's Cliffe. The fame of the Community was considerable until its suppression in 1646. Visitors came daily, including Charles I, and some from overseas. The literary productions of the Community were famous throughout England. We may imagine that Law's pious parents had heard about Little Gidding and William may have heard them speak about it. He almost certainly uncountered the name of Ferrar in Walton's biography of Herbert and as the translator of Juan Valdez's *Divine Consolations*. Again, Nonjurors were prominent in rediscovering Ferrar's work, especially Hearne, Turner, Peck, the Cambridge historian Baker, and Jebb of Steeple Gidding. Peck had made an extract of Ferrar's *Life* in 1733. Baker and Turner also made extracts. All these men were Law's contemporaries. Other Ferrar manuscripts were in private hands and at Clare College, Cambridge, where Ferrar had been a student. Bishop Ken certainly knew about Ferrar and Robert Nelson probably did. Such circumstantial evidence falls short of proof but it seems likely that Law knew of Ferrar's experiment and consciously allied himself with the ancient and Anglican expressions of monastic life.[7]

The move to King's Cliffe was as definitely an act of service to God and humanity as Wesley's decision to become an itinerant evangelist. Let us see how the household spent its time. Mrs Hutcheson's income was about £2000 a year, Hester's £5000–£7000. As the domestic requirements were few and the money was not allowed to accumulate a large sum was available for charity. Inhabitants of King's Cliffe, remembering the trio after their deaths, informed Tighe that their 'acts of charity were boundless'.[8]

In 1745 Mrs Hutcheson founded a school for the education and clothing of eighteen poor boys and the salary of the master to teach reading, writing, and arithmetic. In 1756 the school was enlarged to care for twenty boys, and she directed that every successful scholar should be put to some trade. She bought a schoolhouse for the master and had four tenements built for four old and poor widows of King's Cliffe, and provided a weekly allowance for them.

In 1756 Law built a schoolhouse and school, and two tenements adjoining the school for two old and poor widows or unmarried women, and provided a weekly allowance. In 1752 he founded the King's Cliffe Library. Above the lintel thereof we have Law's inscription, 'Books of Piety are here lent to any Persons of this or ye Neighbouring Towns.'

The only holidays permitted the school children were

Christmas, Easter, and Whitsun. Prayers, accompanied often with the chanting of a psalm, were said six times a day. Periodically the children went to church. On leaving school the children were presented with a Bible and Prayer Book. The girls were examined in the catechism twice a week. For a reward of a shilling the children tried to learn by heart certain passages of Scripture, including the Sermon on the Mount, John 18 or 19, and 1 Corinthians 15.20 to the end. Any girl discovered lying, cursing or undutiful to her parents stood chained for a morning and then knelt to ask forgiveness. If this happened three times, she was expelled.[9]

Law rose at 5 a.m., spent some time in devotion, and breakfasted on a cup of chocolate in his bedroom. After study came a deed of charity. The domestic needs for milk being satisfied by his four cows, he gave the rest to the poor. At 9 a.m. the bell rang for family prayers, the collect and psalms for the day forming part of the devotion. Law studied then for the rest of the morning. A window from his bedroom overlooked the courtyard so that needy persons had immediate access to him. Broth was kept warm on the kitchen fire and, in winter, ale and wine in addition. Among the clothes supplied to the indigent were coarse linen shirts. In order that he might not be tempted to give away what he could not thankfully receive, he customarily wore them, and then washed them before distribution.

Paupers gathered in the wake of this munificence. They brought difficulties for the parish. Eventually the rector preached directly against Law and the ladies, and a paper of complaint signed by many parishioners was presented to the local Justice of the Peace. The trio (1753) responded with the threat that they would leave the parish and stop their charitable works unless some good reason for their not doing so should emerge. If opposition continued they would notify the bishop and local gentry with a list of their charitable works. Law, at sixty-seven, could still be formidable! The complaint died away and the year following the rector became trustee of the charities.

Dinner was served at noon in winter and at 1 p.m. in summer. Law ate moderately and drank one glass of wine. He is reputed to have eaten from a wooden platter, the reason being either a whim that plates are injurious to knives, or, as seems more likely, his desire to assist the local trade of turnery. Devotional exercises were observed after dinner.

Then Law returned to his study, rejoining the ladies for tea. He would stand, eat a raisin or two from his pocket, and indulge in 'cheerful conversation'. Devotional exercises were resumed and the servants took turns reading a chapter from the Bible. Law took then a sharp turn in the fields for refreshment and meditation. There followed a snack, family prayers, and bed at 9 p.m. Two places in the hearthstone of Law's room are worn, suggesting that he sat there often and moved his feet when cold.

Walton tells us that 'Mr Law and his companions . . . were constant in their attendance at church, whenever divine service was performed'. After morning service on Wednesdays and Fridays they rode for an airing; Law and Hester on horseback, Mrs Hutcheson and friends in a carriage. Their neighbours, the Misses Hatton, dined with them on alternate Fridays. The ladies passed some of their time copying passages from devotional writers. Walton noted extracts from Tauler, Lee and Madame Guyon, which suggests Law's tutelage.

Mrs Hutcheson had a reputation for kindliness, but she and Hester did not always agree. For this reason, it was said, they were separated in burial: one lies at the feet, the other by the side of Law. Nor does it seem that their master's command respecting simplicity of dress was observed after his death. Hester bought some yellow stockings and Mary Law (William's favourite niece, who had previously heeded his advice) appeared monthly in a new dress. Meeting Hester in 1774 Gibbon found her a great curiosity, exceeding anything in a masquerade. Her language and ideas were those of the previous century, but she behaved with cordiality and '*in her way*, expressed a great regard'.[10]

Exaggeration may mar such reports. What fragments of letters remain to us from Law to Hester suggests only the warmth and affection binding the three together. In 1742 he writes:

After I received Mrs Hutcheson's letter, I ordered cheese-cakes to be made by way of Rejoicing—I can say no more than that I belong to Mrs Hutcheson and yourself, and have no human pleasure like that of pleasing you both . . . Antient Acquaintance. Adieu.

Another letter ends 'Je suis *en Dieu* tout à vous'. In a 1742 letter he apologizes for troubling her by asking her to procure some pills for him, comments on the beautiful countryside and requests that she sends him the *Gospel according to the Arabians*. In 1743 he remarks about a certain horse, 'He is wild enough for a wild Maid of Honour'.[11]

Such benevolence seems to have been typical of the older Law. Hartley, rector of neighbouring Winwick, recorded that he was used to see company, was free in conversation, had a warm and loving heart and universal charity. Langcake often watched him sporting with his nephew's children after a meal, tossing them up and down on his foot. George Law enjoyed an intimate relation with William. Writing to his aunt, informing her of William's death he referred to his younger brother as 'father'.[12]

Law seems to have been fond of music and on occasions such as the entertainment of the Charities Trustees Hester would play the organ.

He was troubled at the sight of a captive bird and would procure its release if possible. Dean Inge considered this an example of misplaced kindness, for such a bird would fall prey to the nearest cat. But Law, no less than the owners, were countrymen, knowing the ways of cats and birds. He most likely interceded for linnets or nightingales, caged when adult.

His study was a small recess about four feet square, parted from his bedroom by a wainscoting. It contained a chair, writing table, Bible, the works of Boehme in German with a few English translations, the manuscript writings of Freher, the papers of Francis Lee, and other authors. Of course he read more than these. A resident recalled that his books were sold in 1800–1 and that 'boxes, upon boxes, full of volumes' were to be seen. With time he read less. Sometime after 1750 he wrote to a friend, 'Reading is *eating*; and therefore I only read such books as have food suited to the state of life and hunger that is in me. I leave learning to the learned, and reasoning to those that seek help from it.' In 1752 he returned two books to

Langcake, as being so contrary to his inward feeling that they remained unread. His remark in 1740, 'I seldom see the newspaper' suggests that he was somewhat indifferent and they somewhat unavailable.

That sanctity is not debilitating is clear from an altercation in which Law became involved, between Hester and Catherine Elliston, Hester's close relative and godchild. Catherine had become friendly with the Mallets, who were infidels. A quarrel in London led to Hester's lonely departure from the city. Catherine wrote to say how shocked she had been by Hester's words about her friends and that she might break relations with her. An effusive, ungrammatical reply was composed by Hester. She hoped Catherine would soon be loosed from the '*bands* of blasphemy, hypocrisy, and infidelity' in which she was enmeshed. Law was called in and promptly redrafted the letter. Catherine's rudeness, and Hester's twofold relation with her are mentioned. She is shut up with infidels who honour Bolingbroke. Her friends are barefaced, blasphemous scorners of Christ. It were better for Catherine to tend a dung-cart for bread than be seated in a carriage with them. Though deluded Hester will continue to pray for her.[13] It will be remembered that Bolingbroke united loose, even scandalous living, with free-thinking. Whether Hester had private knowledge of iniquity on the Mallets' part we do not know, but association with Bolingbroke would seem iniquity enough.

A visit by Byrom to King's Cliffe in 1743 and briefly recorded in his *Journal* suggests the breadth and topicality of Law's reading and his mental alertness. They spoke of Dodwell's *Christianity Not founded on Argument*, Mandeville's *Free Thoughts on Religion*, Freher, Bertot, Byrom's poetic renderings of Law's later writings, and Silesius' *Cherubinisher*, and he noticed a copy of Ruysbroeck on a table. Law spoke about the ambiguity in the word 'reason' in that although Christianity is not founded upon it, if there is a rational motive for believing we must believe; about those who build spirituality and speculation on unmortified lives; about the limitations of Quakers.

The usefulness of Law's removal to King's Cliffe must be stressed. Commentators have sometimes thought it a removal from life. Neither the monastic tradition, here liberally inter-

preted, nor the portrait of Law's life at King's Cliffe, allows us
to think so.

A geniality emerges from the portrait. Evidently Law lived
better than he wrote. How much more attractive his writing
would have been if it had permitted the theological principles
involved in purchasing cheesecakes for celebration and tossing
an infant on the foot! The forbidding quality of his character
showed on at least two occasions. He reacted too strongly,
surely, to the petition of parishioners and to the letter of
Catherine Elliston. The introvert's tendency to misconceive an
adversary's position seems to be in operation here.

Despite the valuable features of the education provided by
Law we have only to compare his ideas with those of Commenius (1592-1671) to see how unseeing he was in this venture.
Commenius united religion and liberality. His pupils were to
receive a wide education, often by means of pupil-participation
through questioning, acting etc., and everything learnt had to
be understood; punishment was virtually abolished and sport
was included. It is true that Commenius had few immediate
followers and that Law's regimen would have been widely
approved, but the fact that Commenius was able to realize
such excellent educational method indicates that Law exhibited
no genius in this field.

In a letter to his wife dated 27 May 1749 Byrom mentioned
a '12d piece about prayer' recently published by his friend.
Lady Huntingdon had ordered a hundred copies for distribution among acquaintances. The book had been a long time at
the press and Law had another piece ready.[14] To *The Spirit of
Prayer*, for such the 'pieces' were, we turn now.

# 17

## 'THE SPIRIT OF PRAYER'

Our suggestion that the main reason why nine years elapsed between the publication of the *Appeal* and *The Spirit of Prayer* was that Law felt no inner compulsion to write is strengthened, not only by the rhythmic, numinous quality of the sentences of the later work, indicative of a source deeper in the personality than that of the discursive reason, but by two particular remarks of Law. During Byrom's visit in 1743 (mentioned on p. 174) he said that Freher's works should not be published since Freher admitted that he wrote 'historically'. Law could see no particular use in extending Boehme's influence by mere critical, rational writing. The presumption must be that published writings of Law were not only 'historically' written. Not even the *Appeal* had been written in this way. When Langcake offered to send him objections to the *Appeal* that he had received Law disarmingly replied, that he was 'incapable of disputing with anyone in the defence of it. I wrote it only for those who want such light as is there discovered.'[1]

The present work opens with an account of the importance of prayer. Most people are asleep and have no consciousness of the eternity within them. Celestial life has been breathed into natures otherwise ruined by the Fall.

He dwells in a familiar way upon the story of Adam. He imagines God addressing Adam and informing him that the command not to eat from the tree in the Garden is no arbitrary command but 'loving *Information*' necessary to preserve his state.[2] Angels had once occupied the Garden. Standing in the order of creation, meek and resigned, 'Perpetual Scenes of Light, and Glory, and Beauty, were rising and changing through all the Height and Depth of their *glassy Sea*, merely at their Will and Pleasure'.[3] But they began to think that the power to produce such marvels was their own and that subjection to God hindered the full use of these powers. They meditated revolt and 'in the Swiftness of a Thought Heaven was lost'.[4] Heavenly materiality degenerated into the four elements of this world. The 'beautiful *Figures*, and *ideal* Forms of the endless Divisibility, and Degrees of Life' in heaven degenerated into the gross shadows of the creatures we see about us.[5] The devastation would have proceeded but for God's creating fiat commanding the creation to bring forth creatures according to their kind.

The fallen angels lost their heavenly nature but not their eternity. This root of life is now torment. They could only fall into 'the horrible Depths of their own strong self-tormenting Nature', and that they did.[6] They had desired, and they received, the life of self.

Adam did not fall into hell, but into the power of his body which had been taken from this world. Further, since he had only lusted after knowledge of this world his fall was less terrible. But we live on the brink of hell. Without the new birth we must fall into the region of devils when the body drops from us.

Those who say that the new birth is only a figurative expression are therefore 'hurtful' teachers. No passage of Scripture need be taken figuratively unless a literal interpretation is impossible. Such is not the case here. Our souls need reviving as much as our bodies would, deprived of light and air. Scripture and systems of divinity recognise that natural man is eternally lost. Jesus Christ can only truly be a redeemer if he helps us to regeneration.

The truth doubtless surprises us, but then the Incarnation 'astonishes Angels'.[7] Such is the love of God that we may well be so affected. Nor must emphasis upon the inward Christ be taken as

setting up an *inward* Saviour in Opposition to that outward Christ, whose History is recorded in the Gospel. No: It is with the utmost Fulness of Faith and Assurance, that I ascribe all our Redemption to that blessed and mysterious Person, that was born of the *Virgin Mary* and will assert no inward Redemption but what wholly proceeds from, and is effected by that Life-giving Redeemer, who died on the Cross for our Redemption'.[8]

The outward Christ is the cause of the inward experience in the same way as the outward sun is the cause of the life-giving sun within vegetables.

The pre-eminent need is to turn to God and to discover the riches of our souls. Regeneration is the whole of religion. But we lack progress in it 'because we have *No Will* to it'.[9]

Christ's birth in the soul is already begun. The '*second Creator*' entered Adam after the Fall and is the light lighting every man entering the world. 'See here the Beginning and glorious Extent of the *Catholic Church* of Christ, it takes in all the World.'[10] It is to the heart we must look, then, in seeking God. What does introversion mean?

> Thy natural *Senses* cannot possess God . . . thy inward Faculties of *Understanding*, *Will*, and *Memory*, can only reach after God, but cannot be the *Place* of his Habitation in Thee. But there is a *Root*, or *Depth* in Thee, from whence all these Faculties come forth, as Lines from a *Centre*, or as Branches from the Body of the Tree. This Depth is called the *Centre*, the *Fund* or Bottom of the Soul. This Depth is the *Unity*, the *Eternity*, I had almost said, the *Infinity* of thy Soul; for it is so infinite, that nothing can satisfy it, . . . but the infinity of God.[11]

This centre was the place where the Trinity unfolded itself in unfallen Adam. It was the place where God inspoke the Bruiser of the Serpent into fallen Adam. This spark of God 'has a natural, strong, and almost infinite Tendency, of reaching after that eternal Light and Spirit of God, from whence it came forth'.[12] As God and man are so closely related we should not be surprised that 'so many eminent Spirits, Partakers of the Divine Life, have appeared in so many Parts of the Heathen World'.[13]

When the heavenly seed takes root in our lives a true knowledge of the mystery of godliness becomes ours. It is known experimentally and is not dependent on books.

> All that the Gospel teaches of Sin and Grace, of Life and Death, of Heaven and Hell, of the New and Old Man, of the Light and Spirit of God, are things not got by *Hearsay*, but inwardly known, felt and experienced in the Growth of his new born Life.[14]

This pearl of eternity is the Church within us. Here we may worship in spirit and truth. All 'outward *Forms* and *Rites*, though instituted by God, are only the *Figure* for a Time, but this Worship is Eternal'.[15] Here the 'Supper of the Lamb' is kept and the Process of Christ is not merely remembered but inwardly found. Resignation to God and dependence on the Light within are the means by which the new birth proceeds. The Church is supposed to be a spiritual society where every member is governed by the Spirit of God. But '*Self* got footing in the Church' and it suffered degradation'.[16]

Neighbourly love is practised by all who have turned to God. The rule of neighbourly love is: '*That God alone is to be loved for himself*, and *all other Beings only* in *Him, and for Him*.'[17]

There is no intrinsic use in mortification, but as it removes 'the Impediments of Holiness' it is very useful.[18]

Part I of the book ends with an oft-repeated phrase. 'There is but *one Salvation* for all Mankind, and that is the *Life* of God in the Soul.'[19]

The Second Part of *The Spirit of Prayer* (published in 1750) is divided into three dialogues, with *Academicus, Rusticus, Theophilus*, and *Humanus* as the participants. Overton characterized them as follows:

*Theophilus* represents Law's own views, and is completely master of the situation, as Law himself always was; he is an adept in the art of shutting up, as Law also certainly was; but there is an earnestness, a tenderness, and a thorough reality about him which attracts far more than his occasional asperity repels us, and in these respects he exactly resembles Law. *Academicus* is a professing and, according to his lights, a sincere Christian, but he is so hampered by his 'letter-learning', that he finds many obstacles to the reception of Christianity according to Behmen. He is, therefore, continually laying himself open to severe snubs from *Theophilus*; and is still more often being set right by *Rusticus*, who, being unable to read or write, is in a far better position to receive the truth in its fulness and simplicity. Humanus is a learned unbeliever, a friend and neighbour of *Academicus*.[20]

N

The same acquaintances reappear in *The Way to Divine Knowledge*, and *Theophilus* is found in *The Spirit of Love*.

We are told that spiritual writers are 'Friends of God, entrusted with his Secrets, and Partakers of the Divine Nature'.[21] But *Academicus* is advised not to read them too eagerly. To read for intellectual stimulation is to be affected more by nature than grace. Every spiritual book is really a call to give up self and embrace God, which is the first step in religion.

Theology should convert and inspire. For this reason *Theophilus* repeats his doctrine of the angelic Fall and the creation of this world. He refers to Genesis 1. God sees the darkness on the face of the deep and the chaos into which the fallen angels have brought creation. The Spirit of God moves on the face of the waters and transforms it into what we now see. His command, 'Let there be Light', could not refer to the creation of the sun for that appeared on the fourth day. It refers to 'a Degree of Heaven, that was commanded to glance into the darkened Deep' to impart 'its quickening Virtue' to all things, so that progressively the darkness which is death might be transformed into the light which is life.[22] We thus perceive the 'Uniformity of the Divine Procedure' in the restoration of nature and the regeneration of man.

Darkness is the ground of fallen nature. '*Fire* is its Life; and *Light* is its glorious Transmutation into the Kingdom of Heaven; and *Spirit* is the Opener of all its Wonders.'[23] In this way nature is the manifestation of the Trinity in a triune life of Fire, Light, and Spirit.

We are saved by neither faith nor works. 'Faith and Works are at first only *preparatory* to the new Birth; afterwards they are the true *genuine Fruits* and Effects of it.'[24] It is the new birth itself which saves us.

*Theophilus* is challenged to show that this doctrine agrees with the plain letter of Scripture. He quotes his remarks about the new birth as clear evidence and proceeds to his views on Adam. On the day that he ate the fruit he died. He died to his angelical life. St John refers to this when he says that he who does not have the Son does not have life. In his account of the angels' fall no Scripture doctrine is omitted or opposed. Indeed the letters of Scripture are opened to reveal their full meaning. We discover 'the *Ground* or *Philosophy* of the Christian Faith'.[25] This teaching has its authority from Scripture but not so openly as 'Matters of Faith and necessary Doctrine are'.[26]

If the question of proof is raised *Theophilus* might well ask for proof of the doctrine of creation *ex nihilo*. There is no biblical proof and it even violates the Bible. It is plain from Genesis what Adam and Eve were made from and on two occasions St Paul tells us that all things are out of God (1 Cor. 9.12; 8.6). To proceed by birth is the only procedure of nature, but if things are created out of nothing they must be separate from God and have nothing of him in them.

The Second Dialogue begins with a discussion of Adam. That he was meant to be a restoring angel, with power over the world to prevent its evil being known or felt, is borne out by Genesis where we learn of the great distinction between man, made in the image of God, and the rest of creation; and where we learn that all nature was affected by Adam's fall.

He proceeds to a discussion of man's sexual nature. According to Genesis man was male and female in one at first. Christ tells us that in heaven we shall be as the angels and not marry. We may infer from this that angelic perfection unites the two natures. When Genesis says that it was not good for Adam to be alone we see that Adam had altered his first state and 'brought some *Beginning* of Evil into it'.[27] God divided Adam into male and female to prevent greater evil afflicting him. God had wished Adam to propagate his offspring as he himself had been propagated. But Adam had desired to propagate out of himself. By this adulterate love his first virginity was lost. He fell into a deep sleep and during it God divided his overcome humanity. Thus God brought good out of evil, wishing the mutual love of Adam and Eve to prevent them lusting after the world. As things turned out, God in his steadfast love had to raise out of woman, without man's help, Christ the Second Adam. In his humanity Christ had the perfection Adam had at his creation. He has to do all that by a birth of redemption from himself that mankind should have had by a natural birth from Adam.

Clement of Rome, 'who lived in the very Time of the Apostles', relates that Christ was asked when his kingdom would come. He answered, 'When two things shall become one, and that which is outward be as that which is inward, the Male and the Female, and neither Man nor Woman'. Clement of

Alexandria quotes the same words with some alteration, and also an answer of Christ to Salome, who also asked about the kingdom. 'When ye shall have put off, or away, the Garment of Shame and Ignominy, and when two shall become one, the Male and the Female united, and neither Man nor Woman.'[28] Thus Scripture and Tradition are in agreement.

But marriage in this fallen world is lawful as God's appointed means of raising a sufficient number of offspring to Adam. We are born into this world in order that we may be reborn to the life of heaven. Nor must we think that women brought evil into the world. The fault lay in the '*Division*, and that which *caused it*'.[29] Women may indeed be comforted by the fact that Christ had his birth only from the female part of our divided nature.

The Dialogue ends with further remarks on prayer. Prayers from books or at certain hours are of little importance compared with the 'continual Panting or Breathing of the Heart after God'.[30] Of course the soul rightly delights in hours of prayer, but they are only an expression of a more fundamental attitude.

The '*Heresy* of all Heresies, is a *worldly Spirit*'.[31] An orthodox believer full of pride is at the greatest distance from God. Life is a '*working Will*'. Let us therefore will the right.

The Third Dialogue opens with the recognition that *Humanus* has been affected by the previous conversation. He confesses that his sceptical equanimity has been upset and that his objections to Christianity are of little avail against the theology now proposed.

*Theophilus* interprets his state as the mortal torment nature must pass through before it can succeed to life. It is the state of conversion, and those experiencing it realize that they have been enticed by Love, the strongest of facts.

He will prescribe no rules that might enable men to obtain the Spirit of God. Strong desire is alone requisite and our will-spirit might even be called the spirit of prayer. We can pray to idols as well as to God.

The recommendations of the *Serious Call* are mentioned none the less for only '*heartless Form*' does harm and Christ used the same words three times in Gethsemane.[32]

We can test the error of the belief that proficiency in reason prevents prayer by retiring from the world for one month and

then praying earnestly for deliverance from self and the gift of
the Holy Spirit. Not to be willing to do this indicates a defective
heart, not lucid reason. The folly of a religion of reason is
pressed by an extract from the *Demonstration*.

Three levels of prayer are specified. At first penitence,
confession, and humility predominate. Then, uplifted by the
mercy of God, thanksgiving and hymns. When this fervour has
melted away all earthly passions and left no inclination in the
soul but to delight in God prayer changes again.

> It has now come so near to God, has found such union with
> him, that it does not so much pray as live in God. . . . This is
> the last State of the Spirit of Prayer, and is its highest Union
> with God in this Life'.[33]

Each stage has its trials and purification is continual. Always we
must turn from self and cleave to God. Tribulation is of more
use than joy for it gives 'Means and Power of exercising an
*higher* Faith, a *purer* Love, and *more perfect* Resignation to God,
which are the best State of the Soul'.[34] The value of understanding the theology just described is that it will breed a
dissatisfaction with our present state and a desire to undertake
the high adventure of prayer to attain our first perfection.

This theology is not pantheistic. Our good spirit 'is the *very
Spirit* of the Deity, and yet not God, but the Spirit of God,
breathed or kindled into a creaturely Form'.[35]

We can distinguish the movement of the Spirit of God in our
hearts as clearly as wrath, guile, or covetousness. If we are
meek, patient, merciful and universally loving, we are moved by
God's Spirit. If we concentrate on Christ's two great command-
ments we will be led aright.

The teaching of Boehme has passed now through the fire of
Law's own life. This book pulsates with the prayerful spirit of
the author. An autobiographical tone pervades even the
description of the highest reaches of prayer. Commentators
remarking Law's statement that he was a stranger to revelation
forget that he spoke thus in 1735.

He believed that prayer and thinking assist each other and
that theological truth should reform life. For this reason he is
never tired of reiterating his new-found beliefs concerning

creation, fall and redemption. This theological method is practised especially by Orthodox theologians, but in the west Augustine, Anselm, and Karl Barth are amongst those who have pursued it.[36]

The Bible retains its importance, but Law has become idiosyncratic in the use of tradition. The primitiveness of Clement of Rome and Clement of Alexandria lent them importance in his eyes. But Clement of Alexandria is quoting, in fact, from *The Gospel According to the Egyptians*, a Christian Gnostic work. Also, Clement's Second Epistle was written by a Christian Gnostic, not by Clement as Law supposed.[37]

The literary sources informing this work are those we have noted previously. We shall notice later that his concern with fire, air, and light reflect the scientific concerns of the day, as well as traditional mystical concern with fire and light.

The simplicity of Law's teaching on prayer reminds us of the Quakers and the seventeenth-century French school, though its roots are purely traditional. Thus Origen categorizes three ways of spiritual progress: the purgative, the illuminative, the unitive. In her description of the Mystic Way, Evelyn Underhill, drawing on the tradition of the Christian mystics, gives these stages: the awakening of the self, the purification of the self, the illumination of the self, the dark night of the soul, the unitive life.[38] If we turn to a French contemporary of Law, Père de Caussade (d. 1751), we find him teaching much the same method as that of Law, Boehme apart. Reason is no help for penetrating the divine mysteries; when moved by God we should forsake books; argument is indecisive, obedience to God is not; we must care for our spiritual progress and keep away from society; evil must be cleared away before God's good can come to the soul.[39]

At least one contemporary event seems to have been woven into the prose of the Second Part of the book. In 1750 Britain had an earthquake. It was thought that a recurrence would obliterate London and that it instanced God's anger. A pastoral letter by Bishop Sherlock sold 100,000 copies. Charles Wesley preached for hours without intermission. Law uses the crisis to enforce the need for repentance.[40]

A notable defect of the post-Cartesian world was the belief in the dichotomy between body and soul. A consequence of this belief was that the relation between the individual and society was underestimated. We find this defect in Law, and the older he grew the more prominent it became. The traditional Christian idea that man is a body-soul unity is only partly appreciated with the result that the body, society, sacraments and institutions receive less than their due.[41]

Law put the essence of his mature belief very succinctly in a letter to a Customs Officer, who had long been a reader of his works: '*truth* is to be lived . . . nothing lives in us but our heart; and the heart has but one life, and that is *love* with all its *fruitful workings*. Expect no light, therefore, but from the love of God.'[42]

Not the least interesting visitor to King's Cliffe in 1749 was George Whitefield. Despite their strong differences of opinion their meeting went well. His ironic comment upon Law's later theology is:

> His scheme upon the Fall, etc., I think is quite chimerical; but he says many things that are truly noble, and which I pray God to write upon the tables of my heart. Several things at the end of his treatise on regeneration, in my opinion, are entirely unjustifiable: but the sun hath its spots, and so have the best of men.[43]

Whitefield must have echoed the views of many, but not those of Wesley, who never visited Law and who was to attack him again in six years' time.

# 18

## 'THE WAY TO DIVINE KNOWLEDGE'

Law's deep piety is inadvertently indicated in a letter he wrote to Byrom in May 1749. They had been speaking about some plan—possibly that of Byrom turning into verse some of Law's later writing—but the day following he wrote to condemn the proposal 'as coming from myself'. He had realized this as soon as Byrom had left him and had continued to repent, believing that his proposal had

> some degree of self, or self-seeking in it, and therefore I renounce it as such. An assistance that comes in unlooked and unsought for, I can rejoice in, as coming from God, but I have the fullest conviction that I ought to be as fearful of desiring to be assisted as of desiring to be esteemed.[1]

His humanity seemed to have blossomed at the same time as his piety increased. In 1751 he wrote to Byrom to congratulate him on becoming a grandfather. He adds the humorous post-script: 'I begin to have some jealousy about your verse. You indeed sing for me, but so sweetly, that you may (for ought I know) sing my prose out of date.'[2] Replying to Langcake, who had sent him some chocolate, he said that it 'was exceeding good'. An undated fragment shows Law standing by the rights of a lad in service who had difficulty with his master.[3] It was in 1752 that he sent ten guineas for the relief of the Nonjuror, Dr Deacon, with the promise of more if it was required.

In 1752 was published *The Way to Divine Knowledge*. It is sub-titled, 'As preparatory to a new Edition of the Works of Jacob Behmen; and the right Use of them'. But Law never prepared the edition, divine compunction being wanting. The book takes the form of three dialogues. It is a continuation of *The Spirit of Prayer*.

*Humanus* breaks the silence he has so far maintained by

admitting his conversion. *Theophilus* welcomes him as a Christian and warns him that if he is to progress he must renounce self.

To make converts *Theophilus* believes that appeals to reason and antiquity wander from the point in question. A Deist so convinced would not be changed inwardly, he would have only changed his mind respecting certain facts. The purpose of the Gospel is to change the heart of fallen man. The ground for debate is the axiom: '*Life* is God, living and working in the Soul; *Death* is the Soul living and working according to the Sense and Reason of Bestial Flesh and Blood.'[5]

Goodness is rightly called angelic for it comes from God, was what unfallen Adam practised and is prayed for in the petition, 'Thy Kingdom come; thy will be done on earth, as it is in heaven.'

Necessity for the Bible lies in the fact that man is fallen. Moses tried to counteract the bestial life of men and the Law was promulgated to enable men to resist wrong. The prophets declared coming glories, awakening men so that they could be drawn out of the mire of life. Questions in the Old Testament that do not relate to the new birth are no longer relevant. The New Testament is pre-eminently about the new birth and commentaries are superfluous.

Moses only gives the history of facts which experience proves. Our mortality and inability to live as we know we should indicate our fallen condition. Contrast the deformed and helpless condition of a new-born child with the beauty of a new-born chicken. The former is born in sin the latter without it. A similar wrongness attaches to the efforts of reason. All natural knowledge is '*sensible, intuitive*, and *its own Evidence*'.[6] Opinion, reasoning, doubting only appeared when man's state grew confused.

*Theophilus* is asked why Adam should have revolted from God, the origin of all goodness. The reason lay in Adam's inexperience, freedom and ability to conjecture. Much the same reason lay behind the angels' fall.

A question frequently asked concerns the restoration of the fallen angels. Neither ancient nor modern writers have touched the heart of the problem. Appeal to the attributes of God can no more settle it than texts of Scripture. We must ask whether it is

possible. Can diabolical nature be changed? Darkness cannot
be turned into light, it can only be suppressed. If it can be
shown that the devils are accidentally, and not essentially, dark,
their restoration will happen. *Theophilus* thinks this question
may not be resolvable.

The conversation reverts to the approach to the Deist.
Argument is unavailing. Those who will listen to the Gospel
are those who sense the vanity and misery of life and have some
hope in God for a better state. To be in this condition is to
believe in original, universal Christianity. Fallen Adam, the
Patriarchs, and Prophets believed as much. Gospel Christianity
adds the contribution of Jesus which was to 'finish all the
Wonders that belonged to our Redemption'.[7]

The proper proof of Christianity is its spiritual life. 'The
Spiritual Life is as much its own Proof, as the natural Life, and
needs no outward, or foreign Thing to bear Witness to it.'[8]

*Academicus* opens the Second Dialogue by remarking that
Boehme's works need a commentary to make them plain.
*Rusticus* objects that scholars must learn to read with the heart
rather than with the head. To know what Boehme communi-
cates we must stand where he stood. The same applies to
Scripture. Reading Matthew 5 with a commentary dilutes its
force. Whatever the obscurities in Revelation 4 our hearts can
be raised to worship with the elders.

Not that learning is an enemy. *Theophilus* answers:

> I esteem the liberal Arts and Sciences as the noblest of
> human Things; I desire no Man to dislike or renounce his
> Skill in ancient or modern Languages; his Knowledge of
> Medals, Pictures, Paintings, History, Geography, or Chrono-
> logy . . . But . . . Science and Arts . . . belong solely to the
> *natural Man*; . . . Christian Redemption is quite of another
> Nature . . . it . . . is purely for the Sake of an *inward, heavenly*
> Nature, that was lost . . . under the Flesh and Blood of the
> earthly, natural Man.[9]

*Academicus* accepts this point. He recounts his own efforts to
understand Christianity as a scholar. He mentions a number of
the points with which Nonjurors were concerned. Law seems
partly to have his previous experience in mind.

Boehme has two special virtues. He is the most awakening writer in discovering the antichristian Church and the mysteries of the Kingdom of God. In addition he is a 'Relater of Depths opened in himself, of Wonders which his Spirit had seen and felt in his *Ternario sancto*'.[10] In this office he wrote as did St Paul, after having been in the third heaven, things not possible to be spoken in human words. Boehme himself recognized the two kinds of people who would misunderstand his writing; those who were uninterested in the new birth, and those who regarded reason as the touchstone of religious truth.

The word 'mystery' is particularly appropriate to describe what Boehme laid open. It means 'the *deep and true Ground* of all Things'.[11] It embraces doctrines particular to Boehme as well as Christian ethics. As everything is its own proof the mystery of Eternal Nature must be opened in a man before he can philosophize about it. 'Life . . . is only known by Life', we can have no genuine knowledge of an '*unpossessed*' thing. Reason, working on images and ideas brought to it from without, is of little use.[12]

Thus 'the Seed of everything that can grow in us, is our Will'. It is 'the only Workman in Nature'. Nor should we underestimate its importance. As the freewill of man is a genuine birth from God it has the nature of divine freedom, eternity and omnipotence in it. There is no contradiction here to the idea of salvation being the gift and work of God since the will is 'the only Spark of the Deity in us'. It is given by the free grace of God.[13]

This will can be called otherwise faith, hope, love or godly desire. Whilst faith can be defined as assent to a proposition, to be creative we must describe it as 'that *Power by which a man gives himself up to anything, seeks, wills, adheres to, and unites with it, so that his Life lives in it, and belongs to it*'.[14] It is thus wrong to think of the Christian as the man of faith and the Deist as the man of reason. Both are men of faith.

A few days' retirement are recomended so that the friends may absorb what they have learnt and improve their souls before next they meet.

The Third Dialogue opens with an assurance to *Academicus* that reason cannot hurt true religion which is 'a *self-evident Growth of Nature and Life within*' him.[15]

Nature is manifested inwardly. It is *'all the working, stirring Properties of Life'*.[16] These Properties comprise the desire to which reference has already been made. There are seven Properties. The First Property has as its peculiarity 'to compress, inclose, shut up, etc.'. From this characteristic comes *'Thickness, Darkness, Hardness, etc.'*. As soon as it begins to work it brings forth its own enemy, 'For it cannot *compress* or *thicken*, but by drawing or attracting'. This is desire's Second Property. Each one is of equal strength and opposite intention. So the Third Property is generated as 'a *whirling Anguish*'.[17] The ground of every created thing lies in these Properties. As their origin lies in Eternal Nature they will endure. Untouched by any other power they constitute the horrid life of hell.

Common experience suggests the truth of the foregoing analysis. Desire and pain begin together. This means that two properties are resisting each other. Unconsummated desire we experience as hellish. This answers to the Third Property of Whirling Anguish.

Only God can change this painful natural state. So the second group of Properties transforms the first. The first group act as the necessary Something in which the other Properties can manifest themselves. As light needs something thicker than itself to receive and reflect it, so Spirit needs something in which to work. The thickness of the first Properties is not matter as we know it, but it stands in the same place and is distinguished from light and Spirit in the eternal world as matter is in this world. The materiality of this world is the materiality of the eternal world brought into a further degree of thickness and darkness. The variety of ores and jewels in the world is explained by the fact that God spoke his creating Word when good and evil were locked in strife. They became compacted into the visible universe.

Between the three lower and the higher Properties is Eternal Fire. It changes the wrathful Properties into the glorious higher Properties. In the same way the sun stands in the middle of the visible universe sending forth light and fire until the universe be dissolved. Boehme proved the truth of this much more profoundly than Copernicus. This Fire is also the Fourth Property. It 'is not God, *but is* that which *wants* God, or its true Good'.[18] This Property is born in the soul by God and the soul longing for one another. We find the same throughout nature. Wood and candle give fire and light because of the oil and water in them. When the Properties of Nature in them are put in strife and work in darkness they open an entrance for the Light Properties in the water and oil to mix and unite with them. By the union of dark and light fire is kindled and turns the darkness of the wood and candle into light.

The Fifth Property is Light and Love, or Christ who is the life of heaven. The Sixth Property is Sound, or Understanding. These two Properties indicate the gradual entrance of the Deity into nature.

*Theophilus* believes it unnecessary to read all Boehme wrote. Because he was untrained in literary composition he repeated his doctrine in successive books. We are advised to read to the tenth or twelfth chapter of the *Three Principles*, or to the sixth or eighth chapter of the *Threefold Life* and let the teaching so take hold of us that our hearts stand in conformity with what we read. When a self-evident sensibility to the workings of nature and grace has grown in us we can proceed to other portions of his work.

Boehme's teaching became necessary because of the worldliness of the Church. Learned reason brought only disaster and perplexity. We do not find Boehme's doctrine in the Early Church because faith and Christian living were adequate to defend the mysteries. To exemplify his meaning *Theophilus* refers to the controversy over the freedom of the will by Augustine and Pelagius. Both assumed that the will was created out of nothing and therefore could not arrive at the will's constitution. The problem is resolved only when we realize that the will is an outbirth from the eternal will.

Law's involvement in the spheres of intellect and spirit is interestingly shown by the significance he gives Boehme in the divine economy. Though Boehme gained his understanding by revelation, that understanding answers the intellectual perplexities in which religious men have become embroiled.

Whilst Law was alive to the distinction between revelation and the report about it, it is curious that he makes little use of the fact in respect of Boehme. Yet he can silently differ from the master. In contrast to Law Boehme did not expect that fallen

angels or unregenerate men might find salvation after death.[19]
Whilst Boehme can say conflicting things about God, as either
all-loving, or as having wrath, Law believes him to be all-
loving.[20] Law's emphasis can also differ from that of Boehme.
The latter loves to speculate, but Law has an eminently practical concern. He returns continually to the idea of the new
birth and in his uneven explication of the Seven Properties
concerns himself especially with the dark ternary and the
Fourth Property.

Hobhouse and others have quoted Law's favourable remarks
concerning the liberal arts as evidence of his progressive
liberality.[21] But Law remains a rigorist at heart. As an educated
man, using the fruits of education and living in a Christian
civilization that valued it, he was bound to make concessions to
it. But his doctrine of the Fall and of the Properties makes a
disjunction between nature and grace. Because of this he remains
suspicious or antagonistic towards the liberal arts as funda-
mentally an unregenerate activity.

The contrast between the two ternaries and their relation to
experience of the external world enables us to see hints of a
teaching developed in the east. It is easy, for example, to see
the similarity between words of the Buddha and Law's idea
that pain and desire begin together.[22]

A literary source worth mentioning here is the writing of Dr
Francis Lee. Lee's work, as we have noticed, eventually gained
a special place in Law's study. It is voluminous and we may
imagine Law refreshing himself with it from time to time. Here
is a summary of Lee's ideas on the relation between faith and
reason.

Faith signifies the principle of receiving and apprehending
whatever is communicated to the soul by another being,
through testimony of the Bible, or by the Holy Ghost upon the
inward sense, and experience of his operation. Reason signifies
cognition in general, the active intellect. Thus human reason is
not the image of God. It is not the essential part of the soul and
the soul can be happy without it. It may have no portion in the
Kingdom of Heaven. It is a superficial, sterile faculty giving
superficial, sterile knowledge. Its origin is no higher than
nature. It is derived from the secondary intellect or soul of the
world, through the operation of the seven lords and spirits of

nature. Its authority cannot extend beyond its original. Even in natural things there is a certainty higher than that of reason. The evidence of faith is superior to that of reason and not subject to uncertainties as is the evidence of reason. Divine certainty is obtainable only by faith. The more we have of faith the sounder is our reason. Reason can be illuminated by faith and is dark without it.[23]

# 19

## 'THE SPIRIT OF LOVE'

Contact with various Christian groups continued. In 1753 Law wrote to Langcake to say that while in London he obtained a volume of the sermons of Zinzendorf, the founder of Moravianism. He had read them with difficulty. He does not doubt that the Moravians, like other sects, have good people among them, but these sermons were full of inventions and showed excessive attachment to particular phrases concerning the blood and suffering of Christ. The Moravian, Mr Gambold, used to visit him often. Because of the infected condition of his eyes he cannot say more, but he counsels Langcake: 'stop your ears to all religious tales'.[1] In a further letter to Langcake (1757) he distinguished the humble manner of a Moravian's speech from its poor content.[2]

Whilst valuing Ruysbroeck he cannot use him much.

> I could never go through the divine Rusbrochius, in his spiritualizing the Mosaic tabernacle, and all that belongs to it. His illuminated eye saw Christ figured and typified in every part, and what he saw he told the world . . . I cannot go back to search for the *shadow* of the mystery, under its types and figures, because the substance itself is come. . . . Next to the Scriptures, my only book is the illuminated Behmen. And him I only follow so far as he helps to open in me that which God had opened in him.[3]

Though few books were now of much use to Law, his books helped others. Byrom preserved the testimony of John Lindsay (1753) that through Law he came to see the harm done to the Church in Queen Anne's day by the controversy between Anglicans and dissenters. He believes that 'human craft' caused the controversy and this spirit is still strong with the clergy.[4]

The first part of *The Spirit of Love* appeared in 1752, the same year as *The Way to Divine Knowledge*. It took the form of a letter to a friend and is subtitled, 'an Appendix to *The Spirit of Prayer*'. The second part came out in 1754 and the publication was delayed because of difficulties caused by Law's inflamed eyes.

The friend to whom the first part of the book is addressed has been affected by the spirit of love breathing through Law's writing. But he is disturbed by the fact that he cannot enter into that spirit himself and he suspects that the biblical idea of God makes him just and wrathful, rather than merely loving.

Law replies that in himself God is 'an *eternal Will to all Goodness*'.[5] He can only give goodness and happiness and men will only find peace when his spirit of love has entered into them. So fundamental is divine love that we must appreciate that all nature was brought forth only so that boundless love might have room in which to live and work.

We misconceive things because we pay too much attention to what is about us. We are bidden to imagine the transformation into which all things will one day enter. Everything dissolves in water, water is changed into air, air into aether, aether rarified into light. Such a consummation will result in the glassy sea of which St John wrote. By such imagining we can give substance to the thoughts of the transformation of matter to its first state and the sin of angels bringing forth matter. Sin is the father of matter and by the conquest of sin matter will be vanquished also. How superior is this scheme to that of modern metaphysics, represented by Descartes, Malebranche, and Locke. They cannot account for things as they are and must even posit a separate body and soul, essentially contrary one to the other and held together by the arbitrary will of God.

He reviews the working of the Seven Properties. The last is the joy and peace attained by spiritual development. It is what Boehme called his *Ternarius Sanctus*, the place in which he received revelation.[6] The work of Fire, as the Fourth Property is to turn the natural quality of the Properties into a heavenly quality. Purification and exaltation is the work of fire in the visible, no less than in the invisible, world. The shock of conversions is the entry of Fire into the soul.

o

The First Dialogue in the Second Part of *The Spirit of Love* is
between *Theogenes*, *Eusebius* (a local vicar), and *Theophilus*.

*Theophilus* praises the boundless love of God. No wrath can
enter into God for no new thing can begin to be in God.
*Theogenes* appreciates the forces of these sentiments, but recalls
words of the Bible mentioning the 'vindictive Vengeance of
God', and the satisfaction made to God for our sins.[7]

To resolve this difficulty *Theophilus* examines the word
'wrath'. Its nature is discovered in a tempest or bodily sore. It
is found where disorder or impurity exist. As God is perfect,
and close relation subsists between matter and spirit we can
agree that he has no wrath in his nature. Wrath may also be
called evil; as evil can only begin in the creature wrath cannot
be in God.

Nor does a true understanding of the Atonement suggest that
there is wrath in God. All creatures have a twofold life, drawn
from nature and from God. For Christ to be the effective agent
in our redemption a union of the divine and human had to meet
in him. We cannot redeem ourselves, as Deists suppose, for we
are *Emptiness, Want, Insufficiency*.[8] As God is goodness and
happiness salvation must come from him and be his life in the
soul. All the helps God has given man in Law, prophets,
Scriptures and ordinances are assistances to a holiness they
cannot give, enabling men to turn from the corruptions of
earthly life and hunger for that union with God which was lost
at the Fall.

This being so we must speak of the *'perpetual Inspiration'*, and
not of the occasional inspiration, of the Holy Spirit.[9] As we
cannot live without God he must be always inspiring us. A
common sign of his activity can be seen in instances of human
goodness. The Prayer Book supports this position when we read
the prayer, 'we, who cannot do ANYTHING that is good WITHOUT
Thee . . .'[10] Wherever we look we find that outward effects of
creatures come from their inward spirits. The sun only stirs up
the growth and life of creatures. Our sensations are inward,
dormant things, until they are brought into a state of sensibility
by some outward occurrence. When we smell something beautiful an outward object has stirred up the 'delightful Smelling'
state of the soul.[11] We can only show love or hate because these
are within the soul. Thus the part of observances is to stimulate

inward sentiments. Similarly, we do not need a new Luther or Calvin, 'the *Oracle* is at Home'.[12]

The immutable distinction between God and nature is that 'God is an UNIVERSAL ALL; and Nature or *Desire* is an UNIVERSAL WANT'.[13] Wrath, as we understand it, has no place in God. His vengeance must be strictly an act of love. Thus the love of God kindled the flames of Sodom to prevent a more horrible fire. Scripture puts the principle like this: 'Whom the Lord loveth, he chasteneth.'[14]

The Second Dialogue deals fully with the question of atonement. The purpose of the Atonement was to remove the wrath between God and man. If the wrath was in God, Christ made atonement for God. This is blasphemous. Again, atonement suggests the removal of something which should not be there. But nothing in God requires alteration. Hell, wrath, darkness, misery and eternal death are, according to Scripture, synonyms for the same reality. They cannot be in God. What needs atoning for is that sin into which we are born.

*Eusebius* mentions contemporary schemes of divinity demanding the satisfaction of Christ to a wrathful Father, and the debtor and creditor scheme. Theophilus counters with such biblical phrases as, 'God so loved the world that he gave . . .'. Thus love, and not wrath, was the motive for the Incarnation. The mercy of the Saviour is 'the *free antecedent* Gift of God'.[15]

Scripture indicates that Christ's office is to remove the wrath in us. His sacrifice furthers the work of regeneration. St Paul says that the Second Adam became a Quickening Spirit. He revives in us what Adam lost. 'Christ given *for us*, is neither more nor less, than Christ given *into us*'.[16] Righteousness is satisfied by Christ's death in the sense that he brings it back into human nature. Christ expiates the sins of the world by restoring to man his lost righteousness.

The pain of sin can be understood as the arrows of God's love to draw us back to himself. His punishments awaken us to the significance of his love.

By contrast to this scheme, that of the schools only helps the unbeliever to substantiate his case. The notion of the infinite value of Christ's sacrifice, satisfying God's wrath, even when expounded by a Stillingfleet, only increases objections to the mystery.

We must think of the process of Christ, beginning with the Word inspoken into Adam and continuing until now. Incarnation and crucifixion are alike necessary.

> For the Children can have no other State of Life, but that which their Father had first . . . Christ, as the Father of a regenerated human Race, must first stand in the Fulness of that human State, which was to be derived from him into all his Children.[17]

To be a father of humanity Christ had to be divine. Having become man it was necessary that he should die. 'A crooked Line cannot become straight, but by having its Crookedness given up, or taken from it.' Christ took upon himself fallen human nature to bring it out of its crooked state. The glorious power of his sufferings consists in this: 'they were that, in and through which Christ himself came out of the State of fallen Nature, and got Power to give the same Victory to all his Brethren of the human Race'.[18] His Resurrection and Ascension were the consequence of his suffering and death, an entering into that which his death had gained for him. Thus Christ did not suffer 'in *our Place*', but '*on our Account*'.[19]

*Theophilus* emphasizes that this teaching marks Christianity as an unarbitrary religion working in accordance with the powers of nature. Inevitably it contains mysteries because man, in his fallen state, needs the revival of his divine life and expectation of bodily resurrection.

The Third Dialogue opens with the observation that *Eusebius'* delight in the theology just expounded stems from its accord with his natural complexion which 'has a great deal of the animal Meekness and Softness of the *Lamb* and the *Dove*'.[20]

The Calvinist scheme of election and reprobation errs in applying the doctrine to different men. Its significance is for what is in each man. God elects in us the Seed of Life. He reprobates our fallen human nature. Scripture represents this to us in outward figures. Cain and Abel were the consequence of what Adam was in himself. They represent the contrary principles in us all. This matter has been obscured since St Augustine's day.

The great question remains, How are we to obtain the Spirit of Love? All outward observances and teaching can help no more than the Law, which is a schoolmaster to bring us to Christ. If we get no further than this we shall find humility begetting pride, charity nourishing self-love, and our hearts unpurified from 'the Bottom'.[21]

To state the essential problem *Theophilus* speaks about darkness and light. Darkness will never be abolished. It may be swallowed up by light, but even then it enables light to become visible. In the same way the Natural Properties are contrary to the divine life but necessary for its communication.

*Eusebius* objects that traditionally it has been held that darkness is the absence of light and not any positive, necessary quality, antecedent to light. *Theophilus* is convinced that his description is orthodox. When the Bible says that God is Light and in him is no darkness, light is declared to be separate from, and eternally antecedent to, darkness. 'Light, as it is in itself, is only in the *Supernatural* Deity.'[22] By means of darkness men can become sensible of him. Science says that light is material. What the scientist really encounters in his experiments is the 'Body of Manifestation' for light.[23] If light itself were material, all nature would be light, for matter is of one nature. Different degrees of brightness in light are really different qualities of darkness through which light manifests itself. Light is the power that illumines the mind as well as the earth. It is all things and nothing. All things, because every perfection is from it; nothing, because it is supernatural.

Light and darkness do all that is done by man. Darkness is the evil and misery perpetrated by fallen angels and men. As it is from God this darkness is without evil. It is the ground of good. It is the strife of Properties permitting the supernatural good to come into sensibility. It is also the self which allows the incomprehensible perfections of the Deity to be possessed of 'Qualities of *an own Life*' in creaturely beings.[24]

This self comprises covetousness, envy, pride, and wrath (cf. p. 142 above). It is hell or nature. The fallen soul must covet because that is a desire proceeding from want. It must envy because that is a desire turned to self. It must be proud because

that is a desire founded on a real want of exaltation. Wrath is
born whenever any of these qualities are contradicted. The self
must desire and therefore want. From such a contradiction self-
torment is bred. Such is darkness as we experience it separated
from God.

By the operation of the powers of eternity, light is born in the
soul, and reconciliation with God achieved. Thus we stand in
the midst of heaven and hell with the thin wall of matter
separating us from them.

The new birth will be obtained by patience, meekness,
humility and resignation to God. A multiplicity of rules obstruct
the all-important '*Simplicity* of Faith'.[25] Christ is as able now to
assist 'his Church, his own Body' as once he assisted the
publicans and sinners.[26] Nothing is the way to God but the
heart. Let us 'sink down' into the four virtues mentioned and
progress in the spiritual life will be made. The '*Marriage Feast* . . .
signifies the *Entrance* into the highest State of *Union*, that can be
between God and the Soul, in this Life'.[27] It is the birthday of
the Spirit of Love in our souls and whenever we attain it we
feast on such peace and joy as blots out the remembrance of
what was called by these names previously.

This is perhaps Law's greatest book. The concluding remark of
*Theogenes* that *Theophilus* may not be seen more in this life
suggests that it represents a kind of final statement of belief.
Much of the expository portion reads like a literary transcript of
experience. This leads us to the speculation that Law may have
known the state of union with God, which the mystics describe
as the earthly summit of the spiritual life.

A major theme of the book is that the theology described
accounts for facts of nature. So it may well have seemed in the
eighteenth century. The applicability of Newton's findings to
his teaching has been mentioned. We may add the name of
John Freke, Fellow of the Royal Society and well known surgeon
at St Bartholomew's Hospital, London. He was influenced by
Law's remark that 'all is magnetism', and began his experiments after meditating on this theme. In 1752 he sent Law his
treatise *On the Nature and Property of Fire*. In this book he says
'the Element of Fire can only be Subtile and active enough, not
only to create motion, but to produce life throughout all

Nature'.[28] Fire agitates all the world. By dispensing it the sun maintains the world. This we can prove by seeing the rays of the sun concentrated by a magnifying glass produce fire. If a cat and a lighted candle are put in a closed space the cat lives little longer than the flame. Fire is thus necessary for life. It is sometimes contained in objects that are not burning. The melting of heated iron is due to the fire couched between the particles of iron making it 'flow with fire'.[29] Air is 'replete with fire'.[30] Fire is never found in an airless container because air is the medium of its activity. An animal is usually felt to be warm. The warmth comes from the fire dispensed throughout the body, originating from the air it has inhaled.[31]

The eighteenth century fascination with fire is clear from the case of John Wesley. Having observed electrical experiments he recorded, 'fire lives in water . . . flame issues out of my finger, real flame. . . . It is all mystery.'[32]

Speculations not dissimilar to those of Law respecting fire, light, and air can be found in Berkeley's works, especially in *Siris*. He can write of 'This pure fire, aether, or substance of light' as a fundamental cause and pervasive influence in the universe, and finds in this and similar concepts 'bright and lively signatures of a Divine Mind'.[33] Berkeley united genius with erudition (including scientific knowledge) and a Platonic temperament.

Law's interest in the phenomenon of light has its root, as we have noticed, not only in St John's Gospel and the mystics, but in the work of Newton.

It seems likely that Law was a closer student of scientific findings than we have direct evidence for supposing. Freke's work in particular indicates the bad scientific and philosophical conclusions that could be drawn from evidence. Such has been the advance of science, and such is the peril of wide-ranging conclusions, that today we would be unwilling to see more than valuable, even definite, hints and signs of truth where Law thought he saw a more plain manifestation.

His view of Christ is in several respects remarkable. Calling Christ 'Father' is exceptional, probably because the New Testament reserves this name for the First Person of the Trinity, and Trinitarian theology has distinguished the Father from the Son with some definiteness. But Law's attribution is perfectly logical and orthodox. It follows from his idea of Christ, the Second Adam. Significantly, Irenaeus uses the word of Christ, but only once. The nearest parallel Hobhouse found is in Julian of Norwich's *Revelations*, where Christ is called 'our very Mother'.[34] To these we may add the name of St Gregory the Great, who often referred to Christ as our Father.[35]

Also exceptional is Law's belief that Christ assumed fallen human nature at the Incarnation. Madame Bourignon, P. Poiret, and A. Freher taught the doctrine and they were probably influenced by Boehme. H. Johnson, who has examined the question in recent times, believes that the New Testament favours the idea. He gives as a likely reason for most theologians' suspicion of it the belief that it may detract from Christ's divinity. Their hesitation is understandable in view of the numerous heresies denying that divinity.[36] The anti-Gnostic character of Law's belief is worth noting.

His atonement doctrine obviously owes much to Irenaeus, as well as to Boehme.[37] But in the eighteenth century it must count as a *tour de force*. J. K. Mozley has observed that, with the exception of R. Barclay, there was no fresh contribution towards a rationale of the Atonement in the seventeenth century. The century following was even more sterile in soteriological thinking. But a restatement of doctrine was needed to counter, at least, the Deists' probing of Hooker's statement that an infinite wrong demanded an infinite recompense.[38] In real measure Law provided this restatement.

Barclay's atonement teaching and that of Law are very similar. Barclay says that Christ is the Light in all men, despite their corruption due to the Fall. The Atonement only occurs finally in what Christ does in men. But unlike Law he affirms an objective element as well. Christ removes the wrath of God for us, in addition to that wrath in us.[39] Law was aware of Barclay's teaching, of course, and may well have known something about the work of Osiander, Schwenkfeld, and Weigel, whose tradition Barclay and he maintained.

# 20

## THE SECOND ENCOUNTER WITH
## JOHN WESLEY

In 1754 John Freke answered a query by John Byrom respecting Law's idea that light and fire are not material. He believes
that iron expands when heated because the material of fire
passes into the iron to produce the well-known effect. Further,
Villett's mirror destroys bodies most effectively, and since its
power is derived from the sun, darkness can have nothing to
do with it and light must itself be considered to have body.[1]
It is doubtful if Freke had understood Law's ideas on this
question.

In 1755 he allowed George Ward, a London friend and
acquaintance of Langcake, to prevail upon him to prepare a
second edition of *The Case of Reason*. This time 'Part the First' is
omitted from the title-page.

In January 1756 there appeared suddenly John Wesley's *Open
Letter* to William Law. It took the form of a radical criticism of
Law's later theology, expressed in *The Spirit of Prayer*, *The Way
to Divine Knowledge*, and *The Spirit of Love*. Law did not relish it.
Almost a year previously he had commented to Langcake that
the Wesley brothers had no foundation other than zeal. He
found the present *Letter* poorly argued and in bad taste. He
refused to write an answer and urged others not to do so, for he
did not want the world to see Wesley in a worse light than his
own pen made him.[2]

Not all his allies agreed with Wesley's publication. In
Charles' *Journal* for 21 October 1756 we read, 'I drank tea with
Dr Byrom, and was hard put to it to defend my brother's book
against Mr Law. At last we got to a better subject, and parted,
not without a blessing.' Writing to Lady Huntingdon Whitefield said that although he did not agree with Law's theological

speculations, Wesley should not have written. 'I think it a most ungentlemanlike, injudicious, unchristian piece. However, Mr Law knows too much of the divine life, not to see some call even in this cross.'[3]

When Wesley visited Byrom in the year of the *Letter*'s publication, Byrom taxed him to 'repent of that wicked Letter'. He promised to soften some expressions if it should be reprinted. They spoke again about the *Letter* in 1761 'but to no more effect' than previously'.[4]

At least obliquely, Law did permit public comment on the activities of the Wesleys. In 1760 he allowed Langcake and Ward to publish edited letters of his. A 1756 letter says that Methodists have no foundation but zeal and that no one could object to his principles, except on personal grounds. Though John Wesley is an ingenious man his *Letter* is a 'juvenile Composition of Emptiness, and Pertness' that no one could have written who had been serious in religion for a fortnight. He tells his correspondent to let any communication respecting Law and Wesley to die with him and wish Wesley Godspeed in all that is good. The Pope and he have the same reason for condemning the mystery revealed in Boehme.[5]

Law's relation with Wesley had not been helped by some of Wesley's followers. Despite its good, excess had attended the revival. Again, Law read some published sermons by a Methodist Lecturer, in which words of Law, 'If your heart cannot give itself up in this manner to prayer, be fully assured you are an infidel', were quoted with references. But the words were not Law's. He described the incident to Langcake as forgery and stated that Methodists 'seem to have a fire that has as much of nature as of grace in it'. He decided not to publish any correction.[6]

It was perhaps necessary that Wesley should state the differences between Law and the Methodists. They were associated in the public mind. Trapp had seen a connection between Law's writing and the Methodists. Warburton could declare: 'Mr *William Law* begot *Methodism*, and Count Zinzendorf rocked the cradle'.[7] As Law's later theology was publicly suspect, and in Wesley's eyes dangerously false, it was important both tactically and evangelically to oppose it. But the tone of his *Letter* and that of Law's indirect comment suggest that there remained unresolved personal conflicts between the two men.

We have noted likely references to Wesley and his associates in various publications of Law since 1738. He had reservations about the character, theology and method of evangelism of Wesley.

Though Wesley chose not to visit Law after 1735, he never forgot him. In the published *Journal* for 1739 he comments on *Christian Regeneration*, 'philosophical, speculative, precarious; Behmenish, void, and vain! Oh what a fall is there!' Though *The Spirit of Prayer* was sometimes masterly, he believed it to be another gospel. Without the idea of divine wrath Christianity falls. However, he edited versions of *Christian Perfection* and the *Serious Call*, and even a large portion of *Trapp*, though he added in a footnote that the mystical parts were not supported by Scripture.[8]

The *Letter* begins with a generous tribute to Law's language, thought, and sometimes his sentiment, as a writer. He wrote for the glory of God and the benefit of men. But Wesley doubts if Law thinks anyone in England can instruct him. He blends philosophy with religion and in his later theology the philosophy is superfluous; piety has no need of it; it is unproved and uncertain; it is dangerous as tending to take men away from the practicalities of religion; it is contrary 'to Scripture, to reason, and to itself'.[9]

He proceeds to a criticism of the philosophy. It includes things antecedent to creation, the creation itself, Adam in Paradise, and the Fall of man. As he cannot conscientiously use his time formally to refute Law, he will only raise a few questions.

Respecting things antecedent to creation Law says that all that can be conceived is either God, nature, or creature. But there can be no medium. Nature is either creature or God.

Law says that nature is a hungry, wrathful fire of life. He says also that it is the outward manifestation of the invisible glories of God. Are not these statements contradictory?

We are told that nature has no evil and all evil in it, and that nature, self or darkness have no evil in them, and are the only ground of all good. 'O rare darkness!'

He can make no sense of the Seven Properties. Why must

there be seven? How can the conception be proved? If the
Fifth Property is Light and Love, are Light and Love the same
thing?

Respecting the creation he puts into God's mouth words
drawn from his philosophy concerning the fall of angels. Is not
this taking liberty with God and trying to be wiser than
prophets and apostles? How can we prove what is affirmed?
The proofs offered are worth little. It is useless to say that the
devil cannot be called the Prince of this world except he once
had his kingdom here. He might be so designated 'because he
*now* reigns therein'.

Wesley believes in creation out of nothing. Genesis 1 and the
Church affirm it. Law says that nature is the first birth of God.
Did he create it or not? If not, how did it come out of him?

If the angels had heavenly flesh and blood how can they
remain spirits?

The picture of the Glassy Sea continually bringing forth new
figures of life, ideal forms different from the gross species of this
world, is nonsense. What are figures of life? Are they dead,
alive or in-between?

How can it be proved that all life is desire? Can Behmen or
Spinoza prove that fire in the soul and in the body are but one
nature?

What are the proofs respecting Adam's constitution in
Paradise?

Wesley can discover no meaning in the idea that the good
spirit in us is the Spirit of God, or rather, that Spirit kindled
into a creaturely form.

He cannot believe that Adam was originally an herma-
phrodite. It is no proof to refer to Luke 20.35, 36. We are
likened to angels in that we shall be immortal. Law's conception
of Eve is unbiblical, denigrates marriage, and is without proof.

Law says that the Tree of the Knowledge of Good and Evil
grew as a result of Adam's desire. The Bible says that God
planted everything in the garden.

Bad philosophy has led Law into bad divinity. To this he
turns.

He denies God's omnipotence by saying that God works
according to the powers of nature. God is antecedent to nature.
Are we to think that nature gave God extra powers? To say that

matter could not be but for sin makes God dependent on Satan in order to create matter! Why could not God have created man without nature antecedent to man?

It is a very poor omnipotence that must abide by Law's axiom that nothing can rise higher than its original.

He denies God's justice and establishes Deism while pretending to overthrow it.

Denying the wrath of God strikes at the credibility of the Bible. Allow one falsehood there and it may be that there are a thousand. If falsehood is allowed then the Bible does not come from God.

Wrath and justice are almost synonymous terms. If justice is included in the idea of the good then God may will pain in his creatures. According to Law, if God is wrathful now, he must have been so always. Rather, God has always been just, and this was expressed as wrath when man fell. Wrath is not manifested in bodily sores or raging elements.

Law may say that Adam's miserable state is not a punishment, but the Bible says it is. It is nonsense to say that raining manna and fire on the earth manifests the same love. The text, 'whom the Lord loveth he chasteneth', bespeaks a love which is mercy mixed with justice. Wesley quotes forty-two passages from the Bible to disprove Law's contention that there is no vindictive, or punitive justice in God, and that his wrath is not visited on man.

Wesley doubts if Law understands the doctrine of justification by faith. How else can he say that regeneration is the whole of man's salvation, and that redemption is the life of God in the soul?

He is shocked that Law dares to speak of the folly of the debtor and creditor scheme of atonement. It was believed by Christ as the parable of the king settling accounts indicates (Matt. 18.23f). This parable also indicates that God will hand some over to the tormentor.

The Bible teaches that Christ died first to atone for our sins and only secondly to extinguish hell within us. To say that by dying Christ got power to give the same victory to us suggests that he did not previously have this power. He adds the testimony of the Quaker mystic, Anna Maria Schurman, supporting the doctrine of justification by faith.

Wesley proceeds to examine Law's doctrine of the new birth. Christ is said to be our Redeemer because he alone could bring life to the celestial body and spirit that died in Adam. In fact, Christ is our Redeemer because he offered the necessary sacrifice for sins. Being born of water and spirit does not mean that as we have lost our heavenly spirit and body we must be born anew of spirit and water (since water is what the heavenly body is made from). Man must be born of the Spirit because he has lost the image of God. He must be born of water because baptism is necessary.

Law says that we are saved by neither faith nor works. Paul says that we are saved by grace through faith. Law defines faith as a desire to come to God and of being made one with Christ. But faith is not desire. Paul says it is the evidence of things not seen, things that are revealed in God's Word.

He cannot believe that Christ is the universal seed in men. If men are dead in their sin that seed cannot be present. If all men are members of the Catholic Church, Deists and heathen are relieved of the difficulties in unbelief. Such words as 'centre', 'fund' or 'bottom' cannot be applied to the soul.

It is not necessary to think that a sinner can only respond to God if Christ is antecedently in the soul. If God so wills he can give his love to one who has never loved him.

Law's advice to one seeking salvation (to isolate himself, attempt introversion, and thus discover faith, since every good impulse is from God) omits the need of public worship and Bible. In any case Satan might work in the man to make him believe a lie. Nature can easily be mistaken for grace. The new birth and external helps must complement each other.

To deny everlasting punishment is to deny revelation. Body and soul will be punished in hell. The punishment of the wicked is unimaginable. According to the Bible hell is literal fire without intermission.[10]

Whatever value attaches to this examination of Law's later theology it is clear that it is written unsympathetically. Almost inevitably, therefore, it is unfair. Thus, the word 'nonsense' appears too frequently, there is a tendency to take impressionistic words and phrases literally, there is a failure to notice how some words, 'nature' for example, mean something different if understood as being subject to God or in rebellion towards him. Differences in temperament and breach in their relationship account for the unfairness that Byrom, Whitefield, Charles Wesley, and Law himself noticed.

This *Letter* was the most rigorous examination of Law's thinking that he ever received. He was never gregarious, and accident and design had removed him from the situation of neighbourly criticism that he so much needed. But it is doubtful if he and Wesley would ever have found intellectual agreement. Wesley stands in the tradition of those who find a virtual sufficiency in the Bible. Tertullian, Luther, and Barth have done the same. Law stands in the tradition of those who admit the the supremacy of the Bible, but look for help in natural theology also. Origen, Aquinas, and Tillich have done this. On earth these attitudes will not be reconciled. Mutual criticism helps each, however, and Wesley's common sense and Law's soaring vision could have profitably interacted. To this theme we shall return in the final chapter.

An uncharacteristic harshness remained in Law's attitude to Wesley. Thus he called Wesley's published advice to the clergy 'empty Babble, fitter for an old *Grammarian*, that has grown blear-eyed in mending Dictionaries' than for one who has tasted the powers of the world to come. The reference is to Dr Johnson, whose famous *Dictionary* was published recently, and who suffered from eye trouble. Law allowed this remark to appear in the 1760 edition of his *Letters*. An objective and subjective importance lies in Wesley's remark to Byrom in 1761: 'I do not treat him, with contempt, as he does me.'[11]

J. Orbical correctly notices that Wesley was open to the influence of the mystics before 1738 and after 1765.[12] But he fails to connect this fact with William Law. In 1757 he could write to a lady and say that she may receive more hurt from Law's writing than any he knew. In 1761 he was so officious in conversation with Byrom about Boehme, Law, and Methodists who read them that Byrom called him 'Pope John'.[13] By 1771 we find him recommending Law in part.[14] In 1787 he informed Ann Taylor that after the Bible she would profit most from Law's *Works* and his *Sermons*! He commended most of Byrom's poetry, which was inspired by Law's later theology, and edited volumes of Law's later writing. He admitted the force, in

1783, of Henry Brooke's criticism that his comments on the mystics were too strong: 'The words you mention were too strong. They will never more fall from my mouth.'[15] It seems likely that Law's death enabled Wesley to appreciate his writing and sources from which it came, over and above the easing of his mind respecting mysticism when the dangers of Quietism subsided.[16]

Law could be less than just to Wesley and Wesley underestimated the evangelical value of Law's writings. We may end this chapter fittingly by mentioning an encounter of Law with Thomas Yeates, which shows Law's personal excellence and his writings' pastoral use.

Yeates wrote to Law in November 1756 to say how much the loving spirit in his books moved him. He spoke of his need. When young he had passed through numerous religious experiences. He had also sinned much. At eighteen he was disappointed in his ambitions. Great conviction was wrought in his heart by hearing Wesley preach. He felt the desire to commit suicide and did not want life everlasting. In this state he continued for six years. He continued to read good Christian authors and to experience the reproach of conscience. But lust and other sin continued to conquer. He fornicated and drank heavily. In Law's *Regeneration* he came upon the idea that God is all love and without wrath. 'How my peevish angry soul melted into love! My misery fled away in a moment.' Though temptation and sin returned he persevered in reading Law's later works and he has been benefited, though sin remains.

There is no shock or condemnation in Law's reply. He expresses heartfelt, brotherly love. Desolation teaches us that salvation is of God. He should contrive nothing and have absolute faith in God. He should offer God his sins 'to be consumed in that blessed furnace of love, which made God become a suffering, dying Redeemer . . . to this faith everything must yield'.

Yeates should live as temperately as he can, avoiding temptation as he is able. He should place nothing in his own care, but do everything in dependence on God. He writes a prayer for Yeates to use and counsels him to remember the infinitely loving nature of God, of whom he must often think.[17]

As Yeates published his letter in 1787 it is reasonable to

suppose that he found stability and Christian progress. It seems likely that for some bruised souls, Law's theology was more helpful than Wesley's. We might also wonder whether a secular psychiatrist could have helped Yeates so effectively as Law seems to have done.

# 21

## THE 'CONFUTATION' OF
## DR WARBURTON

Law's next work indicates that his critical faculties had not been blunted by age and affective mysticism. *A Short but Sufficient Confutation of the Reverend Dr Warburton's Projected Defence . . . of Christianity, in His Divine Legation of Moses* was published in 1757.

William Warburton (1698–1779) held many of the principles that Law disliked and considered dangerous to vigorous faith. He was the son of an attorney, and although he became a clergyman and eventually Bishop of Gloucester, he retained a measure of the attorney's habits. A man of eminent abilities, he read widely and deeply and could make good use of what he read. As a Latitudinarian he accepted the Enlightenment's deference to reason, recommending students of theology a daily reading of Locke's *Essay* so that they might think logically.[1] He scorned mysticism and shared in some degree the Deists' distrust of church tradition. He challenged Lowth and Gibbon respecting their beliefs, and offered to challenge Hume. He was the friend of Pope, edited Shakespeare and Pope's works, and wrote a preface for the novel *Clarissa* for his friend Richardson.

The overweening regard for reason shared by many eighteenth-century men meant that deeper and darker emotions were suppressed. Sometimes they erupted, and Warburton's truculent and vulgar manner expresses this. In addition he held livings in plurality and was ambitious, and slack in the performance of clerical duties. But he opposed the Slave Trade when Wilberforce was only eight years of age and stated that men should not be persecuted for holding unorthodox views. Johnson and Gibbon paid tribute to his learning and abilities.[2]

His *Divine Legation* was the mature fruit of his mind and

character. The first volume was published in 1738, the second in 1741. Corrections to new editions were still being made when he died. He grappled with the problem of the danger of the decay of the state when religion decayed. According to G. R. Cragg, the *Divine Legation* was one of the century's important books.[3]

The immediate question preoccupying Warburton was that as there is no mention of the afterlife in the Pentateuch, that belief must have formed no part of the original religion. It was forced on the Jews later. We shall outline his argument, using the recapitulation of his position made by himself in Book vi.

Absence of mention of the doctrine of the afterlife and presence of an extraordinary Providence prove the legation of Moses to have been inspired. Religion gives force to the rules of the state and religion needs the doctrine of the afterlife to give credit to God's moral government of the world. That Moses instituted a republic and a religion without reference to an afterlife proves the extraordinary Providence watching over the Jews. The matter can be expressed syllogistically:

Whatsoever religion and society do not have a future state for their support, must be supported by an extraordinary Providence.

The Jewish religion and society had no such support:

Therefore the Jewish religion and society were supported by an extraordinary Providence.

Freethinkers deny the major statement, divines often deny the minor. He notes that Moses resisted Egyptian teaching on the afterlife and risked his authority in claiming to have a divine mission. An impostor would have been foolish to have argued an extraordinary Providence. Old Testament writers teach temporal, and not future, rewards and punishments. Ordinary people clearly know nothing of a future state. God's full dispensation dawned gradually on Jewish leaders. He almost grasped the idea of evolution in religious knowledge. For Judaism to be the rudiment of Christianity it is important that the doctrine of a future state is suggested but not openly taught in the Old Testament. Secondary meaning can be often no longer attributed to prophecy if we postulate belief in an afterlife to Old Testament writers.

An anonymous defence of Warburton, which took the form of attacking Dr Sherlock, who had opposed him, was the means of Law entering the debate. The pamphlet was published in 1756 by Archdeacon Towne and claimed an almost magisterial authority for Warburton.[4]

The *Confutation* took the form of a letter addressed to Sherlock. It begins with Towne, but quickly comes to grips with the main antagonist, Warburton. He begins with sharp ironic thrusts, which remind us that at seventy he might have written as in *The Fable of the Bees*, had not piety discovered a higher path.

He notices that Warburton gives most weight to the New Testament in seeking authority from the Bible. He will prove, therefore, that there is not a New Testament text that does not assume universal, primitive belief in the immortality of the soul. He will show also that the doctrine was openly taught, and believed in, by Old Testament people. He may proceed to his work with some confidence since 'the whole Christian Church of all Ages' opposes Warburton's thesis.[5]

Warburton quoted various New Testament texts (such as 2 Tim. 1.9–10; Titus 1.2–3) to prove that Christ taught the doctrine of immortality for the first time. That he was sent to 'show light' to Jews and Gentiles refers to the gospel of immortality. Zacharias spoke of the same light at the birth of John. When Peter spoke of turning people from darkness to light they must have been ignorant of immortality for the idea to be meaningful.

But the new light was 'the *one whole Process* of Christ'.[6] How can the mystery of the Gospel be anything other than the being and action of Christ? The Gospel mystery had to remain secret 'till what was contained in it came into *actual Existence*, and thereby manifested itself'.[7]

Nothing Christ said or did suggests that men did not already believe in the immortality of the soul. At the Fall men lost the life of God in their souls. The immortality they preserved is 'their Capacity . . . to receive the never-ending, but always increasing Manifestation of Divine Glory in, and through all their natural Powers'.[8] It is a supernatural gift rendered possible by the Process of Christ.

According to Towne, Paul says that Christ abolished death

because before Christ the Jews had no knowledge of the after-life. Law counters that it is the quality of the afterlife that is new. New Testament immortality is the life of Jesus begotten in the soul. He supports his case with relevant texts (Rom. 8.1, 2, 6; Gal 2.21; Rom. 5.17; 1 John 5.11–12; 2 Pet. 1.4).

It is incredible that God should have wished to hide the doctrine of immortality from Old Testament people, for they had need of its benefit. The types and figures of the Old Testament do not obscure but reveal a portion of the light. They resemble the sacraments, which are types meant to teach; imperfect, yet opening the gospel to us.

Not a word in the New Testament is said about the natural immortality of the soul. But it assumes this doctrine and what it teaches demands this belief. A similar belief is demanded by Old Testament teaching. The doctrine of the new birth implies the immortality of the soul 'in the Power that we have to receive it'. Similarly, an ever-enduring holiness can only be received by an ever-enduring creature.[9]

In the Old Testament we find God entering into covenant with man after the Fall. Only if man believed himself to be immortal could he want, or be able to receive, this covenant. It was itself an assurance of redemption, or return to the first glory of life. Moses recorded the history of Abel and Enoch for our instruction. Had Abel not gone to another life we would conclude that he lost the covenant's benefit merely by being good. In fact, the records of Abel and Enoch give proof of 'Victory over Death, and Ascension into Heaven'.[10] Old Testament religion is identical with Christianity except for the Incarnation. Even so, Christ was the redemptive seed in men before his appearance in the flesh. Thus Paul says that our forefathers drank of the supernatural rock, Christ (1 Cor. 10.3–4). The author of Hebrews (11.13, 16) tells us that our forefathers saw the promises from afar. Christ said to the Jews that their father Abraham rejoiced to see his day (John 8.56). Men hoped for full redemption in some unknown way long before the Incarnation.

With time the covenant lost much of its effect. As men fell away from the truth God introduced to the descendants of the patriarchs, by Moses, a *'Covenant of Care, and Protection over them'*.[11] Like the development of the Church since apostolic

times it was a discipline made necessary because of men's
sinfulness.

It is wrong to separate promise and fulfilment. They are part
of one process. Thus the Incarnation began at the beginning
when God looked with compassion on man.

The rational religion of Warburton and others is useless.
The Fall occurred because man reasoned instead of exercising
faith. Faith is adherence to God. Reasoning is adherence to
self.

We have access to God by no reasoning, but by the Spirit of
Christ working in us. After his process on earth he 'ascended
into Heaven, with *that* fallen, but by him redeemed Humanity,
which he had taken upon him'. The efficacy of Christ's mediation thus reaches back to Adam and is available to all. No
arbitrary imputation is involved, only the real working of his
Spirit.

Experience also confutes Warburton's claim. Knowledge of
God and of immortality are found in man because these things
impinge upon him. They,

> make themselves to be *livingly* felt, and found within us . . . to
> seek a Proof of them, by *abstract Reasoning*, is but like seeking
> in the same Way for a Proof of our Thinking, Seeing, and
> Feeling. For as these Qualities of Mind can only manifest
> themselves, so to seek for a Proof of them, from anything else,
> but our own sensibility of them, can only proceed from
> Ignorance both of them and ourselves . . . nothing can prove,
> or be a Proof of any Thing, but that which partakes of the
> Nature of the Thing to be proved.

Abstract reasoning cannot establish God since it does not
partake of him.[12]

For man to be made in the image of God means that the
divine life is manifested in him. Though man is defaced by the
Fall rudiments of the image persist. Locke is mistaken to insist
that the soul is a *Rasa Tabula* in its first created state. Man is a
'*Microcosm* of all the Powers, that are in the great World, of
which it is a Part'.[13] How could a soul destitute of knowledge
develop into a philosopher? If the soul is dependent on the
body for development, an infidel might say that the soul will
become a blank paper again when the body dies. Even a clod of

earth is composed of invisible riches which it gives forth through the plants that are rooted in it.

In searching for the divine image of man, Warburton says that as it cannot be his body it must be his reason. According to Law, it must consist in something peculiar to God. Man's body is like that of animals but as the *'Effect*, and *Form* of his *heaven-born* Spirit, and Life, then it is a glorious Distinction from all the animal Creation'.[14] With reason as his highest principle man might have resembled a fox. Bolingbroke had as much reason as St Paul. Are we to conclude that he was as godly? Warburton is wrong to think that God's command to Adam to rule creation resulted from the dignity of his reason. The similar situation of Christ giving power over all things to his disciples, included the promise of the Spirit (Mark 16.17–8). According to St Paul those who are ruled by God's Spirit are his children. The divine image in man is God's Spirit reduced to a creaturely form.

Warburton misconceives the method of Adam's creation in thinking that God shaped clay and breathed life into it. Many wonders were compressed in the dust from which Adam was made, and his creation was not in two stages.

> Spirit can have no Place, but its *own Body*, nor can be anywhere but in *That*, which proceeds from itself. The Life of the Soul is generated in, and from the Body, and the Body has its Birth, and Growth in and from the Soul, and therefore neither of them can be before the other, in the Formation of the Creaturely Life.[15]

When we consider the importance of the doctrine for religion, it is a shocking suggestion of Warburton's that Moses hid his knowledge of immortality from the Israelites. Without this knowledge men are removed from the sphere of the divine and that of sin. Sin is rebellion against God immanent in man. But God cannot indwell perishable creatures.

Warburton believes that the speech of the first humans was confused sounds and that they began their life in a condition of forlorn brutality. These are blasphemous ideas. Even the speech of animals is not confused and is intelligible to members of the same species. Genesis teaches the high dignity in which men came from God. We must now learn language because we have

lost the heavenly power of speaking which was natural before
the Fall. Literary works are possible only because man's real
good has departed from him.

Genius and industry are present in Warburton's book. But he
has mixed hellish with Christian elements in the composition.
Confronted with the question, 'What must I do to be saved?'
Warburton's defence is driven out of our heads.

> There are *two Ways* of embracing Christianity, the one is, as a
> *Sinner*, the other as a *Scholar*; the former is the Way taught by
> Christ and his Apostles, the latter is the invention of Men,
> fallen . . . under the Power of natural Reason.[16]

The parable of the Prodigal Son contains the whole matter
between God and man.

This is as able a book as Law wrote, close and subtle in
argument, succinct and sufficient in expression. Commentators
have wondered if the comparative freedom from Boehme-type
expressions means a departure from dependence upon him, but
the comparative absence of such expressions stems only from the
nature of the book. His concern is to argue for essential
Christianity, so the essence, but not the developed statement, of
Boehme's system is alone relevant. That essence clearly pervades the book.

Present-day scholarship would agree with Law rather than
with Warburton on the question of the knowledge of immortality in the Old Testament. Of course the Jews would say that
men really died at death and that God raised them up; the
concept of resurrection being preferable to that of immortality.
It is also most likely that the implications of the covenant only
dawned slowly on Jewish minds, so that belief in eternal life
came spasmodically and in the later history of the people.[17]

What Law says about the image of God in man is also preferable to Warburton's idea because it preserves better man's
relation with God. In the earlier phase he would have regarded
reason as the image, now it is the Inner Light. It falls short of
the biblical conception in not taking into account sufficiently
the I-Thou relation in which God and man stand. D. Cairns
writes, 'Every man is in relation with the Logos, and that
relation is one of confrontation. This confrontation involves an

act of response on the part of man.' But the image is partly endowment, so that man's self is endowment in action, or gift response.[18]

The idea that everything in the universe is alive somehow with the life of God, and that man is a micrososm of the universe reminds us of the Platonic cast of Law's mind, as well as his debt to Boehme. Thus John Smith, whose *Select Discourses* is in Law's library, writes, 'God made the Universe and all the Creatures contained therein as so many Glasses wherein he might reflect his own Glory'.[19] Sir Thomas Browne agrees that man is a microcosm.[20]

# 'DIALOGUE ON JUSTIFICATION'
# AND THE PUBLISHED 'LETTERS'

Law was still seeing a variety of people and, despite what he said sometimes, he still read a variety of books.

He mentions to Langcake visits paid by Gambold and other Moravians and how they tried to influence his views. He believes their humility feigned and that they must answer the criticisms of Rimius about their sect before he can treat them seriously. He thanks Langcake for a book by Norris and returns one by Menoza which he did not like.[1]

The fly-leaf of what seems to be Law's copy of Madame Guyon's *Moyen Court* has remarks apparently in Law's handwriting. We can only judge ourselves or others if we get out of ourselves. Everything is 'dead husk' where the Spirit is not acknowledged and experienced. Both these remarks come from Henry More.

Law evidently read the Cambridge Platonists. Besides the *Select Discourses* of John Smith, three works of More, Whichcote's *Sermons*, and two works by John Norris lie on his library shelves. Points of identity and similarity between Law and these Platonists are frequent. A theological emphasis on mysticism, ethics, and simplicity of dogma, an opposition to Calvin, belief in the divine seed, and mystical analogy are common to them all. What they call reason is very similar to what Law calls the Inner Light. It is likely that they confirmed rather than helped to form Law's later belief. It is significant that he nowhere mentions them in published work, though the value of doing so to a public sympathetic to their descendants, the Latitudinarians, is obvious.

Against More, indeed, Law unleashed an abusive tirade reminiscent of his criticisms of Wesley. He allows, in 1759, that More was pious and learned. But he was a bigot to the Cartesian system, believing in the pre-existence of the soul and in the *Divine Dialogues* he was given up to heathenish babble dashed with flashes of piety. More, alas, had criticized Boehme![2]

Law gave slight credit to Swedenborg. He may have been introduced to his works by Mr Hartley, vicar of Winwick, who was his acquaintance and the friend and early translator of Swedenborg. Walton quotes two letters, supposedly by Law, in which he rejects Swedenborg for diverging from fundamental Christian doctrine.[3] Neither the style nor the contents of these letters suggest Law's pen. A Mr Clarke wrote to Henry Brooke in 1772, reporting that Law had called Swedenborg the greatest visionary he had read.[4] Clarke seems to have interpreted a word which Law often used in a pejorative sense contrarily! From a reliable source, and conveying a genuine tone, is the remembrance of Langcake, who in 1776 reported to Brooke that Law considered Swedenborg 'very voluminous, and that *was not his worst fault*'.[5] Interestingly enough, in 1758 Law wrote to Langcake asking for the eighth volume of *Arcana Coelestia*, probably for his village library, for he says he will never read the volumes.[6] As the authorship of this commentary on Genesis and Exodus was only acknowledged in 1768 to be Swedenborg, Law never learned that he could appreciate him.

He approved the Quakers much more completely than the Moravians, More, or Swedenborg. A 1758 letter declares that he likes the spirit of the Quaker writer, Isaac Penington, and that he wants his works for the library. In 1776 Langcake wrote to Brooke to say that although he could not remember having spoken with Law about Penington he knew that he had read Penington with 'great approbation'. He adds that Law had a regard for the primitive Quakers and their writings.[7]

In the letter to Langcake in which he criticizes More his mature attitude to questions raised by the Quakers is clarified. Langcake should not concern himself with the discussion concerning proper and improper use of external observances, or about the external pale of the Church. It is enough that he loves 'the *sign* and the *figure*, till you find them to be an hindrance to that which is higher', and such a time may not come. 'If it was not for the traditions and practice of the Church, the *washing of feet* would appear from Scripture, to be a perpetual Gospel ordinance; it has every mark of it.'[8]

The relativism of external practices may also be gathered from the fact that the Lord's Supper in the primitive Church was always accompanied by a feast of love. With time it fell into disuse because of abuses. Quakers object to sacraments because of the bad use to which they are put and the carnal trust they inspire. 'Gospel signs and figures are not supposed to be so regarded. Thus Boehme called the two sacraments *'hidden seals'*. Those who use and disuse the sacraments may both be right.[9]

It would seem that Law valued the Quaker witness, no less than that of traditional Christianity. In 1759 we find him thanking the Quaker bookseller, 'friende Hinde' for the offer of *'George Fox'* (*Journal* or biography?). But he has no time for folio reading, though the man who wrote the book has Law's esteem.[10]

His fidelity to the letter of Scripture is suggested by his expectation of the end of the world. However, he has no faith in *'scripture arithmetic'* to determine the time. Scripture indicates general conditions, but the forerunner[s] of the event would have signs besides Scripture. Further, they would be 'original' as were the old prophets, and people of great spiritual distinction.[11]

Always unwilling to stir up idle religious curiosity, Law in his writings says little about the vexed question of universal restitution. According to Walton he even deleted some passages from his published correspondence bearing on the subject.[12] We might deduce the drift of his argument were it not for the recollections of Langcake in 1790, which make the matter plain:

> Not only the whole human race, but even the fallen angels, would all be delivered out of misery, but not until the last judgement day. He said there would be a chasm in the creation without their being taken into happiness. But that could not be, until they saw the whole creation made happy before them. When they saw this, and felt the eternal fire fully operating upon them, it would produce the blessed effect of awakening that goodness that lay dormant within them . . . and so they would be made happy, to the full display of God's love and goodness to all his creatures.[13]

As he aged Law became more convivial and his humour more sweet. In 1760 he wrote a most cordial letter to Byrom who had

intimated humorously that he was made a prisoner by illness.
He hopes 'you say this only to make us laugh when we shall see
you and your jailer became fellow travellors'. He prefers
earnest conversation with Byrom to the choicest honours of
Church or state and the ladies often mention 'the good Doctor'
and hope he is well.[14]

Twenty-five *Letters* were published in 1760. Those that are dated
show them to have been composed in the 1750s. Amendments
to the originals were sometimes made and the publication was
made by Langcake and Ward, under the supervision of Law.
We shall treat them summarily since little fresh insight into
Law's character or belief can be gleaned from them. (The same
method will be followed for the remaining productions of Law,
for the same reason.)

'Church Communion is . . . *external* and *internal* . . . the one
is the *outward Sign*, the other is the *inward Truth* signified by it:
The one never was, nor ever can be, in its true State, without
the other.'[15] The inward truth is regeneration, the outward
sign is the manner of life witnessing to it. Christ is the origin-
ator of the inward and the outward Church.

After being in the world a few ages the Church received
patronage and gifts and was strengthened by power foreign to
its nature. Thus, where State and Church are incorporated
together, unregenerate passions are bound to find expression.
But there is good hidden in the situation and we must resign
ourselves to it, knowing that God will work benefit.

Suppose a Church where baptism is mimicked by sprinkling
water on the face; wide differences of belief respecting the
Lord's Supper; the prohibition in worship of Spirit-inspired
utterances and the establishment of tedious man-made worship
led by a hired person who has control of church and churchyard,
prayers for success in unchristian wars. Should we retain
communion in such a Church (he has the Anglican church
immediately in mind)?

We should. The truth aimed at in the sacrament can be
realized in the heart. Injurious prayers need no more be ours
than the cursing psalms. Law joins in public worship, not
because of its perfection, but because of what it intends. The
services are 'the *venerable Remains* of all that, which once was,

and will, I hope, be again, the Glory of Church Assemblies, viz.,
the *Ministration of the Spirit, and not of the dead Letter*'.[16]

He believes a new day is dawning. The formation of new sects
testify to the dissatisfaction felt with established forms. In the
meantime he remains full of love for all Christians and is
neither Catholic nor Protestant.

He defends himself against the charge of encouraging
Quietism.

> I recommend to you Stillness . . . etc., not to make you life-
> less, and indifferent about good Works, or indeed with any
> Regard to them, but solely with regard to your *Faith*, that it
> may have the proper soil to grow in . . . all . . . Haste either
> with regard to God, or ourselves, are not only great Hind-
> rances, but real Defects of our Faith and Dependence upon
> God.[17]

Particular significance should be given to Pentecost in our
understanding of the divine plan. There are expressions in the
Old Testament that might cause offence to an unwary reader.
They are words used in the economy of time to impress men
until a new dispensation could declare the fuller truth.

> *Pentecost* alone was That, which took away all Veils, and
> showed the Kingdom of God, as it was in itself, and set Man
> again under the immediate, essential Operation of God,
> which first gave Birth to a holy Adam in Paradise. Types and
> Shadows ended, because the substance of them was found.[18]

Langcake had been struck by the devotion of the Desert
Fathers, but criticized them for not performing charitable acts.
Law believes that God blessed the Church with them and that
they were the salt of the earth in their time. The particularity
of their lives should no more concern Langcake than the particularity of John the Baptist's life.

Later in 1760 Law published a tract entitled *Of Justification by
Faith and Works*. It takes the form of a conversation between
Churchmen and Methodist. The occasion for the pamphlet was
provided by a Calvinist Methodist clergyman, Mr Berridge,
who had expounded his beliefs to another clergyman. These
were published as *A Fragment of True Religion* (1760). Using

rather intemperate language Berridge enforced the idea that men are saved by faith and not by faith and works. Law admitted that he wrote as 'one who has grown very old, in much haste, through various interruptions'.[19] The pamphlet is not, in fact, very remarkable. Nor does it add to our knowledge of Law's views.

Churchman (who represents Law's opinions) believes that we can no more separate faith and works than the love of God and the love of neighbour. Indeed, the Sermon on the Mount is an inculcation of good works that will one day be rewarded. Methodist answers that the 'very great Man' (Wesley?) who often said that Churchman did not have the right notion of justification must be correct.

We are justified, says Churchman, when we walk by the Spirit of God. Faith and works beget each other. Humility and penitence, for example, are the fruit and the seed of faith.

When Paul opposes faith to works, he includes the whole Gospel religion under the idea of faith. By works, he means the works of the Law. He is thus contrasting Christianity and Judaism. Nor should we denigrate good works. Jesus and the Prayer Book bids us do them. Paul even says,'I can do all things through Christ which strengthened me'.

There are three doctrines that are a scandal of the Reformation: faith without works; the outward imputation of Christ's merits; absolute election and reprobation. In place of these Churchman puts, on God's side—free grace; on man's side—works, or 'the *one Law of Life*'.[20]

# 23

## 'ADDRESS TO THE CLERGY'
## AND GLORY

By January 1760 Law was experiencing rheumatic pain daily, But it seemed not to spoil his temper. In 1763 Francis Okely recalled visiting Law three years' previously. He was a Cambridge graduate and preacher for the United Brethren. Law had been uncommonly open with him and left a very 'tender' impression.[1] Another member of the United Brethren (a Moravian group) wrote to say that they held Law's writings in high esteem, but they were disturbed by his criticisms of them.

Mr Payne, working in the publishing trade, wrote to Law in 1760. He recalled the crisis of his life when the sponsors for his worldly success turned against him and he lost three children in one week. Law's writings became the means of discovering peace with God. He delighted in his mystical works and asked for his prayers.

Law had corrected all but the last few pages of *An Address to the Clergy*, when he died. It is fitting that his last formal utterance should have been addressed to the ministers of the Church for which he felt affection as well as disappointment. It is also fitting that this utterance should exalt the love and glory of God and his care for men, with little apparent reference to the system of Boehme.

He addresses the clergy especially because they affect so many for good or ill. He will treat only the essence of religion which is 'the SPIRIT OF GOD brought again to his FIRST POWER OF LIFE IN US'.[2]

All goodness comes from God and religion must then be built on the supernatural ground of the immediate workings of the divine nature within us. The Gospel itself is a ministration of the Spirit, for it only reaches its completion when the outward

226

teaching of Jesus 'was changed into the *Inspiration*, and *Oper-ation* of his Spirit' in the souls of men.[3] There is no middle ground between belief in the continual inspiration of God and exclusion of the divine. To speak with Warburton of God's Spirit occasionally assisting the faithful is to suggest an oc-casional God and a God who co-operates with human goodness. But God and goodness cannot be divided. Goodness in man is the seed of God struggling to come to birth.

Nor is there religious safety in particular doctrines and opinions. These can lead us from the worship of the living God within to 'an *Idol* of Notions to be worshipped', at least in part.[4] Pride in definitions becomes the error of such people. Learning and scholastic theology become important and alignment with the Pharisees easy. Hence comes the *'Religion of Self'*. Now 'Self is the Fulness of Atheism . . . nothing else but the Creature *broken off* from God and Christ'.[5]

A proper emphasis in religion does not make one an enemy of reason, as Law has been called. As reason chiefly distinguishes us from beasts, the call to deny ourselves must mean that reason must be denied. When Scripture speaks of the flesh and all its works, what does it mean but 'our *rational and Intelligent* Nature?'.[6] A religion springing from reason is satanic. Genuine theology can flow only from the converted heart. A long quotation follows from the *Demonstration* indicating the use and limits of reason. Literature, the arts and science can be useful like the common labours of life. 'It is *literal Learning, verbal Contention, and critical Strife* about the Things of God, that I charge with Folly and Mischief to Religion.'[7]

He cites particular evils in the contemporary Church. Mammon is alike served by Christian, Jew, and infidel. Christians make *'Church Sale* . . . [of] . . . *Cures of Souls, Parsonages* . . . etc.'[8] Ministers of religion are often the chief buyers and sellers.

The swearing of oaths is another evil. Our Yes should be Yes, our No, No, and nothing added. But we have law-oaths, Office-oaths and other oaths, and despise the word of Christ against them. Law does not wish Christians immediately to refuse to to take oaths but to indicate how unchristian Christendom's laws are. Unless they are wicked we may take oaths, since Christ's condemnation shows that the evil lies in that from which the oath normally proceeds. But he cannot fault those who refuse all oaths. He hopes that all Englishmen will one day follow their lead.

The third evil cited is that of the Antichrist, war. He denounces the 'Army of Church Wolves' in the Crusades. Since the Reformation matters have been, if possible, more diabolical.[9] The duellist and his second must be condemned for the same reason as we condemn war. The difference is only between the murder of one person or many. At the moment European nations kill and seize possessions in *both the Indies*.[10] Thus we tread underfoot the natural rights of man and the supernatural virtue of Christ. To kill a young man, for example, threatens his chance of obtaining the new birth.

He does not advise immediate pacifism. His task is only to prove Christendom's fallen state. He quotes texts to show that it should be a place of peace and piety so that all nations might be drawn to it.

Behind these errors lies the worldly spirit of men and the rule of Antichrist. The learned have given many marks of the true Church. The real mark is 'Being dead unto all Sin, and alive unto all Righteousness'.[11] He ends with an exhortation to progress in the new birth or 'heavenly Church'.[12] The book ends with the following words of Christ, written in capitals: LO, I AM WITH YOU ALWAY, EVEN UNTO THE END OF THE WORLD.

The Latitudinarian spirit in religion, with Warburton as one of its representatives, thus received Law's passionate apology. Warburton rejected Law's estimate of his theology, stressing that he believed the Holy Spirit to illuminate our understanding and rectify our will. But Law caught the main tone of Warburton's theology, and with it that of many. If we read on in his *Doctrine of Grace* we find him saying that the 'primitive abundance of the Spirit' is not needed now that the peace and ordering of the Church have been secured. The character of inspiration is given by James as 'the wisdom from above . . . first pure, then peaceable, gentle, open to reason, full of mercy and good fruits, without uncertainty or insincerity'.[13]

There are no grounds for thinking that Law's debt to Boehme was waning because it is not obvious here. The devotional emphasis of Boehme is pervasive and as Law stressed at the beginning, it is the essence of Christianity alone of which he writes. The relation he sees between self-centred men and

Antichrist is paralleled in Boehme. Thus, 'The Antichrist is he who claims that God is outside this world; so that he may rule the world as a God'.[14] Boehme also concerned himself much with the social outworkings of the Faith. Indeed, E. Herman has spoken about 'The passion for social righteousness that is deep-rooted in the brooding heart of Jacob Boehme'.[15] He frequently castigated lovers of Mammon and wranglers over creeds and opinions. Law's mention of oaths and war as instances of worldliness, reflects his preoccupation with the Sermon on the Mount and admission of the importance of ideas for which Moravians, Quakers and other minority Christian groups, stood. Though opposition to oaths seems trivial compared with the iniquities of the slave-trade, capital offences, the depressed state of the poor, etc. It is worth remembering that when Law opposed war, England was especially appreciating its benefits for trade and Empire. Battles had been fought which would enable England soon to subjugate India. The conquest of Canada had just been completed.[16]

Law died a few days after the last words in *Address to the Clergy* were written. At the annual Easter audit of the King's Cliffe schools in 1761 he caught a cold. This led to inflammation and he died in pain, possibly from nephritis.

Hester recorded some words of his the day before his death. 'He said he had such an opening of the divine life within him, that the fire of divine love quite consumed him.'[17] Another record, which may have been taken down hurriedly (since, where I substitute 'life' it reads 'literature' which is impossible, unless Law was unlucid), reads: 'Oh what hast thou done? Thou hast awakened such a spark of divine love that quite devours me. Who would have thought that all my life should end in my dying a martyr to love!'[18]

He experienced much pain, but just before his passing to Glory, at 8 in the morning of 9 April he sang in a loud clear voice some words from a hymn:

> And let the Church with one accord
> Resound Amen, and praise the Lord,
> Hallelujah, Hallelujah,
> Hallelujah, Hallelujah!

# 24

## LAW'S ENDURING SIGNIFICANCE

Desultory critical comments have accompained the foregoing description of Law's life and writing. We must now add these comments to others to give a final evaluation.

His life was continuous with his writing. The change in his views must be seen therefore as development rather than as revolution. Whilst Boehme gave him a particular framework, many of the thoughts expressed in that framework had been lighted upon prior to his first reading the Teutonic theosopher. This fact should be remembered in the pages that follow.

Law was less a stranger to his century than Overton thought. The dominant cultural form taken by the Enlightenment was that provided by reason and science. Law reflected his age in various ways: in the first period he has high admiration for Newton and Malebranche; he refers constantly to reason and his literary style embodies typical Enlightenment features. Throughout his career he exhibited a distrust of 'scholasticism' and speculation. His concern in writing is either to defend or expound the Faith, or to encourage men in the practice of their religion. Whilst he rejected Locke's conclusions in *The Reasonableness of Christianity*, he agreed with the general programme of stating the essence of religion, eschewing profitless argument and speculation and concentrating on practicalities. In his later period he championed Boehme partly because he thought he answered Enlightenment man's religious and philosophical problems. It is significant that the age considered mathematics to give the ideal form of truth, and that Boehme's system lends itself to diagrammatic representation. Law treasured Freher's drawings of it. Voltaire would have applauded his inculcation of tolerance and condemnation of war.

His single-minded concern for religion and the visionary quality of his later writing are certainly untypical of the age.

230

But every age is complex, and the appearance of William Law in the company of Bolingbroke, Butler, and Pope only means that we must not conceive the Enlightenment too narrowly. Law testified to qualities in men that the Romantic Age was to improve upon.

He was a remarkable person even apart from his literary productions. He may be taken as a Christian *type*, whatever our reservations about certain idiosyncrasies. In the first period strength and integrity are particularly evident. He can be witty and humorous, and the sunlight of divine grace and personal charity relieve the bleakness caused by rigoristic belief. An ungenerous quality clings to his idea of God and man and makes him slightly unhuman and anti-humanistic. Advance in the ascetical way and the peace afforded him by Boehme's system brought a flowering of Christian life. Joy and love flooded his heart and it seems that he was raised to the state of union in prayer. An intermittent vituperative element marred his life and seemed to have its source in his introvert personality, the cramped theology of his first period, and perhaps a homosexual strain.

It is instructive to compare the *type* of humanity developed in Law with that developed by, for example, secular humanism. The autobiography of Leonard Woolf enables us to do this. Together with an unflinching respect for reason and stoic morality we notice the barrenness of his world-view and tendency to despair. He ruminates over 'a kind of fatalistic and half-amused resignation . . . in the end nothing matters'.[1] The difference deification makes to a man is that the universe is fertile with glorious meaning and that joy and love progressively invade the heart.

We may curtail critical assessment of Law's pre-Boehme phase as he follows broadly the High Church Anglican tradition. A limiting factor here is his belief in the verbal inspiration of the Bible. The work of Origen and the renewed critical work of the late seventeenth century had indicated that the Bible was not uniformly inspired. Law's study of mysticism had enabled him to distinguish inspiration from the verbal report of it. But his youthful training and incomplete humanism held him in thrall. Instead of questioning the text we find him reconciling criticisms of it by recourse to Boehme.

In doing this he reverts to the allegorical method exemplified by Clement of Alexandria and Origen. In addition to literalistic interpretation some texts are penetrated to yield a typological, philosophical, or mystical meaning. The dangers of subjectivism are obvious and R. M. Grant significantly believes Clement used 'scripture to illustrate his already formed thought'.[2] Boehme and Law succumb to this danger.

Until the 1730s we may regard Law as a successor of the Carolines divines. He draws on Catholic and Reformation principles and the theological method he adopts gives supreme authority to Scripture, appeals to tradition—especially that of Antiquity—as interpretative of Scripture, and respects reason as authoritative in its proper sphere. His *Three Letters to the Bishop of Bangor* illustrate well his use of the method.

We have noted previously that he was not an academic writer, and that the occasion to which he addressed himself and his personality influence his writing (Waterland makes an interesting contrast to Law in this respect.) His orthodoxy can therefore be underestimated. This is often done in the evaluation of *Christian Perfection* and the *Serious Call*, where he deals with subjects of personal importance. As he assumes that his readers are communicant members of the Church, it is wrong to charge him with Pelagianism and unconcern with external religion. He is particularly insistent that believers must respond fully to the divine initiative. McAdoo rightly groups Law with Taylor, Scougal, and More and comments:

> The devotional works of the period display a remarkable unanimity of method on combining moral theology, prayer, meditation and sacraments, in such a way that devotional practice and practical divinity are seen to be two aspects of the same thing. In this way they are parallel to the general disposition of theological method and faithfully reflect the characteristics of theology in the seventeenth century.[3]

None the less, we can discern the theological strains to which Law was put, especially by the cultural developments that led to the Enlightenment. Apart from this he appropriates the Caroline method in theology in a distinctive way. The Carolines with the exception perhaps of Taylor, were more indebted to Aristotle and therefore to Aquinas, than to Plato. Law was a natural

Platonist so that theological unease always threatened him, and since the Enlightenment generally was much nearer to Aristotle's mentality than to Plato's we should not be surprised at Law's later development. To a degree it was a compensation-fantasy to which a reflective, introverted and artistic mind is always liable. [4]

Secondly, whilst the Bible, tradition, and the Carolines taught the tragedy of life without God, we find a particular stress on this fact in Law. His own nature was passionate, his reading of the mystics and Bible had deepened his insight into the 'chasm' in life that existentialists have understood again in our own century, [5] and he was conscious that Christian debate had moved from problems within the Church to those concerning belief and unbelief. His witness only deepened with time and it remains disturbing.

He exceeded other Carolines in the rigoristic quality of his writing and his personal style of life. Though used to other-worldly teaching, his audience frequently criticized this excess.

In part he was reacting to the religious slackness of the age, but certainly he believed in rigorism. It has deep biblical roots of course and a perennial strain in Church tradition has maintained the same emphasis. It develops strength and integrity of character, recognizes the pervasive element of temptation, and is a means of responding to the surpassing worth of God. He is profoundly conscious of the fallen condition of the world and therefore wishes to transcend it. Already in the *Fable of the Bees* he bids us aspire after *angelic* perfection.

There is nothing essentially unrobust in his attitude. Tough, world-directed Puritans would have agreed with Law. So would Dr W. E. Sangster, whose religious development probably owed something to him. His son, who does not identify himself with this view, commented that: 'His puritanism was not negative but, like everything else about him, dynamically positive. He did not deny; he affirmed.' [6]

The defect of rigorism is that it reflects only a part of the Christian vision. Kirk has pointed out how even the parables of Jesus suggest the community of character between the earthly type and its heavenly archetype, and how St Paul may be considering a storehouse of Christian humanism. [7] At its best

Christian tradition embodies rigorist and humanist values. Ascetism and mortification have not been allowed to kill the cultivation of learning, art, or the social graces and domestic felicities as part of the Good Life. Against Law we may quote such examples of the mingling of both values as St Thomas More and the 'devout humanism' Bremond discovered in the French monastic tradition.[8] The Caroline divines also were deeply interested in the creation doctrine of St Thomas, St Francis, and St Victor.[9]

Experience as well as doctrine rebels against Law's excess. Grace must complete rather than supplant nature. It is useless to try to make into men angels: we must become genuinely human. Inevitably Restoration laxity succeeded Commonwealth rigour. Law would have approved the austere convent school in which the novelist, Antonia White was educated. But she reflected that 'Years of blue serge, stiff high collars, and no looking glasses make you much vainer than nice clothes do . . . my two daughters who have always had gay and comfortable clothes don't care a fig what they look like'.[10]

Criticism of Law's teaching on the Atonement has been formulated well by H. Lindström, who writes: 'The struggle for sanctification is . . . regarded as a necessary condition of justification. The idea of atonement is modified in Law, as it was in practical mysticism in general, by the notion of man's own mortification.'[11] Whilst the tradition of Christian mysticism escapes Lindström's criticism more than he supposes it may be applied justly to Law. But we must discriminate.

Justification by grace through faith is stated by Law occasionally.[12] The liturgy he loved and the Bible he pondered daily taught it. That he never emphasized it and opposed any separation of justification and santification resulted from his Catholic rather than Protestant complexion, preference for medical rather than forensic theological categories, and realization of the ineffability of God. Furthermore, as we have mentioned, in *Christian Perfection* and the *Serious Call* he is concerned with the development of spiritual life among formally believing Christians, not its beginning.

The value of Wesley's doctrine of penal substitution lies in its recognition of God's initiative and love, and in the relief it brings the sinner who learns that he need not be good to be accepted by God. Its defect lies in the fact that the model of penal substitution scarcely conveys the truth of atonement with anything like the exactness Wesley imagined.[13] The idea of God emerging from the conception is usually narrow and vindictive; the loving relation between Father and Son is often obscured; the importance of sanctification is often missed; it is difficult to believe that God requires such payment for man's sin; the New Testament has a wider and more complex reference than this model suggests.

The value of Law's doctrine is that it maintains the link between what God has done for us and what he must do in us. Nor does he run the risk of reducing the mystery of Atonement with verbal over-precision. Its defect, as Lindström pointed out, is that mortification is permitted to qualify the idea of atonement. God is conceived too much under the the category of *eros* rather than of *agape*. His belief that God can only love what is lovely is significant.[14] A sinner might well find despair instead of peace confronted with Law's teaching.

Even as a student Law had been interested in mysticism. During the 1730s that interest so increased that he came to consider mystics the Church's best teachers. What value are we to attach to the mystical tradition? A representative description of mystical experience is given by von Hügel:

> The ontological presence of and the operative penetration by the Infinite Spirit, within the human spirit. This Spirit's presence would produce, on occasion of man's apprehension or volition of things contingent and finite, the keen sense of disappointment, of contrast with the Simultaneous, Abiding, and Infinite.[15]

Like others with knowledge of Christian mysticism, Law made acute distinctions between those who confused nature with grace, illusion with divine reality. We cannot be concerned here with the whole cult of the supernatural.

The mysticism referred to admits the value of discursive reason and verbal expression for man's sensory-intellectual consciousness, but insists that supernatural spiritual reality can be communicated to man at the spiritual point of his being. We find St Thomas stating that knowledge can be infused into the mind with such clarity as to transcend the use of images. St John of the Cross believed he received an intimate understanding of the Incarnation. Ruysbroeck was admitted to the vision of the three divine Persons and penetrated to the primary unity of the Godhead.[16]

Naturally more authority must be given to the mystic's experience than to his verbal report of it.

The case of Boehme is surely one of a brilliant and spiritually sensitive Christian with genuine mystical experience interpreting his experience without guidance, without an adequate cultural belief to help him, and without sufficient academic training. A. B. Sharpe comments upon the 'strange transcendental imaginations of . . . Boehme'.

> His mind [he writes] appears to have been constantly fixed on the idea of God; and by a purely natural process there arose in it, together with many sane and devout reflections, a kind of philosophical statement of the problems of existence, transferred in strange and bizarre phraseology to the divine nature. These ideas Boehme declared to be 'opened' to him; they came, he could not say how, into his mind, and had upon him the effect of a communication from an external source . . . there is no possibility of accepting his explanation of their origin. A meditative and abstractive mind, without authoritative guidance or restraint, will naturally and almost inevitably find in the abstract idea of the divine nature a repetition of the influences it sees at work in the surrounding world.[17]

We may qualify Sharpe's account in two ways. There was more genuine experience of the divine in Boehme's life than he allows. After all, there is much sound theology and spiritual wisdom in his work, he was a wonderfully pious man and Law himself was too acute to be hoodwinked by an unconscious fraud. Secondly, account must be taken of the influence of persons, books, and discussion on the thinking of Boehme. Though it argues against some of Law's precious preconceptions, Boehme was no unlettered peasant gaining wisdom only by revelation.

We may conclude that all that the Bible tells us makes us expect for some the kind of revelation about which mystics testify. But the experience can be misunderstood, and without the restraint and proper encouragement of dogma, Church and reason fantasy will mingle with fact.

It is probable that we should include Law among the mystics. In *The Spirit of Prayer, The Way to Divine Knowledge,* and *The Spirit of Love* he writes with such directness about God and sanctification and makes autobiographical hints indicative of deep penetration into God that any other description seems inadequate. We must also remark upon his use of Boehme. He never simply copied out Boehme's revelations. It seems that he absorbed them, meditated upon them and came to see things in terms of them. Law himself became a visionary. Kathleen Raine has commented upon the imaginative geniuses who have created a world of their own. She mentions Blake whose 'work, as he believed, represents "portions of eternity" seen in imaginative vision'.[18] Boehme can be included in this class and Law reminds us of them. The extent to which we believe Law's vision depends upon its coherence with Christian truth. We turn therefore to leading ideas in his later writing.

The Law of Contraries, as he stated it, says that nothing can be manifested without contrariness. Only by means of darkness can light become visible. The idea has been important for such philosophers as Nicholas of Cusa, Schelling, Hegel, and Berdyaev. The ancient Chinese conception of *Yang* and *Yin* expresses it.[19] There seems no reason to reject the idea especially as Law refuses the thought that God somehow becomes more himself through the contrasting medium of Eternal Nature.

The Platonic idea that nothing can rise higher than its original also seems to answer to experience. A dog cannot become a man, nor sin goodness. Wesley was simply being hypothetical in saying that only a poor omnipotence could not raise a thing above its original. God's working is lawful.

The importance he attaches to the doctrine of the Trinity is admirable though an abritrariness and lack of clarity attaches to his treatment. There is a danger of tritheism in the designation of the Father as Fire, Son as Light and Spirit as Spirit. The idea that the Son quenches the Father's Fire can also lead to unworthy conceptions of the Father. It seems arbitrary also to discover an outbirth of the Trinity in the fire, light, and air of this world. In what sense can air be said to proceed from fire and light? Nor does there seem to be any necessary conjunction between the Trinity and the Seven Properties. With Wesley we ask how Law knows all this? We may agree with St Augustine that there are 'vestiges' of the Trinity in the created order, and that creatures exist by participating in God. But sound theology asserts no more than it must.

Light is an apt symbol to express the idea of God—but not just Christ. According to Law it is more than a symbol, derivatively it is the Fact. It seems presumptuous to say so much. The development of the idea of God as uncreated Light has been undertaken most by Orthodoxy. But they safeguard against confusion by the doctrine of creation *ex nihilo*.[20]

The notion of emanation as Law develops it is suggestive. The doctrine of creation *ex nihilo* was formulated to protect the idea of the sovereignty of God. All things depend on him and he is dependent on nothing. It has negative value and is open to the criticisms Law mentions. The Bible hardly decides the matter.[21]

Law does not regard God as giving form to pre-existing material, or as necessarily giving birth to creatures. He distinguishes God from his creation and believes that God created to share the bounty of his nature. He adumbrates the idea because he finds the traditional conception unintelligible, the problem of evil more satisfactorily answered if emanation is true, and an analogy between the working of nature and human creativeness and divine creativeness. He would have agreed with Frank that

> God is not a particular content, but an all-embracing and all-determining unity.... His creativeness, like all creativeness, consists on imposing form upon material, but the difference is that he posits the material himself.[22]

The idea of Eternal Nature easily follows from belief in the Law of Contraries and in emanation. We might relate the biblical idea of 'glory' with it.[23]   Martensen remarks on the suitability of God having uncreated glory as a dwelling place. Without corporeity and externality mention of the beauty of God remains an abstraction. If there is Eternal Nature we can postulate God not only thinking and willing, but imagining, and figure- and image-making.[24]

The Orthodox distinguish God's essence from his energies.

The former is unapproachable, the latter are active in the world as deifying grace and divine light.[24] Law would have been very sympathetic to this doctrine considering what he writes about Eternal and Temporal Nature, but as he develops it in terms of the conception of the Seven Properties it seems to be unlucid, confusing and mistaken. He is more articulate about the dark than about the light ternary. He refers to both the dark ternary and the Fourth Property as Fire. With Wesley we ask, why are there *seven* Properties? What do 'Light and Love' and 'Sound of Understanding' mean applied to two Properties? Their relation to the Trinity seems artificial. Why should the Father be connected with the dark ternary?

A difficulty with the Properties is that they tend to remove antinomies and contrasts from God to an outbirth from him. Can we believe that God is merely overflowing Love? Although he does not follow Boehme, who in one passage seems to rate Love above God,[26] his tendency is in this direction. All that we know of ethical personality suggests that it depends on the balancing of different qualities. The Bible refers robustly to the love, wrath, justice, and majesty of God. Law's doctrine of God seems to fall partly under Forsyth's criticism that those who speak of God as Love draw more from their own sentiment than from the Bible. He concludes: 'An effusive God cannot be a holy God, and such love is not divine.'[27]

Recourse to the Seven Properties scarcely solves the problem of evil. If evil results when the dark ternary is no longer governed by the light ternary, how is it that God could posit such a contrast to himself as the dark ternary?

There is also the problem of how an angel of light could succumb to temptation. Law refers to Lucifer's immaturity. But he was mature enough to conceive rebellion. This must have been a vast, brave thought, especially as he was surrounded with a host of spirits paying homage to God. Again, if God foresaw the rebellion can he be relieved of ultimate responsibility for it? If he could prevent Lucifer's kingdom falling into hell and make of it earth, could he not have helped Lucifer more?

The notion of an angelic fall is referred to in the Bible, though Law identifies his speculations too easily with those references.[28] Of the different ideas of the origin of evil in the Bible only one (Gen. 6.2–4) assumes iniquitous angelic beings and we are told

very little about them. Von Rad, at least, believes it 'linguistic-
ally and objectively impossible' to draw the theory of a pre-
mundane Fall from the opening verses of Genesis.[29] It is irresponsible to erect an important edifice upon so shaky a foundation.

There were other sources. At the periphery of the New
Testament we find Jude (v. 6) mentioning the Watcher legend
and 2 Peter 2.4 referring to fallen angels. Plato speaks of a
pre-mundane Fall and the idea is found in various apocalyptic
writings.[30] In antiquity Origen and Basil of Caesarea employ the
idea and since the Orthodox Church favours an allegorical
interpretation of Genesis 3 the question is not foreclosed. But
the condemnation of Origen meant the end of speculation on
the angelic Fall story and the triumph in the Church of the
Adam Fall story. Law's visionary treatment is interesting in
suggesting some limiting factor upon God prior to the creation
of this world. It has little substance beyond that.

A commonplace of medieval speculation was that Adam was
created to fill the gap in creation left by the Fall of angels. Law
seems to accept this idea. An interesting objection of Anselm is
that on this theory Adam's praise of God must have been a
perverted joy, since it included a realization that he was
blessed only because of the downfall of other beings.[31] Eventually, Law believed that the devils would be saved. In this case
the reason for man's creation is unclear. But if the devils are to
be saved Adam could praise God innocently.

Nothing in the Bible necessitates the idea that Adam was a
magnificent creature. In his typically spiritualizing way Law
makes Adam an angel, so unconscious of his body that the
biblical idea of the soul/body constitution of man is impoverished. He follows the Augustinian type theodicy in
construing Adam as perfect, and evil only making its appearance consequentially to the Fall. But in the person of Irenaeus
antiquity had another conception of Adam. He was created like
a child and God willed that he develop into maturity by the
responsible use of his freedom. He fell through weakness. The
appropriate divine response was pity, not wrath as in the
Augustinian idea.[32] Whilst Law tries to improve the Augustinian
type theory, not least in relating God's reaction to the Fall, we
must surely agree with Hick in considering the story of Irenaeus
less fantastic and more useful for rational deliberation today.

Law's thinking might have been deeper if he had tried to explain less. Faith can admit the mystery shrouding the origin of evil. We might even quote Law's Law of Contraries against him and urge that evil was somehow needed in the universe if goodness in man was to be developed. If there are densities of evil where the intellect founders, we are not bereft religiously as the cross of Christ remains as an assurance that we do not suffer alone. In heaven, perhaps, we shall become developed enough to penetrate the divine counsels.

On Law's account we are left with the same problem in accounting for Adam's fall as we had in accounting for Lucifer's: how could so glorious a creature succumb to such temptation?

He seems to be indebted to Greek and Gnostic ideas in writing about procreation in unfallen man. Von Rad comments on Genesis 1.27 that the phrasing 'prevents one from assuming the creation of an originally androgynous man'.[33] The obvious meaning of Mark 10.2–9 is that God ordained marriage for man from the beginning. Perhaps the Bible compelled Law to admit the value of marriage, certainly he is grudging and perfunctory on the subject. At the same time we must remember that antecedently to Law lay a Christian tradition mainly rigoristic in its marriage doctrine. D. S. Bailey believes that Jeremy Taylor was the first theologian to teach the importance of the societal relation in wedlock.[34]

His doctrine of redemption is eloquent and profound. Despite certain whimsical features, it is governed by biblical categories. Aldous Huxley says:

> From the writings of Eckhart, Tauler, and Ruysbroeck, of Boehme, William Law, and the Quakers, it would be possible to extract a spiritualized and universalized Christianity, whose narratives should refer . . . to 'processes forever unfolded in the heart of man'.[35]

A similar extraction could be made from the Bible or St Thomas Aquinas. Christianity is apposite to the human condition. In fact Law is adamant that the Incarnation and salvation-history are essential to redemption. He even states that Christ assumed fallen human nature. This anti-Gnostic feature relates to the belief that Christ could only redeem what he assumed.

The conception of Christ as the Second Adam is most impressive. It enables him to approach the Old Testament typologically and so escape the difficulty of sub-Christian passages. Old Testament writers do expect the Fall and its consequences to be reversed in the new age. New Testament writers see Christ as the Second Adam accomplishing this. They use the Temptation story, Christ's references to Paradise on the Cross, his title Son of Man, direct parallels between Adam and Christ (Paul), and the Eden story (Rev. 20.2, etc.).[36] Irenaeus' theory of recapitulation is essentially the same as Law's doctrine.

By the idea that Christ began to be incarnated with the first gracious word spoken to Adam, and that this process grew more complete with every movement to goodness and truth in the human heart, Law is able to account fairly for the variety of religions in the world better than most of his contemporaries. The best recent thinking on comparative religion assumes this idea.[37]

The essence of Law's later atonement teaching is that at every stage of his incarnate life Jesus successfully reversed the failure of Adam. Thus the fallen human nature he had assumed was purified and enabled to become a channel through which the grace of God could flow to men. Pentecost became a supreme Christian Festival. Contemporary theologians question whether there is any human nature apart from the individual examples of it. If there is not, the value of Law's teaching is weakened at this point.[38]

His rejection of contemporary ideas of the wrath of God was right, though we can question whether his solution to the problem of wrath in God was correct. We can distinguish vindictive and vindicative wrath. It is significant that the Bible speaks of God, not only as Father, but as Judge, Lord, King, and the like. A good case can be made for the fact that grace and not love is the central biblical category. The New Testament uses sacrificial images to describe the Atonement, and occasionally penal words.[39] It is true, so far as it goes, but his atonement teaching is less than completely satisfying. Sentimentality can degrade the idea and no moral precept is disregarded by P. T. Forsyth's reiterated plea that 'The willing acceptance of final judgement was for Jesus the means presented by God for effecting human reconciliation'.[40]

His doctrine of the work of Christ is brought into strict alignment with the doctrine of the new birth. He is constantly illuminating on this theme, to which his writings continually revert.

Whilst justification and sanctification cannot be separated in life they can be separated logically. The biblical idea of δικαιοῦν means that God accepts the sinful. This notion is blurred in the first phase of his writing, but in the second phase, through the notion of God as overflowing love, he teaches it in his own way. He uses medical rather than forensic images.

If we may agree with Berdyaev that 'Mysticism is the soil on which religion flourishes and without which it withers and decays,' Law's emphasis on the Inner Light in the uncongenial social environment of his day was a *tour de force*.[41] He replenished men's understanding of religion's object and sustenance.

Law's later teaching on spiritual apprehension repays careful study.[42] His theory is not new for theistic systems must postulate a means of knowing God; since he is Spirit discursive reason is not primarily helpful. The value of Law's treatment lies in the eloquence and insight of his exposition. He is assisted by what mystics taught him and his own experience, moulded by encounter with the first 'Age of Science'. His error lies in the extent of the breach he makes between the Inner Light and reason. He is influenced partly by the recognition that discursive reason cannot penetrate God, and in itself remains ambiguous to theology; partly by the belief that curiosity leads to infidelity; partly by the Inner Light psychologically enabling him to compensate for a reduced faith in reason and giving a definite position over against his contemporaries; partly by the breach inevitably made between them by the contrast between the light and dark ternaries. This latter reason might only seem to us a further point for rejecting the ternaries.

Although he gives perfunctory credit to the liberal arts, he is suspicious of them and gives no encouragement to his readers to progress in them. Reason came into operation in consequence of the Fall and its use partly precipitated it. In Paradise Adam was obedient to the Inner Light; it is this we must cultivate.

It is notable that the early Church, to which Law appeals, so much rejected the Fideist position. Reason enabled them to defend the Faith from attack, to build a bridge into the

R

opponents' camp and understand their faith better.[43] Augustine, Aquinas, Hooker, Butler employed reason similarly. Had Law been able to give it more scope as the good servant of the Inner Light, his response to infidelity would have been stronger. Part of the answer to criticisms of the Bible lay in linguistic, archaeological, and philosophical study. The eccentricity into which men tend to fall (including Law) when the checks of reason are loosened is notorious. Elements of his system would be called in question, of course, if reason were to be treated more kindly, but all we know of the use of reason suggests that the question must be asked. The reader will remember Law's advice in the *Address to the Clergy*. His essential stress is that the clergy should be sanctified men attentive to the Inner Light. Consider Wesley's advice in *An Address to the Clergy* (1756). The minister should be sensible and rational; he should be able to read the Bible in the original tongues; he should have knowledge of the arts, science, and philosophy; he should understand church tradition; he should have knowledge of the world; he should have prudence and good breeding; he should be genuinely Christian and devoted to helping others to the same state. Such advice Law ridiculed! With typical rigorism he has opted for an either/or choice where a both/and confronted him.

What he says about the Church is consonant with what he says about the Christian's relation to the world, and reason and the Inner Light. He writes impressively but narrowly, undervaluing nature. Dogma and customs are important because of the intimate relation between matter and spirit. They are suited to earth-dwellers. Though they only point to the truth and are never the truth itself, without them truth would grow very dim. It is a characteristic of the mystically inclined Platonist to spiritualize and generalize. But spirit grows in man slowly and fitfully, so that appeal to his proper condition must come often through the physical and particular.

He did not relinquish membership of the Church however. He believed that Christ instituted the sacraments of baptism and Eucharist, and in his late letter describing features of a rejuvenated Church, he proposes reform of baptismal method in accordance with New Testament practice, not its abolition. It would be unfair to say he fell into a figurative view of the sacraments. For him everything had a spiritual reference, so that God must be evident where prayer is offered, Bible and Bible-impregnated liturgy said, and persons obedient to Christ's commands. But as the seat of religion is in the heart of man, there is his best chapel.

Law's words on this subject recall a tradition that has come to prominence whenever the Church has grown worldly. Pre-Reformation groups like the Friends of God, the Brethren of the Common Life, and to a lesser extent the Montanists, Waldensians, and Lollards remind us of Law. Reformation groups like the Anabaptists and a post-Reformation group like the Friends approach Law's belief. They are all perfectionists and, in their longing for a Spirit-governed Church, witness providentially against corruptions in the world and the established Church.

It is worth adding that the tradition of Christian mysticism helps Law less than he imagined. There is an etymological connection between μυστικός and μυστήριον. Inquiry into the early Christian usage of the words 'mystery' and 'mysticism' suggests that mystery is God's eternal plan for history and that this is hidden from us. When St Paul says that Christ is the mystery of God he means that he is the sign by which the plan is divulged and also the plan itself. As E. J. Tinsley remarks: 'Mystery is simultaneously the human sign and the divine reality which it reveals and bestows.' Mysticism is that which penetrates the mystery. The concrete and particular are necessary, not offensive. The mystic is led therefore to the Bible and liturgy. Such visible things introduce him to the ineffable. They are necessary signs by means of which the Reality they signify may be encountered.[44] The majority of Christian mystics have appreciated these truths better than Law.

He is most suggestive on the theme of heaven, hell and purgatory. His own vivid sense of their reality is communicated to his reader. He writes of heaven with imaginative brilliance and he never lingers over the picture of hell. His eventual universalism joins him to the Orthodox. Origen and Gregory of Nyssa had promulgated the same view. Law like Origen, believed that our vices were the fuel to torture us in hell.[45] He seems to have been the first Anglican to be a universalist and to recognize that the Roman Catholic idea of purgatory needed purifying, not denying.

On these great subjects Law is governed more by the notion of Return than of Progress. This desire for symmetry in the cosmos fits the Dionysian out- and in-flow of creation and redemption as well as the natural cast of Law's mind. But it takes insufficient account of history. Something new occurs in the life of grace. Whilst Cullman's teaching on this matter is too stark he rightly stresses that the biblical doctrine of salvation-history is a straight line. By contrast, the Hellenistic is cyclical.[46]

The reader will find a similar atmosphere to the later writing of Law in the Orthodox theologians. Solovyov, Frank, Lossky, and Berdyaev are recent representatives of that Church who often remind us of Law. In the recent Western tradition Tillich recalls him most of all. Tillich was indebted to Boehme, mysticism, and the Romantic philosopher, Schelling. It is interesting to notice that Berdyaev regarded Boehme as one of the greatest Christian gnostics and that he placed him in the group including Clement of Alexandria, Origen, Gregory of Nyssa, Nicholas of Cusa, and St Martin, F. Baader and Solovyov.[47] We may accept this valuation and think that Law, Blake, and Coleridge cannot be placed far from them.

Important for this group is belief in God as Love, pre-occupation with the problem of evil, a tendency to universalism, a consciousness of mystery and absence of forensic categories, mysticism, perception of the limitations of law and unwilling-ness to define, and an apophatic rather than a catophatic approach to theology. We need these qualities.

With the exception of the *Serious Call* Law's writings have largely been neglected. But in his later work especially remark-able ideas are expressed. His conceptions of spiritual apprehen-sion, the Atonement, the Person of Christ, prayer, spiritual progress, and the after-life are richly suggestive. His personality is also distinctive. Whatever eccentricities detract from his witness the reader leaves Law's books enlightened about our common destiny to become '*Flames of Love*' about the throne of God, and conscious that the flames of divine Love penetrated deeply into the soul of William Law.[48]

# NOTES

## INTRODUCTION

1 *Autobiography* (1796), 1923, p. 16
2 J. Boswell, *Life of Johnson* (1794), 1893, p. 216
3 *Works*, e.g., vol. 4, p. 245; vol. 7, p. 297; vol. 12, p. 447
4 *The Fable of the Bee*, Advertisement and Introduction
5 *English Thought in the Eighteenth Century*, vol. 2, pp. 42, 396; cf. Macaulay, *History of England*, vol. 2, p. 104fn, 'In mere dialectical skill he had very few superiors'
6 J. O. Nash and C. Gore, *William Law's Defence of Church Principles* (2nd edn, 1909
7 *Christian Mysticism* (5th edn, 1921), p. 279
8 *The Perennial Philosophy*, 1946, p. 57
9 *The Letters of Aldous Huxley*; ed. Grover Smith, p. 504
10 *Cambridge History of English Literature*, vol. 9 (1911), p. 308
11 R. Tighe, *The Life and Writings of William Law*, p. 16

## CHAPTER 1

1 *Journal* 17–2–1753
2 Quoted in Heaton's essay in Turberville's *Johnson's England* 1933, vol. 1, pp. 225–60
3 Quoted by J. H. Plumb, *England in the Eighteenth Century* 1950, pt. 1
4 Tighe, pp. 1–2
5 Plumb, op. cit., ch. 1
6 *Letters of Laurence Sterne* (1966), ed. L. P. Curtis, pp. 1–5
7 See W. Cowper, *Letters* (1817) 1926, p. 361; J. L. & B. Hammond's essay in Turberville's *Johnson's England*, vol. 1
8 See his poem *The Village*
9 Walton, pp. 344–5fn; cf. Trapp. vol. 2, p. 185
10 Walton, pp. 345–6fn
11 *The Vision of God* (1931), pp. 67, 85f
12 P. A. Welsby, *Lancelot Andrewes* (1958), p. 152fn. 4 cf. H. R. McAdoo, *The Structure of Caroline Moral Theology*, pp. 98, 119–20, etc.
13 p. 2
14 Sunday 7, xxiv (1661); Sunday 15, xvii
15 Sunday 8
16 Sunday 9, viiif
17 See M. Thornton, *English Spirituality*, ch. 20
18 Bk 1, ch. 21
19 P. Hazard, *The European Mind*, p. 215

20 *Autobiography*, pp. 36–7
21 See Hazard, op. cit., pref.
22 See V. H. H. Green, *Religion at Oxford and Cambridge* (1965), ch. 6; *The Young Mr Wesley*, p. 40
23 J. Byrom, *Remains*, 10–2–1730
24 A leather notebook of Law's contains a digest of patristic writers, including Justin Martyr. One date in 1718. The Fathers are specially mentioned in another fragment. Walton Collection, 186, 8, 5–6
25 Trapp, 11, p. 203
26 Byrom, vol. 2, pt 2, p. 363
27 V. H. H. Green, *Religion at Oxford and Cambridge* (1965), ch. 6
28 *Moral and Religious Aphorisms* (1753) 1930, no. 2
29 Byrom, vol. 1, pt 2, p. 337
30 The writer is grateful to R. W. Church's *Study in the Philosophy of Malebranche* for help with this summary
31 See for the foregoing paragraph A. Cuvillier, *Essai sur La Mystique de Malebranche* (1954)
32 Tighe, p. 1
33 As Law was an M.A. at this time it is possible that the record is mistaken and that he was not Tripos but Praevaricator, playing the Lord of Misrule, or Abbot of Unreason at the Masters' Commencement; see C. Brigg, *Introduction to the Serious Call*, pp. viii–ix
34 Byrom, vol. 1, pt 1, pp. 20–1
35 Walton
36 Walton, pp. 344–5
37 See Byrom, 3–1–1731; 31–12–1734; Tighe, p. 2fn; S. Hobhouse, *William Law*, pp. 388–9

## CHAPTER 2

1 *Ecc. Pol*, VIII (1907), ch. 2, 13
2 The ground is well covered by Macaulay, *History of England* (1889 edn), vol. 1, p. 523; vol. 2, pp. 97f
3 *A History of the Nonjurors*, pp. 223–4. See also J. H. Plumptre, *Thomas Ken* (2nd edn, 1890), vol. 2, pp. 44–6; N. Figgis, *The Divine Right of Kings* (2nd edn, 1914)
4 *History*, p. 277
5 H. Broxap, *The Later Nonjurors*, pp. 39–40
6 Ibid., p. 47
7 P. Gay, *The Enlightenment* (1967), vol. 1, p. 231
8 *The European Mind*, p. 47
9 *Essay* (1690) 1949, III, ch. 4. 8; IV, ch. 19
10 *Essay*, I, ch. 4.16
11 *The Philosophy of the Enlightenment* (1969), pp. 5–7
12 Quoted by H. T. Hughes, *The Piety of Jeremy Taylor* (1960), p. 25; cf. Patrick's remark quoted by Tulloch, *Rational Theology and Christian Philosophy in England in the Seventeenth Century*, vol. 2, pp. 41–2
13 *From Puritanism to the Age of Reason* (1950), pp. 42–4
14 Quoted by J. Tulloch, op. cit., vol. 2, p. 185
15 J. Birch, *Life of Dr John Tillotson* (1752), p. 407
16 Birch, p. 74
17 *Church and State* (1934), p. 362
18 J. M. Creed and J. S. Boys Smith, *Religious Thought in the Eighteenth Century* (1934), p. 249f

19 *English Thought*, vol. 2, p. 156
20 p. 3
21 p. 5
22 p. 6
23 p. 7
24 p. 9
25 pp. 12–14
26 pp. 14–15
27 p. 19
28 p. 20
29 p. 22
30 p. 27
31 p. 33
32 p. 41
33 p. 47
34 p. 57
35 p. 78
36 p. 80
37 p. 80
38 p. 106
39 p. 107
40 p. 118
41 p. 144
42 p. 151
43 pp. 195–6
44 See T. W. Manson, *The Church's Ministry*; J. Knox, *The Early Church and The Coming Great Church* (1957)
45 See the undated fragment for a trenchant assertion of this: 'a doctrine of an Author, condemning, despising, rejecting, and contradicting that which every saint, every Church, every Liturgy from the days of the Apostles to this hour have said and taught about this matter?' Walton Collection, 186. 3(8)
46 See *The Library of Prophesying*; Tulloch, *Rational Theology*, vol. 1, p. 337f

## CHAPTER 3

1 Walton, pp. 346–8fn, 351–3fn
2 *Preces Privatae* (1675) 1903, p. 25
3 P. E. More and F. L. Cross, *Anglicanism* (1935), p. 513f; Plumptre, vol. 1, p. 78
4 See F. B. Kaye in *The Fable of the Bees*, 2 vols, for the best assessment of Mandeville
5 P. Hazard, pt 1, ch. 5
6 Or early in 1724, see Kaye, *Fable*, vol. 2, p. 401
7 *Fable*, vol. 2, p. 401; cf. W. R. Sorley, *A History of English Philosophy* (Cambridge 1920), p. 163
8 p. 3
9 p. 4
10 p. 4
11 p. 9
12 p. 12
13 p. 13
14 p. 18
15 p. 20

16 p. 23
17 pp. 34-5
18 p. 35
19 pp. 36-7
20 p. 49
21 p. 50
22 *Works*, vol. XI, p. 370
23 1.1.1
24 1.8.6
25 The Charity Schools were founded in 1712; by 1727, 5000 had been educated and 4000 of these had been clothed. 2000 were apprenticed after leaving school. Education included care over manners, reading, writing, arithmetic; and household skills for girls. Boys of unusual ability received special treatment and evening classes for adults were arranged. The movement was supported almost entirely by the Church of England.

## CHAPTER 4

1 Gibbon, *Autobiography* (1796) 1923, p. 15
2 Ibid., pp. 15-16
3 *Edward Gibbon*, p. 13
4 Byrom, vol. 1, pt 2, pp. 337, 411, 421-6, 435
5 See M. D. George, *London Life in the Eighteenth Century* (1966)
6 Porphyry, *Life of Plotinus;* see Plotinus: *The Enneads* (1956 edn)
7 *Life*, pp. 29-30
8 Walton, pp. 359-60; cf. p. 502fn and Tighe, pp. 12-13
9 Walton, p. 502fn; D. M. Low, *Edward Gibbon* (1937), p. 12; Byrom, vol. 1, pt 2: 25.5.1731, 21.2.1729
10 *Works*, vol. 4, p. 245
11 Walton, p. 616fn
12 Byrom, vol. 1, pt 2, p. 337; vol. 2, pt 1, 13.4.1737
13 Walton, p. 500fn; Byrom, vol. 1, pt 2, 4.1.1730
14 Walton, p. 26fn; cf. also F. Law's note to William thanking him for only asking £40 for a quantity of books he sold him. Walton Collection, 186.8.1
15 Hume, *Essays* (1903 edn), p. 122; Swift, *Letter to a young poet* (1934) for the foregoing survey, see C. J. Cadoux, *The Early Church and the World* (Edinburgh n.d.); J. Marlow, *The Puritan Tradition in English Life* (1956); P. Hartnoll, ed, *The Oxford Companion to the Theatre* (1967); E. Legouis, *A Short History of English Literature* (1934 edn), p. 189
16 *Stage Entertainments*, p. 168
17 pp. 138-9
18 C. F. Secretan, *Robert Nelson* (1860), pp. 105, 107
19 p. 143
20 p. 155
21 p. 175
22 p. 177
23 p. 177
24 *Works*, vol. 4, p. 20
25 *Works*, vol. 7, pp. 34-5
26 Vol. 1, pt 2, p. 333
27 E. K. Sanders, *Jacques Bénigne Bossuet* (1921), pp. 352-9; F. de Sales, *Introduction à la Vie dévote*, ch. 23

## CHAPTER 5

1 p. 5
2 p. 8
3 p. 11
4 p. 11
5 p. 12
6 p. 13
7 p. 21
8 p. 25
9 pp. 31-2
10 p. 36
11 p. 37
12 p. 39
13 p. 64
14 p. 65
15 p. 67
16 p. 79
17 pp. 79-80
18 p. 80
19 p. 83
20 p. 84
21 p. 99
22 p. 100
23 p. 101
24 p. 106
25 p. 134
26 p. 135
27 p. 139
28 p. 151
29 p. 165
30 p. 196
31 p. 197
32 p. 214
33 p. 217
34 p. 236
35 p. 240
36 Walton, p. 356fn
37 Sunday 3, VIII
38 Secretan, p. 293
39 Plumptre, vol. 2, App. 2
40 E.g. *Theologia Germanica*, ch. 16, 19, 20, 39, 53; H. Suso, *Life*, pp. 36, 88, 120-1, 183, 185, 254
41 By direct and indirect influence Law was indebted to Epictetus. The latter teaches: men are connected to God by reason; sin is ignorance; learning, not moral, is often a trap; if moral it must be shown in conduct; right choice must be a constant concern; possessions and fate are of little importance; eating is a low activity; public entertainments are often a trap. See *Moral Discourses*, p. 21, 39, 80, 108, 124, 170; *Enchiridion*, XXXIII, XLI
42 For the history but not the interpretation of this idea see A. Nygren, *Agape and Eros* (1953). Malebranche agrees with Law, see *Dialogues on Metaphysics*, p. 131, etc.

43 E.g., R. Baxter, *The Saints' Everlasting Rest* (1650) 1962, ch. 15. 2; J. Taylor, *Works*, II, XVIII, XIX; B. Whichcote, *Moral and Religious Aphorisms*, nos. 133, 145, etc.

44 M. Thornton, *English Spirituality*, ch. 20

45 E.g. *Introduction to the Devout Life*, pt 1, ch. 4. 19; pt 2, ch. 14. 20, etc.

46 Fragment in Walton's Collection; Lovel commented to Byrom that Law was terribly perplexed with scruples and wearing dirty stockings. *Remains*, vol. 2, pt 1, p. 113

47 *Introduction*, pt 1, ch. 3

48 In the *Thoughts*, Section 2 is devoted to the theme of man's misery without God; the need for grace, no. 508; the greatness of religion, no. 573; rejection of Descartes' method, nos. 76–80, etc.

49 p. 155; cf. p. 196, etc.

## CHAPTER 6

1 Broxap, p. 313

2 Rawlinson MSS, D. 848

3 Walton, pp. 357fn; Tighe, pp. 6–7

4 p. 7

5 pp. 10–11

6 p. 15

7 p. 20

8 p. 21

9 pp. 24–5

10 pp. 27–8

11 p. 32

12 The strictness with which Law followed this injunction emerges in a letter (1742) to Hester Gibbon about one Betty: "Her Dress was too much . . . she is too fine and seems too pleased with it . . . a girl . . . pleased with Dress . . . is exposed to every Folly—I have often been afraid that I gave too good clothes in ye school, but to prevent all thoughts of finery, I never allowed a white apron or a bit of Ribbon on ye Head.' Walton Collection, 186, 5.25. 1742

13 p. 41

14 p. 43

15 p. 46

16 p. 62

17 p. 63

18 p. 78

19 p. 80

20 p. 100

21 p. 102

22 p. 116

23 p. 128

24 p. 131

25 p. 132

26 p. 135

27 p. 153

28 p. 160

29 p. 163

30 p. 175

31 pp. 197–205

32 p. 216
33 p. 217
34 p. 238
35 p. 258
36 p. 264
37 p. 271
38 Cf. C. J. Stranks, *Anglican Devotion*
39 *English Thought*, vol. 2, p. 394
40 *Works*, vol. 4, p. 157
41 E.g., *Dialogues on Metaphysics*, Dialogues 1 and 4
42 J. Cosin, *A Collection of Private Devotions*, ed. P. G. Stanwood (1967), Introduction, pp. XIII–XXXIX; *The Whole Duty of Man*, p. 295f; M. Thornton, *English Spirituality*, chs 19 and 20; cf. pp. 282–3
43 *The Short Method*, 'at all times . . . the *prayer of the heart*' 1.4
44 10.3
45 20.3
46 2.2; 3.4; 9.1; 14.2
47 vol. 1, pp. 47, 77, 91, 145, etc. Bossuet found it difficult to understand how pious people could read books in which Christ had no place. See E. K. Sanders, *Bossuet*, p. 354
48 See H. R. McAdoo, pp. 146–7
49 *Works*, vol. 4, pp. 214–17
50 *Remains*, 25.4.1761
51 Boswell, (1794) 1893, p. 17: see also p. 216
52 *Autobiography* (1796) 1923, p. 17
53 Walton, p. 360fn
54 *Remains*, vol. 1, pt 2, p. 327, 29.12.1734; 9.1.1735; cf. 4.4.1735
55 *Journal*, p. 47
56 *Journal*, vol 2, p. 278
57 24.5.1738; his preface to the *Plain Account of Christian Perfection*, revised 1777, where his deep offence is unmentioned. Wesley seems to be reading into earlier years his 1738 convictions
58 *Works*, vol. 7, p. 203; cf. p. 297
59 Overton, pp. 110–11
60 S. Hobhouse, *William Law and Eighteenth-Century Quakerism*, pp. 171–2
61 Ed. J. Meister and others (Philadelphia n.d.)
62 Ed. F. Cross (1957), p. 791

## CHAPTER 7

1 Vol. 1, pt 2, 14.5.1727, 4.1.1728
2 See Broxap, pp. 39–40
3 Rawlinson MSS, D. 1254; Brett MSS, vol. 8, c. 24–35; see vol. 8, Sept. 1731, for a letter of Smith
4 *Remains*, vol. 1, pt 2, pp. 428–9
5 *Eccl. Pol.*, bk v, ch. 63
6 See D. Cupitt's article, 'The Doctrine of Analogy in the Age of Locke', in *JTS*, April 1968, pp. 186–202. Of course the incomprehensibility of God was a notion familiar to patristic thought; see G. L. Prestige, *God in Patristic Thought* (1964), pp. 5–6; the idea of analogy is also traditional; e.g., St Thomas Aquinas, *Summa contra Gentiles*, 1. XIV–XXXIV
7 *The Analogy of Religion*, Advertisement
8 *Christianity as Old as the Creation*, p. 10

9 p. 15
10 p. 258
11 p. 61
12 pp. 62-3
13 p. 66
14 p. 71
15 p. 74
16 p. 90
17 pp. 91-2
18 p. 107
19 p. 116
20 p. 129
21 p. 135
22 *Dialogues on Metaphysics*, Dialogues 1 and 11
23 E.g., *Dialogues on Metaphysics*, Dialogue 14
24 *Life and Sermons*, p. 200
25 *The Church and the Age of Reason* (1960), p. 163
26 *Analogy*, pt 1, conclusion
27 *Analogy*, pt 2, conclusion
28 Walton, p. 560fn
29 Walton Collection, 186.11 (1-4); 186.11(2)

## CHAPTER 8

1 Where necessary, reference will be made to the version in the Bodleian Library, which gives the full text. The lady's letters are also there
2 *Life*, p. 130
3 p. 218
4 p. 219
5 p. 219
6 p. 221
7 p. 231
8 p. 233
9 p. 233
10 pp. 233-4
11 p. 235
12 p. 272

## CHAPTER 9

1 See Introduction, pp. 1-2; cf. H. Talon, *William Law* (1948), *passim*
2 *Letters to a Lady*, p. 236
3 *The Fable of the Bees*, ed. F. E. Maurice, Advertisement, p. v
4 *Christian Perfection*, p. 14
5 See *Three Letters*, p. 9; *Christian Perfection*, p. 80; *Serious Call*, p. 116
6 Fable of the Bees, p. 40; cf. Tauler, *Life and Sermons*, p. 133; Suso, *Life*, ch. 25
7 *Christian Perfection*, p. 6; cf. pp. 197, 245
8 *Remains*, vol. 2. pt 1, p. 258
9 *Stage Entertainments*, p. 143
10 *Essays Modern and Critical*, pp. 16-17
11 *Autobiography* (1796) 1923, p. 17
12 *Serious Call*, p. 109
13 Ibid., p. 194

14 *Serious Call*, p. 112f
15 *A Survey of English Literature* (1928), p. 207
16 *The Eighteenth Century Background* (1962), pp. 100–1
17 *A Survey of English Literature* (1928), p. 206
18 *Cambridge History of English Literature*, pp. 323–4
19 *A Survey of English Literature* (1938), p. 209
20 *Cambridge History of English Literature*, p. 323
21 p. 113
22 *The Letters of C. S. Lewis*, ed. W. H. Lewis (1966), p. 143
23 Walton, p. 537fn
24 Walton, pp. 45–6fn


# CHAPTER 10

1 V. H. H. Green, *The Young Mr Wesley*, p. 277 and fn 4; *The Letters of John Wesley*, ed. J. Telford, pp. 161–3
2 J. Wesley, *Works*, vol. 9, p. 466; vol. 12, p. 470
3 *Letters*, pp. 168–9
4 V. H. H. Green, *The Young Mr Wesley*, pp. 187–8
5 Byrom, vol. 1, pt 2, pp. 558–60
6 *Remains*, vol. 1, pt 2, pp. 616–19
7 Walton, p. 26fn; cf. Byrom, vol. 2, pt 2, p. 363, where Dr Cheyne is said to have mentioned the book in which Law found Boehme's name
8 *Sunrise to Eternity*, p. 52
9 *Aurora*, 19.7–12
10 *Epistles*, 12.8
11 p. 60
12 *Aurora*, 8.7
13 p. 61
14 p. 233, 1941
15 p. 93
16 See especially J. J. Stoudt, op. cit.; also H. Brinton, *The Mystic Will*, 1931
17 *Of Grace*, 3.26
18 *Of Grace*, 4.10
19 *Aurora*, 10
20 See H. Martensen, *Jacob Boehme*; F. Hartmann, *Personal Christianity*
21 See S. Hutin, *English Admirers of Jacob Boehme*; H. E. Wildes, *The Voice of the Lord*, pp. 32–5, 59, 104, 389–90, for Fox 1965; H. Talon, *John Byrom*, p. 149fn 22 for Byrom
22 S. Hobhouse, *Selected Mystical Writings of William Law* (1948), pp. 397–422; H. McLachlan, *Sir Isaac Newton, Theological Manuscripts* (Liverpool 1950), pp. 20–1
23 *Les disciples anglais de Jacob Boehme*, ch. 6
24 Quoted by R. Maxse, *The Reception of Jacob Boehme in England*, p. 12
25 In 1756 he informed Langcake that the book of Richard Clarke, the numerical mystic and prophetic writer, could be put to no use other than fire kindling! Walton, pp. 573–4
26 *Works*, vol. 4, p. 625; cf. J. Wesley, *Works*, vol. 9, pp. 509–18; J. Boswell, *Life of Johnson*, p. 216; E. Gibbon, *Autobiography*, p. 16; J. S. Swift, *Works* 1934, p. 319
27 Quoted by T. McFarland, *Coleridge and the Pantheist Tradition* (1969), p. 250

28 For an example of Law's reliance on divine promptings, Walton, p. 562fn
29 Walton, p. 46fn; cf. p. 106 above
30 Quoted G. J. Warnock, *Berkeley* (Penguin 1953), p. 11
31 p. 153
32 P. Hazard, op. cit., p. 489
33 'William Blake', in *Selected Essays* (1951)
34 Walton, p. 157fn
35 A. Koyre, *La philosophie de Jacob Boehme*, p. 13; S. T. Coleridge, *Aids to Reflection* (1913 edn), p. 258
36 *Perspectives in nineteenth- and twentieth-century Protestant Theology* (1970), p. 88

## CHAPTER 11

1 See S. Hobhouse, *William Law and Eighteenth-Century Quakerism*, pp. 87–91. Unless stated otherwise page references in this chapter are from this book
2 *Works*, vol. 4, pp. 27, 42, 44, 127, 278, 119, etc.
3 *History*, vol. 1, p. 248, etc.
4 *Journal*, e.g. p. 23, 101, 43, 94, etc.
5 See S. Hobhouse, *William Law and Eighteenth-Century Quakerism*, ch. 5
6 *Three Letters*, pp. 5, 7, 199
7 p. 63
8 p. 27
9 p. 32
10 p. 37
11 p. 42
12 p. 47
13 p. 57
14 p. 57
15 p. 60
16 See p. 63, fn 1
17 *Remains*, vol. 2, pt 1
18 S. Hobhouse, *William Law and Eighteenth-Century Quakerism*, pt 2, ch. 2
19 p. 206
20 p. 212
21 p. 214
22 pp. 215–16

## CHAPTER 12

1 Walton, pp. 348–51
2 *Remains*, vol. 2, pt 1.13, 15; 17.4.1737
3 Walton, p. 370fn
4 Quoted by R. T. Holtby, *Daniel Waterland* (Thurnam), p. 160
5 Hoadly, *Works*, p. 848
6 *Works*, p. 867
7 p. 3
8 p. 11
9 pp. 11, 18
10 p. 20
11 p. 26

12 pp. 38-9
13 p. 39
14 p. 41
15 p. 44
16 p. 53
17 p. 54
18 p. 62
19 p. 72
20 p. 72
21 p. 73
22 p. 77
23 p. 82
24 p. 88
25 p. 89
26 p. 90
27 p. 90
28 p. 97
29 p. 104
30 p. 117
31 *Works*, vol. 3, p. 296
32 C. W. Dugmore, *The Eucharistic Doctrine in England from Hooker to Waterland* (1942), p. 112
33 The notion of the Inner Light is usual in religious thought, though variously developed. Before reading Boehme Law was sympathetic to the Johannine and early Christian apologists' idea of the Logos in every man. Platonists and Stoics employ the same idea, e.g., Epictetus, *Moral Discourses*, VIII, 2
34 *Theologia Germanica*, ch. 18; Suso, *Life*, ch. 51; Tauler, *Sermons*, no. 19
35 See article by S. Hobhouse in *JTS*, vol. 37 (1936), pp. 350-68
36 p. 2
37 p. 18
38 pp. 136-96
39 pp. 199-200

## CHAPTER 13

1 *Sermons and Tracts*, 1713-43. P.P. 17.4.9.(14) Dr Williams's Library, p. 1
2 *Works*, vol. 12, p. 27
3 *Works*, vol. 1, pp. 101-2
4 J. B. Green, *John Wesley and William Law*, p. 64
5 *Works*, vol. 1, p. 103
6 He said to C. Wesley, 'Was I talked of as Mr Whitefield is, I should run away and hide myself entirely.' Quoted by Overton, p. 90
7 *Psychological Types* (1926), pp. 480-517; cf. D. Stafford-Clarke, *Psychiatry Today* (1952), pp. 151-2
8 *Letters*, p. 240
9 *Letters*, p. 191
10 E.g., pp. 192-3
11 Walton, p. 559fn
12 Walton, p. 579fn
13 Walton, p. 605fn
14 Walton, p. 555fn (1754); p. 610fn (1760)
15 Walton, p. 593fn

16 Walton, p. 534fn
17 *Remains* (1750–1), vol. 2, pt 2, pp. 515, 588–9 (1757)
18 Walton, p. 559 (1757)
19 P. Sabatier, *Life of St Francis of Assisi* (1894) 1930, p. 148; M. de la
   Bedoyère, *Francis de Sales* (1960), p. 186; cf. E. A. Peers, *St Teresa of
   Jesus* (1953), p. 67
20 *England in the Eighteenth Century*, p. 90
21 Quoted by F. L. Lucas, *The Art of Living* (1959), p. 101
22 R. A. Knox, *Enthusiasm* (1950), p. 432
23 Boswell, *Life* (1794) 1893, p. 176
24 G. Lawton, *John Wesley's English*, pp. 238–9
25 *Enthusiasm*, p. 494
26 *Journal*, 13.10.1752
27 *Psychological Types*, p. 416f
28 *Journal*, 3.8.1737–2.12.1737; cf. J. H. Overton, *John Wesley*, pp. 182f;
   R. A. Knox, *Enthusiasm*, pp. 444f; M. Schmidt, *John Wesley*, vol. 1 (1962),
   pp. 195f for a sympathetic account
29 See Wesley's *Letter to Dr Coke, Mr Asbury and our brethren in North America*,
   10.9.1784; A. B. Lawson, *John Wesley and the Christian Ministry* (1963)
30 *Enthusiasm*, p. 454
31 Vol. 1, pp. 84–5, 24.4.1738; cf. H. Harris rebuking Wesley for saying
   the Revival started in 1738 and the 'self that appeared in his writings in
   monopolising the whole of the Methodists to himself and his branch . . .
   all know Mr Whitefield was the first field-preacher in England, and the
   work was in the fields in Wales long before'. J. D. Walsh, in 'Origins of
   the Evangelical Revival', *Essays in Modern English Church History*, ed.
   G. V. Bennett and J. D. Walsh agrees with Harris; in 1740 Whitefield
   asked a correspondent to ask Wesley to 'avoid disputing with me'. He
   later counselled Wesley to be gentle with someone and to guard against
   'irregular warmth' in his temper (*Works*, vol. 1, pp. 185–225)
32 Quoted by Overton, *Life*, p. 90
33 Quoted by J. B. Green, *John Wesley and William Law*, p. 60
34 *Remains*, Vol. 2, pt 1, pp. 181–2; Byrom was no Methodist. In 1752 he
   wrote to Warburton, 'They are mad. I believe they are.' Walton
   Collection, 186/2 (zi)
35 Vol. 2, pt 1, 7.2.1739; 16.2.1739; similarly to the Wesleys Whitefield
   advised a correspondent, 'Look . . . not to the *Mysticks*, but to Jesus.'
   *Works*, vol. 2, p. 300 (1749).
36 Dr Dimond, quoted with approval by A. S. Yates, *The Doctrine of
   Assurance* (1952), pp. 207–8
37 The corrected letter is reproduced by J. Telford, *The Life of John
   Wesley*
38 E. W. Baker, *A Herald of the Evangelical Revival*, pp. 27–8
39 Thus M. Schmidt, in *John Wesley*, vol. 1, p. 9. considers Wesley's stature
   scarcely less than that of the Great Reformers; Lawton's astonishing
   claim for Wesley's *Address to the Clergy*, 'in prose worthy of the Royal
   Society . . . something of Hooker's massiveness, Herbert's sincerity,
   Pope's satire, Chesterfield's breeding, and Burke's passion all in one'.
   *John Wesley's English*, p. 261; W. E. Sangster, *The Path to Perfection*
   (1943), esp. ch. 1; even Wesley's mother can be called a 'formidable
   theologian'; see J. A. Newton, *Susanna Wesley* (1968), p. 183
40 J. B. Green, *John Wesley and William Law*, esp. chs 3 and 7; E. W. Baker,
   *A Herald of the Evangelical Revival*, esp. chs 2 and 9

41 *A Herald of the Evangelical Revival*, p. 32
42 *A New History of Methodism* (1909), eds. Townsend, Workman, and Eayrs, vol. 1, pp. 168–74; R. Davies, *Methodism* (Penguin 1966), p. 168
43 See Byrom's surmise, pp. 133–4 above, and for the impetuosity of Wesley, in addition to this chapter see p. 148
44 *Journal*, 10.8.1739; cf. Byrom, 13.8.1739

## CHAPTER 14

1 *Trapp*, p. 26
2 p. 137
3 p. 138
4 p. 139
5 pp. 139–40
6 p. 140
7 p. 143
8 p. 146
9 p. 152
10 p. 153
11 pp. 153–4
12 p. 156
13 p. 158
14 p. 161
15 p. 162
16 p. 166
17 p. 167
18 p. 171
19 p. 178
20 See A. S. Yates, *Wesley and Assurance*, pp. 65, 67, 69, 71; Whitefield reports 'I am supported under the prospect of present and impending trials, with an assurance of God's loving me to the end; yea, even to all eternity.' To Wesley he writes, 'our Lord frequently manifests himself in such a manner, that it throws me into an agony which my body is almost too weak to bear'. *Works*, vol. 1 (1740), pp. 182, 219
21 A. S. Yates, *Wesley and Assurance*, pp. 150–8; *A New History of Methodism*, eds Townsend, Workman, Earys, vol. 1, pp. 19–26
22 *Remains*, vol. 2, pt 1, pp. 258–9
23 S. Hobhouse, *William Law and Eighteenth-Century Quakerism*, pp. 238–43; *Trapp*, p. 182
24 Walton, pp. 258–492
25 Byrom, vol. 2, pt 1, pp. 258–9; August–September 1739 and 297–301

## CHAPTER 15

1 Overton, p. 295
2 A Mr Gough also remarked upon the similarity between Law and the Methodists; see Byrom, vol. 2, pt 1, 8.9.1739
3 p. 3
4 pp. 8–9
5 p. 17
6 p. 18
7 p. 18
8 p. 20

s

9 p. 23
10 p. 27
11 p. 28
12 p. 47
13 pp. 57-8
14 p. 61
15 p. 62
16 p. 63
17 p. 67
18 p. 68
19 p. 72
20 p. 77
21 p. 81
22 p. 86
23 p. 88
24 p. 89
25 p. 98
26 p. 100
27 p. 110
28 p. 117
29 p. 119
30 p. 121
31 p. 125
32 p. 127
33 p. 133
34 p. 139
35 p. 143
36 p. 143
37 p. 146
38 p. 147
39 pp. 150-1
40 p. 156
41 p. 166
42 p. 175
43 p. 183
44 p. 197
45 p. 204
46 p. 209
47 G. Herbert, *A Priest to the Temple*, ch. 9; P. E. More and F. L. Cross, *Anglicanism*, pp. 667-71
48 p. 34; also Suso's *Life*, p. 242; the *Theologia Germanica*, pp. 2, 128, 197, and Ruysbroek's *The Spiritual Espousals*, pp. 186-7
49 Tauler's *Sermons and Life*, p. 348; *Theologia Germanica*, pp. 62-3, 112-14; à Kempis, *Imitation of Christ*, pt 1, ch. 3; Suso, *Life*, p. 131; cf. A. Baker, *Holy Wisdom*, sec. 2, ch. 1, no. 5
50 *The Book of the Poor in Spirit*, p. 246; Suso, *Life*, p. 121; *Theologia Germanica*, pp. 9, 214; Tauler, *Life and Sermons*, p. 71
51 Suso, *Life*, p. 241; *Theologia Germanica*, pp. 6, 109; Ruysbroeck, *The Spiritual Espousals* (1953), pp. 96, 126 and *The Seven Steps of the Ladder of Spiritual Love* (1944), p. 61
52 *The Apocryphal New Testament*, E.T., M. R. James (1924), pp. 189, 178, 468, 513-14, 321-2, 335, 266, etc.
53 See J. N. D. Kelly, *Early Christian Doctrines* (1958), p. 348

54 Ibid., pp. 172–3
55 See N. Sykes, *Church and State in England in the Eighteenth Century*; S. C. Carpenter, *Eighteenth-Century Church and People* (1959), J. W. Legg, *English Church Life from the Restoration to the Tractarian Movement* (1917)
56 *Journal of the Rev. W. B. Stevens*; ed. G. Galbraith (Oxford 1965), 22.3.1792; 13.5.1792; 18.11.1792; 20.2.1795; 14.8.1794; 24.9.1792; 19.9.1792; 17.3.1792; 15.9.1792; 8.12.1792; 20.2.1795; J. Woodforde's *Diary of a Country Parson*, suggests a stronger but similar life
57 *Extracts from the Diary of Robert Meeke* (1874), eds. Moorhouse and Hulbert
58 His remarks on the Christian use of Law Courts also lack balance. Samuel Pepys was better served by the preacher, Thomas Fuller, who showed, 'we are to go to law never to revenge, but only to repayre, which I think a good distinction'. *Diary*, 3.2.1661

## CHAPTER 16

1 pp. 348–51fn
2 Tighe, p. 9
3 His correspondents included some from overseas. James Read of Pennsylvania asked in 1742 if a lawyer could be in the spirit of Jesus. Walton Collection, 186.4.(12)
4 Tighe, p. 10
5 Secretan, p. 91
6 See V. H. H. Green, *The Young Mr Wesley*, p. 209fn 1
7 See Secretan, *Life of Robert Nelson*, p. 7; Plumptre, *Life of Thomas Ken*, vol. 1, p. 73; B. Blackstone, *The Ferrar Papers* (1938), pp. XVII–XXII, 3–5; A. L. Maycock, *Nicholas Ferrar of Little Gidding* (1938), pp. 126, 146–9
8 *Life*, p. 10
9 Walton, pp. 429–41
10 Overton, pp. 352, 356, 455
11 Walton Collection, 186.5.16; 186.5.17; 186.5.24; 186.5.20; 186.5.26; 186.5.28; 186.5.43
12 Walton Collection, 186.8.22
13 For much of the preceding, Walton, pp. 427–505fn
14 *Remains*, Vol. 2, pt 2, pp. 491–2

## CHAPTER 17

1 Walton, p. 542fn
2 p. 8
3 p. 8
4 p. 9
5 p. 10
6 p. 16
7 p. 21
8 p. 23
9 p. 26
10 p. 27
11 pp. 28–9
12 p. 31
13 p. 33
14 p. 34

15  p. 35
16  p. 41
17  p. 42
18  p. 43
19  p. 45. For wording and sentiment Law probably owed something here to Henry Scougal's famous Puritan tract, *The Life of God in the Soul of Man* (1677)
20  *Life*, p. 313
21  p. 53
22  p. 63
23  pp. 64–5
24  p. 66
25  p. 72
26  p. 72
27  p. 84
28  p. 90
29  p. 90
30  p. 97
31  p. 98
32  p. 120
33  p. 128
34  p. 130
35  pp. 138–9
36  Barth says, 'theology must be an act of prayer'. *Evangelical Theology* E.T. (1968), p. 167
37  See M. R. James, *The Apocryphal New Testament*, pp. 10–12
38  *Mysticism*, pt 2, 1930
39  *Abandonment to Divine Providence* (how Law would have loved this title!), pp. 21, 37, 134, 172, 197, 357, etc.
40  Overton, *Life*, pp. 400–3
41  See W. N. Pittenger, *The Christian Understanding of Human Nature* (1964), esp. chs. 3 and 4
42  Walton, p. 540fn
43  *Works*, vol. 2, p. 359

## CHAPTER 18

1  *Remains*, vol. 2, pt 2, p. 493
2  *Remains*, vol. 2, pt 2, pp. 519–20
3  Walton Collection
4  Byrom, *Remains*, vol. 2, pt 2, p. 545fn
5  p. 153
6  p. 168
7  p. 181
8  p. 184
9  pp. 189–90
10  p. 196
11  p. 199
12  p. 205
13  pp. 211–18
14  p. 223
15  p. 232
16  p. 236

17 p. 238
18 p. 252
19 *Tilk*, i, 267; *Six Theosophical Points*, vii, 37; *Three Principles*, iv, 66; *Mysterium Magnum*, lx, 44
20 See S. Hobhouse, *William Law*, p. 368f
21 *William Law*, p. 117f
22 E.g., *Some Sayings of the Buddha* (Oxford 1925), pp. 38–44; F. Hartmann stresses the kinship between Boehme and Indian religion in *Personal Christianity*
23 Walton, p. 521fn

## CHAPTER 19

1 Walton, pp. 550–1fn
2 Walton Collection, Fragment
3 Walton, p. 123fn
4 Byrom, *Remains*, vol. 2, pt 2, pp. 552–3
5 p. 3
6 p. 20
7 p. 38
8 p. 44
9 p. 45
10 p. 47
11 p. 51
12 p. 53
13 p. 62
14 p. 68
15 p. 73
16 p. 74
17 p. 87
18 p. 89
19 p. 85
20 p. 99; Boehme believed that our inward characteristics can be likened to animals or birds: e.g., *Six Theosophical Points*, vii, 37; *Three Principles*, xvi, 50
21 p. 107
22 p. 111
23 p. 112
24 p. 115
25 p. 123
26 p. 123
27 p. 131; the phrase Marriage Feast and the idea of it are found in Boehme; e.g. *Regeneration*, iv
28 Op. cit., p. 2
29 Op. cit., pp. 44–5
30 Op. cit., p. 49
31 Cf. H. Talon, *John Byrom*, p. 222fn 18
32 M. Piette, *John Wesley and the Evolution of Protestantism* (1938), p. 413
33 para. 169f
34 *William Law*, p. 319
35 J. Leclercq's essay in F. Vandenbroucke and L. Bouyer, *The Spirituality of the Middle Ages*, p. 17
36 *The Humanity of the Saviour* (1962), pt 2, pt 3, pt 4, pp. 131f, 139f

37 J. N. D. Kelly, *Early Christian Doctrines*, p. 170f; Boehme, *Stiefel*, ii, 168; *Threefold Life*, xxi, 21

38 *The Doctrine of the Atonement* (1915), p. 156; Butler's defence of Christ's atonement against the Deists relies upon analogy from nature, rationality, revelation (which must not contradict reason). He argues that mediation is necessary to avoid punishment for sin; Christ mediates because he reveals God's will, establishes the Church and sacrifices himself for sin. Butler can give no *rationale* of sacrifice; that lies in the counsels of God. But he notes that nature exhibits the principle of vicarious punishment. *Analogy*. Pt II. ch. 5

39 *Apology*, Props. 4, 8; 5, 6; 7, 10

## CHAPTER 20

1 Byrom, *Remains*, vol. 2, pt 2, p. 558

2 Walton, pp. 560fn, 561fn; Byrom, vol. 2, pt 2, p. 589

3 *Works*, vol. 3, p. 184

4 Byrom, vol. 2, pt 2, pp. 593, 629

5 *Letters*, pp. 198–9; cf. *Letters*, pp. 167–9

6 Walton, p. 566fn

7 *The Doctrine of Grace*, p. 626

8 Baker, *A Herald of the Evangelical Revival*, p. 46; Whitefield commented on his own edition of the *Serious Call*, 'my abridgement . . . which I have endeavoured to gospelize'. *Works*, vol. 2, p. 144, 1748

9 *Works*, vol. 9, pp. 466–509

10 For two pamphlets of Wesley criticizing and ridiculing Boehme, see *Works*, vol. 9, pp. 508–18

11 *Remains*, vol. 2, pt 2, pp. 593, 629

12 R. Davies and G. Rupp, eds., *A History of the Methodist Church in Great Britain*, vol. 1 (1965), p. 109

13 *Remains*, vol. 2, pt 2, pp. 629–30

14 See E. W. Baker, *A Herald of the Evangelical Revival*, p. 59f

15 Walton, p. 91fn

16 With reference to Law's *Letters*, pp. 136–45, the writer can find no evidence to substantiate Baker's presumption that some or all of it was sent to Wesley. Law probably had a larger audience in mind than Wesley when he permitted it to be published. Nor can he find evidence to substantiate Green's point that this letter shows Law coming closer to Wesley's view of the Atonement. Law reiterates already expressed views, and in interpreting the Matthean parable as teaching the importance of forgiveness, improves upon Wesley. See E. W. Baker, *A Herald of the Evangelical Revival*, p. 53; J. B. Green, *John Wesley and William Law*, pp. 165–6

17 Walton, pp. 570–2fn

## CHAPTER 21

1 *Divine Legation*, vol. 2, p. 90; A. W. Evans, *Warburton and the Warburtonians* (1932), pp. 224–5

2 Boswell, *Life*, p. 545; Gibbon, *Autobiography*, p. 169

3 *Reason and Authority in the Eighteenth Century* (1964), p. 43

4 Evans, *Warburton and the Warburtonians*, pp. 216–17

5 p. 139

6 p. 142

7 p. 143
8 p. 147
9 p. 157
10 p. 160
11 p. 166
12 pp. 179–80
13 p. 186
14 p. 188
15 p. 194
16 p. 212
17 See E. Jacob, *Theology of the Old Testament* (1958), pp. 325–8; A. B. Davidson, *The Theology of the Old Testament* (1904), pp. 402–522
18 *The Image of God in Man* (1953), pp. 188, 190–1, chs 3–7
19 *Select Discourses*, p. 419
20 *Religio Medici*, p. 52; cf. Boehme, *Threefold Life*, xviii, 4; *Mysterium Magnum*, xiv, 8; *Aurora*, xxiv, 7; this is also the position of Orthodoxy; see T. Ware, *The Orthodox Church* (Penguin 1969), p. 225 and some eastern thinkers

## CHAPTER 22

1 Walton, pp. 579fn, 592fn
2 Walton, pp. 599, 162
3 Walton, 158–60fn
4 Walton, p. 492fn; cf. pp. 605–6fn
5 Walton, p. 593fn
6 Walton, p. 592fn
7 Walton, pp. 592–3; Law refers also to the *Godly Life of Luterman*, that he wants from a Quaker bookseller. Hobhouse suggests he might be thinking of J. Lutkemann, a German pastor and theologian. *William Law and Eighteenth-century Quakerism*, pp. 247f
8 In England the king traditionally washed poor men's feet on Maundy Thursday. After the reign of James I a deputy did this. The custom lapsed in 1731. Pepys observed the ceremony, *Diary*, 4.4.1667. The pope has maintained the custom in the church of Rome
9 Walton, pp. 599, 162fn
10 Walton, p. 600fn
11 Walton, p. 605fn
12 Walton, pp. 601fn, 216fn
13 Walton, p. 601fn; cf. pp. 602, 604–5fn
14 *Remains*, vol. 2, pt 2, p. 614
15 p. 109
16 p. 118
17 p. 176
18 p. 210
19 Walton, p. 611fn
20 p. 240

## CHAPTER 23

1 Byrom, *Remains*, vol. 2, pt 2, pp. 648–9
2 p. 5
3 p. 14
4 p. 17

5 p. 20
6 p. 29
7 p. 76
8 p. 78
9 p. 82
10 p. 89
11 p. 96
12 p. 99
13 *Works*, vol. 4, pp. 565fn, 606, 608
14 *Three Principles*, iv, 22
15 Quoted by A. W. Hopkinson in *About William Law* (1948), p. 72
16 See Hobhouse, *William Law*, p. 291
17 Walton, p. 616; cf., p. 609 fn
18 Walton, p. 616
19 Tighe, p. 12

## CHAPTER 24

1 Vol. 1, pp. 23-4; cf. pp. 38-42; vol. 2, p. 192; vol. 3, p. 69
2 *A Short History of the Interpretation of the Bible* (1965), p. 60
3 *The Spirit of Anglicanism*, p. 327
4 Cf., P. Tillich, *On the Boundary* (1967), esp. p. 31
5 The word is used by Tillich, *On the Boundary*, p. 52
6 P. Sangster, *Dr Sangster* (1962), pp. 145-6
7 *The Vision of God* (1931), pp. 66-7, 180-1
8 *History of the Religious Thought in France* (1928), vol. 1
9 M. Thornton, *English Spirituality*, pp. 234-5
10 *The Hound and the Falcon* (1965), pp. 14-15
11 *Wesley and Sanctification*, pp. 56-7; cf. E. W. Baker, *A Herald of the Evangelical Revival*, ch. 8
12 E.g., *Three Letters*, p. 203; *Serious Call*, p. 212
13 The literature is immense, but see A. M. Farrer, *Saving Belief* (1964), pp. 87f; V. Taylor, *Jesus and His Sacrifice* (1937): *The Atonement in New Testament Teaching* (1945); *Forgiveness, and Reconciliation* (1946); J. Knox, *The Death of Christ* (1959): A. Richardson, *An Introduction to the Theology of the New Testament* (1958), ch. 10
14 *Christian Perfection*, p. 101
15 *The Mystical Element of Religion* (1909), vol. 2, pp. 282-3; cf. T. H. Hughes, *The Philosophical Basis of Mysticism* (1937), ch. 2; W. R. Inge, *Mysticism in Religion*, p. 25
16 *The Spiritual Letters of Dom John Chapman*, ed. R. Hudleston (1946), p. 303; C. Butler, *Western Mysticism* (1922), p. 222
17 *Mysticism*, pp. 165-70; Coleridge believed his errors were 'the mistaking the accidents and peculiarities of his own overwrought mind for realities and modes of thinking common to all minds: secondly, the confusion of nature, that is the active powers communicated to matter, with God, the creator'. *Aids to Reflection*, p. 258. Similarly, he believed Swedenborg thought so intensely through the medium of visual and auditory images that they became sufficiently distinct for him to mistake their subjective nature for objective reality. T. McFarland, *Coleridge and the Pantheist Tradition*, p. 284
18 *William Blake* (1970), p. 7; in a remarkable work by the mathematician W. E. Whiteman, *The Mystical Life*, the reader will find a record of experiences sympathetic to much of Law's later theology

19 See E. O. James, *Comparative Religion* (1961), pp. 156–7
20 V. Lossky, *The Mystical Theology of the Eastern Church* (1957), ch. 11; cf. E. Bevan, *Symbolism and Belief* (1938), p. 150
21 Cf. G. von Rad, *Genesis* (1961), p. 47; S. L. Frank, *Reality and Man* (1965), esp. p. 212; Sanday and Headlam, *Romans* (1902), pp. 42–4; H. Martensen, *Jacob Boehme*, p. 120, and fn 14
22 *Reality and Man*, p. 217; R. C. Zaehner records similar ideas in Teilhard de Chardin and Indian thought, the latter speaks also of the Trinity. *Evolution in Religion* (1971), e.g. pp. 55–6, 85
23 See E. Jacob, *The Theology of the Old Testament*, pp. 79–80; U. Simon, *Heaven in the Christian Tradition* (1958), pp. 76–9
24 See H. Martensen, *Jacob Boehme*, pp. 100–10
25 T. Ware, The Orthodox Church, p. 217; V. Lossky, *The Mystical Theology of the Eastern Church*, ch. 4
26 *The Supersensual Life*, pp. 26–34
27 *This Life and the Next* (1918), p. 18; P. Roubiczek, *Ethical Values in the Age of Science* (1969), p. 300, 'The transcendental must transcend even love itself; it must have a reality of its own from which feeling can emanate.'
28 Gen. 6.2–4; Ps. 78.49, etc. See generally F. R. Tennant, *The Sources of the Doctrine of Original Sin* (1903); The *Origin and Propagation of Sin* (1902)
29 *Genesis*, pp. 48–9
30 *Ethiopic Book of Enoch; Visions of Noah, etc.*
31 *Cur Deus Homo*, pt 1, ch 18
32 See N. P. Williams, *The Ideas of the Fall and of Original Sin* (1927), lect. 4; J. Hick, *Evil and the God of Love* (1966)
33 *Genesis*, p. 58
34 *The Man–Woman Relation in Christian Thought* (1959), p. 208
35 *The Perennial Philosophy*, p. 63
36 See J. Daniélou, *From Shadow to Reality* (1960), pp. 11–12.
37 Cf. F. O. James, *Comparative Religion*; R. Panikkar, *The Unknown Christ of Hinduism* (1965); C. Davis, *Christ and World Religions* (1970)
38 See R. B. Rackham, *Acts of the Apostles* (1925), pp. 14–5
39 Gal. 3.13; 2 Cor. 5.21; Rom. 3.25, 1 John 1.7; Heb. 9.08 etc
40 *The Work of Christ* (1910), pp. 163–4
41 *Freedom and the Spirit*, p. 239
42 V. F. Storr, *The Development of English Theology in the Nineteenth Century*, p. 56, gives an appreciative note. There are few others
43 See H. E. W. Turner, *The Pattern of Christian Truth* (1954), pp. 493–4
44 See the stimulating symposium, *Mystery and Mysticism* (1956) and E. J. Tinsley, *The Imitation of God in Christ* (1960), ch. 1
45 See J. N. D. Kelly, *Early Christian Doctrines*, pp. 473–4
46 *Christ and Time* (1951), p. 51f
47 *Six Theosophical Points* (1958), p. v; cf. his *Freedom and the Spirit* (1935), p. xix
48 *Christian Regeneration*, p. 153

# SELECT BIBLIOGRAPHY

Books referred to only very occasionally are fully described at their first appearance in the text. The place of publication is London except where otherwise indicated:

Baker, E. W.: *A Herald of the Evangelical Revival* (1948)
Boehme, J.: *Sämtliche Schriften* (Stuttgart 1955)
  (English translations of Boehme are numerous. Usually the writer has followed F. Hartmann's *Personal Christianity* (N.Y.), which compresses Boehme's voluminous writings.)
Broxap, H.: *The Later Nonjurors* (Cambridge 1924)
Byrom, J.: *Private Journal and Literary Remains*, 2 vols., Chetham Society (1854–7)
Catalogue of Books in Law's Library, King's Cliffe (1927)
Church, R. W.: *A Study in the Philosophy of Malebranche* (1931)
Green, J. B.: *John Wesley and William Law* (1945)
Green, V. H. H.: *The Young Mr Wesley* (1961)
Guyon, Madame: *Œuvres complètes* (Paris 1789–91)
— *Autobiography*, 2 vols (1897)
— *A Short and Easy Method of Prayer* (1900)
Hales, M.: *Magnetismus Magnus* (1695)
Hazard, P.: *The European Mind* (1935; Penguin 1964)
Hobhouse, S.: *William Law and Eighteenth-Century Quakerism* (1927)
— ed. *William Law; Selected Mystical Writings* (1938)
Hooker, R.: *Ecclesiastical Polity*, 2 vols. (1907)
Kaye, F. B.: *The Fable of the Bees*, 2 vols (Oxford 1924)
Law, William. *Works*. As a complete set published in London, 1762; text used here: ed. G. Moreton (P. repr. 1892)
Lathbury, T.: *A History of the Non-jurors* (1845)
Lindström, H.: *Wesley and Sanctification* (1950)
Malebranche, Nicolas: *De la recherche de la Vérité* (E.T., 1692, 1694)
— *Traité de la nature et de la Grâce* (1680); E.T. (1695)
— *Traité de morale* (1683); E.T. (1699)
— *Traité de l'amour de dieu* (1697)
— *Entretiens sur la metaphysique et sur la religion* (1688); E.T. (1923)

Martensen, H. and Hobhouse, S.: *Jacob Boehme* (1949)

McAdoo, H. R.: *The Structure of Caroline Moral Theology* (1949)

— *The Spirit of Anglicanism* (1965)

Overton, J. H.: *The Life and Opinions of the Rev. William Law* (1881)

Stephen, L.: *English Thought in the Eighteenth Century*, 2 vols (1876)

Stoudt, J. J.: *From Sunrise to Eternity* (Philadelphia 1957)

Stranks, C. J.: *Anglican Devotion* (1961)

Talon, H.: *William Law* (1948)

— *John Byrom*, (1952)

Taylor, J.: *Works* (1822)

Thornton, M.: *English Spirituality* (1963)

Tighe, R.: *A Short Account of of the Life and Writings of the Late Rev. William Law* (1813)

Tulloch, J.: *Rational Theology and Christian Philosophy in England in the Seventeenth Century*; 2 vols. (Edinburgh, 1874)

Walton, C.: *Notes and Materials for an Adequate Biography of William Law* (1854)

Warburton, W.: *The Divine Legation of Moses Demonstrated* (1738); 2 vols (1837)

Wesley, Charles: *Journal*; ed. T. Jackson, 2 vols (1848)

Wesley, John: *Letters*; ed. J. Telford (1931)

— *Works* (1829)

# INDEX

## 1. NAMES

## 2. SUBJECTS